TOTTS

FROM THE KOP TO THE KELPIES
THE ALEX TOTTEN STORY

TOTTS

FROM THE KOP TO THE KELPIES
THE ALEX TOTTEN STORY

ALEX TOTTEN WITH JEFF HOLMES

FOREWORD BY SIR ALEX FERGUSON AND WALTER SMITH OBE

First published by Pitch Publishing, 2015

Pitch Publishing
A2 Yeoman Gate
Yeoman Way
Durrington
BN13 3QZ
www.pitchpublishing.co.uk

A CIP catalogue record is available for this book
from the British Library.

ISBN 978 178531-021-8

Typesetting and origination by Pitch Publishing

Printed in Great Britain

Contents

I would like to dedicate this book to my wife, Jessie, daughter, Kay, and son, Bruce.

Also, my two grandkids, Alexander and Jake.

Acknowledgements

WHEN you undertake a project as big as this, there are so many people who help you along the way — whether that be through assisting with photographs, organising things or merely jogging your memory of a long-lost career incident. Every little helps.

First of all I would like to thank Jeff Holmes for helping with the writing of this book. I first got to know Jeff when he interviewed me for his Jock Wallace book, *Blue Thunder*, and we met up around a dozen times to ensure *Totts* was as good as it could be. Thanks for all your hard work and meticulous research, Jeff!

Apart from an initial meeting at my house in Dunipace, these get-togethers all took place at the plush Westerwood Hotel, in Cumbernauld, and for that I am indebted to general manager Paul Bray, who ensured we always had somewhere cosy to sit and chat — and enjoy welcome coffee and biscuits!

I would also like to thank Gordon Bannerman, of the *Perthshire Advertiser*. Gordon was someone I got to know during my days at St Johnstone and he was once again a big help when I was piecing together the chapters relating to my time at Saints.

I would also like to say a big thank you to Paul Camillin, Jane Camillin and the talented team at Pitch Publishing for having faith in this project.

And I must thank two of my oldest pals in football, Alex Ferguson and Walter Smith, for taking the time to pen their forewords for this book. I value our friendships highly and appreciate them helping out.

And a big thank you to Eric Davidson for coming up with our clever sub-title, *From The Kop To The Kelpies*.

I have made so many wonderful friends during a lifetime of loving football and even to this day, I continue to meet new people and the thing we all have in common is our love of the beautiful game. It has been quite a journey, and it isn't finished yet!

Foreword by Sir Alex Ferguson

I FIRST met Alex while we were playing with Dunfermline and I liked him from the start. He was a nice lad and always looked after himself, and was clean-shaven and well dressed. We got on really well and I admired the fact that he was a really good, honest pro who had carved out a very successful career for himself.

While we were at Dunfermline, though, I always thought that if he had possessed a bit more pace, it would have changed everything for him. When I moved into management, I always liked my full-backs to have lots of pace, and that's why guys like Patrice Evra and Gary Neville were such a success. They were obviously both very good players, but they were also very quick.

Mind you, the other side of the coin was full-backs with the approach of guys like Bobby Shearer, who played for Rangers. He certainly wasn't the quickest but boy could he intimidate the opposition!

When I played with Alex in the 1960s, you could tell he truly loved the game – and he still does – but he worked hard at his game and played for some good Scottish clubs after leaving Liverpool. He had obviously picked up some excellent habits working under Bill Shankly at Anfield and he lived his life the right way, which gave him every chance to succeed in his chosen profession.

When we were at East End Park, it really was the perfect time to be a Dunfermline player. Jock Stein got the ball rolling there and Willie Cunningham and George Farm continued in a similar vein. They really were the halcyon days for me. Alex arrived at East End Park about a year after me, but he was always going to have a tough time holding down a full-back slot in the team because we had a cracking defender in John Lunn, who played left-back at the time. John was a speed merchant while, on the other hand, Alex was more of a cultured full-back.

But he was a big part of everything we achieved at Dunfermline and we had some great success there. We had a fantastic squad at that time, which was important, because football never has – and never will be – about just 11 guys.

I was at Dunfermline a little over three years and have nothing but good memories of my time at the club. Alex was a big part of that and we have remained friends ever since, and it is a friendship that will stand the test of time.

When he was at St Johnstone, I took Manchester United up to open their new ground. He had built something special there and I was very proud to have had the privilege to play a small part in what he was trying to achieve. When he asked about the possibility of United going to Perth, it wasn't a problem, because Alex is, and always has been, one of the game's good guys.

Foreword by Walter Smith OBE

LIKE most of those involved in Scottish football, Alex and I had crossed paths many times in the game but it wasn't until I started coaching, at the age of 27, that we really got to know one another. We met one year in Ibiza, while we were both on holiday, and that sort of cemented our friendship. That was when I really got to know him and naturally we stayed in touch.

It was ironic that when I went to Rangers in 1986, I got Alex's job. I was there before Graeme Souness arrived but by that time Jock Wallace, Alex and the rest of the staff had gone. But Scottish football being the size it is, you tend to come across coaches and players regularly and it wasn't long before we were locking horns again.

One of the most notorious occasions – and I use the term loosely – was when I took Rangers up to McDiarmid Park, and Alex was the manager of St Johnstone. We had our infamous bust-up and both got escorted out of the ground – which was an absolute nonsense. We had a wee clash in the tunnel, but there were no punches thrown or fighting, just a wee disagreement, as no doubt we had both done on numerous occasions throughout our respective careers. I recall that we were both utterly amazed at being thrown out the ground and not seeing the second half. We went to one of the St Johnstone directors' houses and had a cup of tea and a chat, and there weren't any problems between us. We were absolutely fine and were able to laugh about it later on, but it was just so preposterous at the time.

Alex has worked under some great managers, such as Bill Shankly and Jock Wallace, and has a steely determination to succeed. He was brought up by some real winners but he is as straightforward and honest as the day is long. What you see with Alex is definitely what you get. When we clashed that day in Perth, Alex had no problem sticking up for his own end, and I was the same, but that is just the sign of two people who love winning.

But when he became ill, it was a really worrying time for everyone who knew him. Alex always looked that fit and healthy, and perhaps the way he fought the illness and the recovery he made was testimony to his fitness and determination. He really loves his golf and is always out and about so I couldn't ever imagine Alex being unwell, but he was very ill at one point, and it just shows you that it can happen to anyone.

Playing-wise, not every one of us can have a sterling career laden with silverware, but for a lot of us, including Alex and myself, having a lengthy career in itself was a measure of success. And picking up all the knowledge along the way stood him in good stead for a lengthy career in management.

Alex has been involved with football since he was just 15 years old and has given great service to the game. Football has been his life and he deserves every single plaudit that comes his way.

1

An Al-Fresco Childhood

A SINGLE end with two small rooms – that's where my story starts. I was born at home – 125 Glasgow Road, Dennyloanhead – on 12 February 1946, a few months after the end of the Second World War which, I suppose, makes me a 'war baby'. I'm sure mum and dad, Mary and John, didn't have their troubles to seek during that awful conflict but they seemed to come through it relatively unscathed.

We had our home comforts, even though they were few, although everything still seemed to be situated outside. If you needed the toilet, you had to nip outside to the almost 'al fresco' cludgie, while the women all went out to the wash house to launder the clothes – and after they had finished, the kids were chucked in for their twice-weekly bath. That was after you had played outside all day, which was customary when I was growing up.

I was an only child and called after my grandfather, Alexander. Mum had wanted to call me Robbie, which I suppose would have been quite a modern name, but my grandparents were incredibly strong individuals and gran got her way. She had apparently come down to the house and said to mum, 'So it will be Alexander then?'

And that was that, although I can't quite imagine the same thing happening today.

Dennyloanhead is a small village near Denny and we had great neighbours. Everyone was really friendly and I didn't have many problems in my early years. Leaving your front door unlocked was the norm, as no one would dare have entered another person's home. Your belongings were 100 per cent safe and that in turn bred a culture that was warm and friendly. People in our part of the village would rather have helped one another out than take what wasn't theirs, and these are values that you then carry through life.

I lived in that house until I was nine years old and went to Dennyloanhead Primary School. When we moved, it was to a bigger council house, and we got our first black and white television, which was quite something. BBC Scotland had started transmitting by then but Scottish Television, which was inaugurated in 1957, was still some two years off, so we were pretty limited in what we could watch. Mind you, it was such an exciting innovation in my eyes that I would've sat for hours on end just watching the test card!

But while I was really taken with television, I was an outdoor boy at heart. We had a large patch of grass quite near the house and that's where I spent the biggest part of my childhood. There might not have been any goalposts but that didn't matter because sticking a couple of jackets down did the trick. Your imagination did the rest. You could have been playing at Hampden, Wembley, or my own personal blue heaven – Brockville, home of Falkirk FC. Since I was able to walk, and perhaps even before that, I was kicking a ball around.

Moving house didn't mean changing friends because we relocated just a mile up the road. Along with the television we had an inside toilet and a bath. Things that people obviously take for granted these days but which were luxury to us back then. We were living like kings, or at least that's the way it felt.

Dad was a shipping clerk with the local foundry and mum worked there as well. They must have been pretty happy with me as I was an only child. They knew I was football mad from the first whistle and every Christmas I would get a ball, a pair of boots and a tin of dubbin to keep the ball and boots in good working order. I was the epitome of easy to buy for. A standing order for the same presents every year, but at least I was never disappointed.

I enjoyed primary school. One of my best friends was a lad called Alan Boslem and we played football in school each time the opportunity arose. Alan was a real character and used to tell everyone his dad was a traveller, when in fact he was a road sweeper! We would use the shed for one of the goals because it was the perfect shape. The other goal was a couple of posts, but I always preferred shooting into the shed because it felt like you had scored a real goal when the ball hit the wall at the back.

I always pretended to be Alex Parker. He played for Falkirk and was my hero when I was growing up. He was a great player and as I weaved my way through the opposition in the playground, in my mind I was Alex at Brockville playing in a Scottish Cup tie against one of the bigger teams, and as I hit the back of the 'net' I could hear the roar of the crowd, appreciating what I had just done for them. Some of the other lads pretended to be other big-name players, playing for the more glamorous sides, but I was happy being Alex. He was the greatest as far as I was concerned.

We also enjoyed playing a game that involved hitting a ball off a wall and you were eliminated if you missed the wall. We would try and make angles and hit it as hard as we could in order to knock the other lads out. It was a really popular game, and good fun, but one we all took deadly serious, although one day no one could move for laughing when an accident befell poor Geordie Sherman. Someone hit the ball off the wall so hard that it went straight over a fence and Geordie jumped over to retrieve it. Sadly, for him, he jumped straight into an old bath that had obviously been dumped quite some time before, as it was filled with stale and smelly water. Moments later he re-emerged, soaked to the skin and smelling to the high heaven – but with the ball tucked safely under his arm and a big smile etched right across his face. It was hilarious.

The whole of the school holidays were always spent at my Aunt Kate's house in Aberdour, which I loved. My mum and dad both worked but I would go there and have a great time playing with the other kids and spending a lot of time on the silver sands.

We played football around the clock in those days: at play time and lunch times in school, we kicked the ball all the way home from school and then it was out straight after your dinner until your dad shouted you in when it was getting dark. And we never tired of it. If I had remained a kid for my entire life I would've been quite happy to play football until the end of time – that's how much I loved it.

When mum went to see the headmaster, he asked what I wanted to be when I left school. Then, without waiting for an answer, he said, 'I know, a footballer!' But it was true. Just about everyone I knew played football all the time, and we wouldn't just play matches. We would practise all the little bits and pieces and, while we all wanted to score goals, we didn't mind taking our turn in goals. In fact, other sports didn't even come into the equation. The likes of golf didn't get a look in. It was football or bust – and that's just the way it was.

I was like most other young lads growing up, and got up to a few dodges, although when the snow fell one year I got more than I bargained for when I decided to fire some snowballs at a passing bus. There was a police car right behind it and when I saw it stop, and two officers getting out, I started to shake with fear. They put their caps on as they were walking across the road and one of them in particular was just staring at me. Running away crossed my mind but Dennyloanhead was such a small place that I soon thought better of it. They were laying into me and telling me how dangerous it was to throw objects at passing vehicles when I started to get this warm and wet sensation in my lower half. I had peed myself. I couldn't wait to get away and I promise you I never even considered chucking a snowball at another bus.

Mind you, that didn't stop me and one of my friends conjuring up our own party piece for those leaving the pub more than just a little inebriated. We would get a piece of rope, stretch it out and one of us would be at either end. When we saw a drunk man coming we would pull it tight, and you can imagine the outcome. We thought it was hilarious, and I often wondered if we encouraged anyone to give up the booze!

In school, I wasn't big on lessons. I enjoyed having a carry-on with Alan more, but we were soon separated for giggling too much. I was more into my football and even though my primary school didn't have an organised team, we made sure we didn't miss out.

We had a thriving school team at Denny High. My science teacher, Mr McGuinness, and Mr MacFarlane, a PE teacher, encouraged me all the way. I played for them on a Saturday morning and in just about every position going; full-back, centre-half, midfield, you name it, but in the afternoon, when I was just into my teens, I played in goals for Dunipace Thistle, and got picked for Stirlingshire between the sticks, and really enjoyed it. Perhaps I should have remained in that position! Seriously though, it was a great feeling representing my Shire, whether it was in goals or outfield.

It was a couple of years beforehand that my grandfather had started taking me to see Falkirk, and I later went with my friends. Brockville was a fantastic ground to watch football at. It was compact and if you stood down at the front you were just a few feet from the players. When they leaned back to take a throw-in you really did get up close and personal. I was about ten when I went to my first game but later went with my friends and we would stand in the Hope Street end where the atmosphere was electric, and where the singing emanated from. These were great days.

When I was 11, Falkirk went on an amazing run in the Scottish Cup and even at such a young age I could sense something special was happening. I went to every game, home and away, and we eventually went on to lift the trophy when we beat Kilmarnock 2-1 in a replay at Hampden Park. I remember travelling to that game on the supporters' bus and winning the sweep thanks to big George Merchant. He scored the first goal and I netted the princely sum of 3/6, which is around 17p in today's money. Never mind a prince, I felt like a king with all that money in my pocket, and with Falkirk winning the cup, it was like a double celebration for me. The victorious team still holds a prominent place in my heart. It was Slater, Parker, Rae, Wright, Irvine, Prentice, Murray, Grierson, Merchant, Moran and O'Hara.

Alex Parker, who was a right-back, the same as me, was one of our important players that season and was simply sensational. A few years later, when I made the move south of the border, I played against Alex and took great delight in telling him that he had always been my hero. He had moved to Everton so to play against him in a Merseyside derby, albeit for the second string, was something special.

He was at my testimonial dinner with his wife and I made sure he sat at my table. It was a great night and after that we became really good friends. Sadly he took ill and ended up in Dumfries Royal Infirmary. He had to undergo an operation to remove part of his leg. It was a real tragedy, and when he died his wife asked if I would take a cord at his funeral to help lower his coffin into the ground. He lived in Gretna at the time and had the Coach & Horses pub in Carlisle, and I went down to see him a couple of times. He was a lovely man, and a great player. I can still visualise him with Everton, pinging precision passes all over the park. He was Falkirk's most capped player and no wonder. I think he won about 14 caps for Scotland.

What was great for me was that when I finally got to meet him, he was such a gentleman. It meant that all those visions I'd had growing up weren't shattered by finally meeting my hero and him turning out to be arrogant or dismissive. No such fears there, although I remember one particular occasion when I was at Dennyloanhead Primary and Rangers were due to play at Brockville. My dad was a big Rangers fan and would occasionally take me through to Ibrox, which seemed further away in those days, as there were no motorways. I loved that as well as there were often 70,000 and 80,000 at matches and the atmosphere was incredible. My favourite Rangers player was Billy Stevenson, who would go on to join Liverpool in a mammoth £20,000 deal, after his place had been taken in the Rangers team by Jim Baxter. One day, we had waited outside the Royal Hotel in Dennyloanhead for ages for the players to come out so that we could catch a glimpse of them. Out they started to filter and we approached them for an autograph. I asked Sammy Baird, a huge player with Rangers in those days, and a local guy to boot, and he told me to 'eff off'. I was only about nine at the time and was devastated. I was just thankful that it wasn't Billy Stevenson who swore at me, as that would have been such a let-down.

I had the best of both worlds at that time, getting to see my hometown team in Falkirk, and also heading through to Ibrox to watch Rangers, a club I was very fond of. In fact, I can still recall that Rangers team. It was Niven, Shearer, Caldow; Davis, McKinnon, Baxter; Henderson, McMillan, Millar, Brand and Wilson.

But your life moves on and when I turned 13, I had a decision to make. Continue to play football or watch it, and as much as I loved Falkirk, it was a no-brainer. You can't beat playing competitive football so the choice really was quite an easy one in the end.

Mr McGuinness and Mr MacFarlane had recommended me to the Stirlingshire Schools FA, and insisted I could do a good job for them at right-back. I was chosen for the trials which in itself was a real buzz, and eventually picked to play for my local county. That was a fantastic honour which made my mum and dad so proud. When you're younger you dream of playing for your favourite team, but representative football is also a great achievement.

When I was 15, a man called Sandy Brown, from Graeme High School, took Stirlingshire and he was absolutely delighted when four of his players were picked to play for Scotland. We were following in good company because big George Young, the former captain of Rangers and Scotland, had come from Stirlingshire, but we created a record for the county when four of us were chosen to represent our national team. It was a tremendous feeling and we all became close after going through the trials together.

The first international match I played was against Wales at Rugby Park and there were three coachloads of family and friends down from Denny High. We won 4-1 and the team played really well. Pulling on that Scotland strip was such a buzz, and you felt like you were representing your entire country, and not just your team-mates, family and friends. The other Stirlingshire players in the squad were William Smith, a left-back, David Cattenach, who played centre-half, and Ian Mitchell, an outside-left.

I remember my parents received a letter from the association prior to the match and one of the rules stated, 'Boys must bring pyjamas, handkerchiefs, comb, raincoat, towel and toothbrush. They must also bring properly studded boots, stockings, shin guards, white pants, a jersey and rubber shoes. These will be required for a practice and a complete strip will be provided for the match.' We were also warned that 'charging the goalkeeper wouldn't be tolerated!' There was a civic luncheon planned to take place before the match at the Co-operative Hall, in Dunlop Street, Kilmarnock.

Afterwards, a match report in a newspaper, written by Jimmy Delaney, the ex-Celtic star, read, 'Right-back Alex Totten kicked well with both feet and used the ball intelligently. For Wales, Jones was a heroic red-shirted defender, but the only Welsh forward with progressive ideas was Humphries, who faced the best Scots defender, Totten.' I was fair chuffed when I read that.

We were staying at the Broomhill Hotel, in Kilmarnock, the night before the game and I'll always remember receiving a telegram which read, 'Mr McGuinness, Mr McIntosh, Mr MacFarlane and your team-mates wish you the very best of luck in tomorrow's game.' It was a lovely touch and very much appreciated.

From there we moved on to Dens Park, Dundee, to play Ireland on a Friday night, and little was I to know that the ground would one day become my place of work, although that night we turned in a first-class performance and again won 4-1.

A contemporary report stated, 'Before the international series, only Mitchell, of the four Stirlingshire lads, had been capped. The selection of Totten, however, was no surprise. He is a talented and versatile young footballer who is equally at home in goal or at centre-half, as well as either of the full-back positions. Indeed, two years ago, he represented Stirlingshire Under-13s as a goalkeeper against Glasgow. The following season he was outstanding as a centre-half and impressed again during trial matches at Stenhousemuir and Linlithgow. Totten is an all-round athlete who has represented his school at the County Sports.' Glowing praise indeed!

The bandwagon was rolling, and I was so glad to be on it... but the big one was still to come. England were *the* team to beat and we knew that only a momentous performance would help us achieve that. The match was originally scheduled to take place at Wembley but the fixture clashed with the English FA Amateur Cup Final so it was switched to Sunderland's Roker Park. I'll never forget that day because just before the game I was standing out on the pitch looking up at my dad in the stand. The national anthem was playing and my chest had expanded a few inches and dad was the proudest man in the stadium. I wasn't too far behind, mind you, because I can only begin to describe the joy I felt at wearing the dark blue jersey.

It was a fantastic game and I was up against a lad called John Sissons, who would sign for West Ham United, but we won 3-2, after being three goals up, and when the final whistle went it was an incredible feeling – not to mention a great relief. We had just defeated England on their own soil and not only that, but had secured the Victory Shield in the process. Mr Reid took the team and when we got back into the dressing room he congratulated us all on a great performance, but said his only regret was that the match hadn't been played at Wembley, and that was our regret as well because I would love to have played there. But we had still beaten England in front of 30,000 spectators, which was a 'decent' consolation.

A match report read, 'This victory helped Scottish fans get over their Wembley headache. The way the boys fought and blended against a more powerfully built English team was a credit to the teacher-talent spotters who chose them. The result at Sunderland was a great achievement because the boys went to Roker as the "no chance team", and after taking a buffeting for five minutes, settled down to give an exhibition of football that the opposition simply couldn't counter. They outwitted their opponents with skilful teamwork and until 10 minutes from time, were leading by 3-0.' The 'Wembley heartache' the report alluded to was the infamous 9-3 game, when the English ran riot in the annual Home International match. We all felt sorry for goalkeeper Frank Haffey that afternoon.

It was 1961, and a centenary year for the association, and as part of the celebrations we played England later in the year at Tynecastle. We drew 2-2, which meant they hadn't managed to beat us that year. I played in all four international games, as did Bobby Watson, later of Motherwell and Rangers, who was our captain. Another team-mate, Denis Setterington, also went to Ibrox so it was a really exciting time for us all.

I'll never forget being called up to the stage at the annual Denny High School awards ceremony and being handed my Scotland Schoolboys' cap by the headmaster. It was a fantastic moment and one that I lapped up every second of. Once again, my proud parents were there to support me.

Because we were such a successful team, there was always a posse of scouts at our games, and I was asked down to Manchester United. The moment I was told that United wanted to see me was incredible. Suddenly, the reality kicked in. Young Totten might just have a future in this game after all. What was it I'd told the headmaster?

Manchester United weren't offering a trial, as such, because the scouts had given a detailed report on each of the players. They wanted to sign me. I remember flying down from the old Renfrew Airport with my mum and dad, who had never been on an aeroplane before, and the first thing you see as you're taking off is a big cemetery, and we all sort of gasped. When we got to Manchester we were well looked after by a guy called Jimmy

Murphy, Sir Matt Busby's trusted assistant. He took us to Old Trafford, and said, 'There is someone I want you to meet.' We walked round the corner and there was Bobby Charlton, probably one of the greatest players in the world at that time. I was only 15 and was totally in awe of this guy. He was by himself and was standing there rattling a ball off this wall, right foot, then left foot etc. It really was a case of practice makes perfect. He stopped though when I asked for his autograph, which he signed on Manchester United headed notepaper. He was the perfect gent – and I still have that autograph to this day.

But it wasn't just United who were keen on me. I had a few clubs, and next stop on the 'Totten Roadshow' was Birmingham City, and then Middlesbrough, and I visited these clubs with my dad. Middlesbrough wanted to sign me there and then, and I was told Arsenal were also keen, but next up was Liverpool, and as I was to meet the legendary Bill Shankly, I thought it might be wise to hold off from signing a contract at Ayresome Park – and I'm so glad that I did.

Meeting 'Shanks' was an incredible experience. As soon as my dad and I arrived at the front reception at Anfield we were ushered in to see Mr Shankly. He was a real character. He stood out straight away, and just like Jock Wallace, he had an aura about him. He must have made an instant impression on me because I chose a Second Division side over top-flight clubs such as Manchester United. He had so much enthusiasm and sold the club to my dad and I in an instant. He would say, 'This is a special club and we are going places,' and of course he was 100 per cent right. When he went to Liverpool, the likes of Bob Paisley and Joe Fagan were already there. He didn't take his own people, like David Moyes did when he took over at Manchester United, he slipped into the way of working they had at Anfield and continued that great continuity they already had at the club, and that would be the way of it for many years to come.

I was so impressed by him and the whole set-up at Liverpool, and they wanted to sign me on the spot. He showed me around and took time out with me to explain all about the club, and when he mentioned signing me, my head was all over the place. Suddenly the offer from Middlesbrough – and other clubs – was pushed to the back of my mind, but I asked for time to think about it and my dad and I headed back up the road to Dennyloanhead.

I spoke to dad at length about all my options. There were no agents or advisors in those days, so my dad's was the only opinion I really valued. He guided me not only in every aspect of my career, but also in my life. We spoke about Arsenal and Manchester United being in the top division and United's manager, Sir Matt Busby, who was also a living legend. They had some fantastic players at the time so it was a really tough decision, but Shankly had impressed me. There was something about him that attracted me almost instantly and I had more or less made my mind up. While my dad had a say in the matter, he made it clear that ultimately the decision was mine, as I was the one that would be tasked with making it happen.

But it was such an exciting time because we regularly had scouts at the door wanting to sign me or asking me to come and take a look at the facilities of the club they were representing. It was that feeling of being wanted, which was fantastic, that I'm sure played a part in me realising that all I wanted to be was a professional footballer. When that level of interest is shown in you, then you start to realise that you must have something to offer.

While mum and dad and I were down at Old Trafford, we were given a tour of the ground, and even then it had the most fantastic facilities. After that we were taken to the cricket, and then off to the pictures to see *Guns of Navarone*, which has stayed with me to this day. It was all part of the buzz and I'll never forget it.

But I had made my decision and went back down to Liverpool a couple of weeks later and put pen to paper, which was an incredible moment in my young life. I went down myself this time and remember leaving Central Station, in Glasgow, and being waved off by my parents and a lot of family and friends. That was probably when the enormity of the whole situation kicked in; when I realised that all my family had travelled through to Glasgow to see me off, I knew it must be something big.

At that time, Dundee and Falkirk were also interested in me, which was fantastic, and to sign for the Bairns would also have been a great honour, but they wanted to give me a job as a draughtsman at a company called Alexander's. They wanted me to stay part-time and turn pro when I was 21, but I wanted it straight away. My only ambition at that time was to be a professional footballer. I couldn't wait, so Falkirk's offer was a non-starter. Looking back, I reckon I made the right decision. I wouldn't change anything about my career. I've been very fortunate with what I've done, who I've met and the places I've been. But I had just agreed to sign for Liverpool, and it was game on.

2

Bill Shankly Calling

THE train pulled into Liverpool Lime Street station and the hairs on the back of my neck stood to attention. For goodness sake, it was only a train station, although not just any old one. I had a couple of pieces of luggage, which I collected from the overhead rack, and made my way on to the platform. Excited and apprehensive, I was looking out for a club employee called Tom Bush.

I felt like a VIP. Nowadays, you go on holiday abroad and there is a line of people at your destination, holding up cards with names on them. This day, there was only one, and it said 'Alex Totten: Liverpool FC'. How good was that?

It was just such a buzz being at a club like Liverpool and from day one I lapped up every single moment. From the second I was met at the station by Tom, following that four-hour journey from Glasgow, during which I thought about nothing else other than being a Liverpool player, to the day I left, I drank in everything.

Tom took me straight from the station to Anfield – a journey of less than three miles – and when the car pulled up at the front door, the enormity of the task lying in front of me started to sink in. I might have been a Liverpool player, but the hard work started here. No one, but no one, waltzed into the Liverpool first team, or probably the second team, for that matter. It wouldn't be easy, but I was a determined kid.

When I walked into the stadium, there weren't many players about – they were all in Czechoslovakia for a challenge match. One man was there, though, and he was the most important. Bill Shankly didn't go to Eastern Europe. He had stayed at home in an effort to sign a number of promising young Scots, but just as negotiations were going well, the International Board barred all English clubs from signing boys from Scotland as apprentice professionals. I was only 15 so I signed as an amateur and went straight into Liverpool's third team, which played in the open-age Lancashire League competition, so you could say it was a real baptism of fire playing against guys my dad's age!

One of the most memorable games I played in for Liverpool was against a very strong Manchester United side at Anfield in the Central League – which was the equivalent of our reserve league. We won 5-2 and the likes of Harry Gregg, David Sadler and Noel Cantwell played for United that day. It might have been a reserve league fixture but it was my cup final, and I was joined in the Liverpool side by Tommy Smith and Chris Lawler, who would go on to become legends at the club.

My 17th birthday was something else. I was called into the office by Mr Shankly and handed a piece of paper and a pen. 'There you go son, it's your first professional contract with Liverpool FC,' he said. That was some moment, but a day or two later, while I was taking part in a training session with the first team, one of our goalkeepers got injured. They were looking for volunteers to nip between the sticks and I stuck my hand up. I pulled off some fantastic saves, and Ian St John came up to me afterwards and said, 'You never told me you were a goalkeeper, you kept that one quiet.' But I had quite a bit of experience of playing in goals, although when I'd played there for the likes of my school or juvenile team, I didn't have guys like the Saint firing in shots at me from all angles, so I enjoyed the compliment.

My first day at Anfield might have been more than 50 years ago but it is still fresh in my mind. Tom took me into the ground and told the receptionist I was meeting Mr Shankly. He came down to the front door with a big smile on his face and I felt like I was greeting my long-lost uncle. I felt so at home. I was shown around the ground and had a chat with Mr Shankly.

Then it was time to see where I would be staying, but I didn't have too far to travel. My digs were just a long throw-in from the Anfield ground – no more than 100 yards, 258 Anfield Road, to be more precise – and I will never forget that address. The landlady was a Mrs Murphy, and there were another three lads in the digs with me, and the good thing was that they had been there the previous season as well, so they had a year's experience and showed me the ropes. They kept me right, and while that was a massive help, that first night in a warm, but strange house will live with me until my dying day.

I started to unpack my case, and as I took each item out, the tears began streaming down my face. I was only 15 and I was really missing home, and my mum and dad. I thought to myself, 'What am I doing here?' But it must also have been equally as tough for them because I was an only child and suddenly my room was empty. I'm sure it left a big hole in their lives at that point. I can say hand on heart, though, that never once did I consider throwing in the towel.

I immediately sat down and wrote to my parents. The letter, which I still have, read, 'Dear Mum and Dad (and Judy), Just a short note to tell you how I am doing. Arrived safely at Lime Street Station at 6.30, and had about two hours sleep on the train. I went to Mrs Murphy's, had breakfast and then went for a walk. At 10 o'clock we went to the ground. I saw Mr Shankly and received my train fare. I met Ian St John and Bert Slater. I am staying at Mrs Murphy's just now, and it may even be a permanent address for me. I will write again on Thursday and mum, can you remember to post the photographs. I am missing you both very, very much. Your loving son, Alex.'

It was really tough at first but my three flat-mates – who were all Scottish – made me very welcome, which was a big help. They were Phil Tinney, who would sign for Dundee at the same time as me; George Scott, who went on to Aberdeen, and a lad called Hamish McKenzie, who came from Cambusbarron, which wasn't too far from Dennyloanhead. I'm still friendly with Phil and George and we go to the occasional match at Anfield together. They both married Liverpool girls so I go down and see them now and again.

But they really helped me settle in to Liverpool life and knew all the local youth clubs and where else to go and what to do. Ian St John signed in the June, 1961, I signed in July and Ron Yeats joined in the August, but they were both first-team players. I was only a kid at the time. The great thing about Shanks was that he treated everyone exactly the same. No matter whether you were a young kid or an experienced guy, he would speak to you just the same.

The youth players would go up to Anfield first thing in the morning and get all the gear ready for the first-team players before travelling by bus to our training ground at Melwood. It was a 25-minute journey and you could sit beside anyone, which was a great feeling. Bobby Graham, who would go on to find fame at Motherwell, was also on the ground staff.

I always remember lifting the *Liverpool Echo* one day and it said 'Shankly signs Billy Stevenson for £20,000'. I couldn't wait to go in the next morning to speak to him. When I watched him at Rangers I thought he was a tremendous player, but he had lost his place to Baxter. I spoke to him not long after he joined and he was as good a guy as he was a player. He was another player who had a terrific range of passing.

At that time, Liverpool were in the Second Division. Shanks had taken over two years previous and had been re-building the team. The season I joined Liverpool they won the league and that was them back up and in amongst the elite. It was a great time to be at the club because you could just sense that it was the beginning of something really special. But it wasn't just the football club where things were happening, but the city itself. This incredible music scene was just taking off and a few of us were regular visitors to the Cavern Club, which was, and still is I believe, one of the most important music venues in the country. I managed to see The Beatles there a few times, but also remember watching The Swinging Blue Jeans and comedians such as Jimmy Tarbuck. Cilla Black, then Cilla White, was another artist we liked. So, between the music scene and the rise of the football club, Liverpool was really emerging and people were beginning to sit up and take notice. It was a great place to be and I'm just delighted that I was a small part of it.

After training at Melwood in the morning, we would always finish with a five-a-side match, with the management against the ground staff. The management side usually included the likes of Shankly, Paisley, Fagan and Reuben Bennett. It was amazing even to be playing against club legends like that. We would have a cup of tea before making our way back to Anfield, where we would unload all the kit into the stadium, and get the training gear into the laundry. We would have our lunch and then it was time for our chores, which included hand-cleaning all the boots.

I used to clean Ian St John's boots before scrubbing the baths and showers. If we had a home game on a Saturday we would get to work on cleaning the stands and terracing – especially the famous Spion Kop – and the amount of money we found was unbelievable. Sometimes we could double our wages just by getting out on to the terracing with a brush in our hand. That was our job on a Monday afternoon, while the first-team players were away home, or off for a game of snooker. Nowadays, a lot of teams are back in for afternoon training sessions but Shankly didn't believe in that. Take Ian Callaghan for example, Shankly reckoned that players such as Callaghan would never have clocked up more than 800 games had they been asked to put in double sessions every day.

But to be working with a manager such as Shanks, and be with a team of that stature, was a great education and one that stood me in good stead for the rest of my career. Shanks was a fantastic manager and always had a word of encouragement for the lads on the ground staff. Everyone was an equal in his eyes, and he gained enormous respect for that.

There was a young lad called John Bennett and he was always immaculate. His boots were the shiniest I had ever seen in my life – you could comb your hair in them. Shanks came up to him one day and said, 'I like your boots son, where do you keep them, on the mantelpiece!' He was great with the one-liners.

I really enjoyed the early days at Anfield and while my flat-mates were fantastic, I did miss home an awful lot, especially in the early days. Twice a week I would sit down and write letters to mum and dad and tell them everything I was getting up to – well most things – and that was my way of making sure I kept in touch. Telephones weren't readily available then so writing was the best option.

I've got two grandsons now – one is 15 and the other is 11 – and I can't imagine them leaving home. When I think about it, Alexander is the same age I was when I headed down to Merseyside. It doesn't bear thinking about, he's just a pup, so it hits home how young I actually was. The plus side, however, is that leaving home at that age broadens your outlook on life and you soon learn to look after yourself – you've no alternative. Naturally you take a few knocks along the way but ultimately it was a great experience and one that I'm so glad I was given the opportunity to live.

Mrs Murphy was a great landlady. She had three bedrooms and really looked after us but she was getting on, and after a year, we went to stay with another lady, a Mrs Carroll, who was originally from Tarbolton, in Ayrshire, and she was also such a lovely person. Mrs Carroll's house was also close to the ground. It was a pre-requisite because none of the younger lads had cars in those days so we had to make sure we were handy for our 'work'. We were also close to a youth club and we quickly made friends with a lot of the local lads. They accepted us readily, which meant we had something to do at nights. Mind you, on one occasion we visited the Blackpool Pleasure Beach, and one of the local lads brought a bottle of rum, and a number of us had a few 'swigs'. I then decided to have a go on the big dipper – which wasn't the best idea I'd ever had. I'll leave you to imagine the outcome! When you're young you're a bit harum-scarum but I quickly learned my lesson. It was definitely a one-off.

In the afternoons, we would go to the bookies and put on a bet. As the youngest in the group, I followed the others a bit. One afternoon I decided that I liked the look of a particular horse and I put £5 on it to win. The others just stood there in astonishment because they would never have dreamt of putting almost half their wages on a single bet. Anyway, the horse came in second and I lost my money. I had to borrow £5 off my landlady and promise her that I wouldn't do anything so stupid again, and I was true to my word. It was a harsh lesson but I never put another bet on in my life.

I was on £13 a week at the time so I soon learned the value of money. At the time, the club set up an account for us with Barclays Bank. It was my first account and having all this money in the bank was alien to me so you can imagine what it was like. I used to make regular withdrawals simply because I liked the feeling of having money in my pocket. The bookies was out but there were plenty of other ways to spend your money in 1960s Liverpool. One day I got the shock of my life, though. I went in to the bank to make a withdrawal and the girl at the counter told me that the manager wanted a word. I walked into his office and he said he was concerned about my pattern of withdrawals. I didn't realise the club had organised an overdraft facility and I was in the red. But that was another good lesson in money management and I soon got the hang of managing my finances a bit better. I also used to send money up the road to my mum so I had to make sure that I wasn't spending it on silly things, just for the sake of it.

I have remained friends with a lot of the guys I was on the ground staff with and met up with one of them, Gordon Wallace, at a recent Liverpool game. I'll always remember watching him make a piece of history when he became the first player to score a goal on *Match of the Day*, when Liverpool beat Arsenal 3-2. He was also the first guy to score in Europe for Liverpool. When we met up, we went out for a few beers after the game and paid a visit to the Cavern, which, as you can imagine, brought back an awful lot of memories. It's nice to keep in touch with players that you were with all those years ago. I remember I was part of the Liverpool side heading to Newcastle for an FA Youth Cup tie. We all met at Liverpool Lime Street and Shanks was there to wave us off. He didn't come with us, but I still thought it was great that he showed such an interest. I'm sure Gordon didn't feel the same way that day. He was out injured and just as he was hobbling on the train, Shanks said to him, 'You've been out injured so long that you've had that walking stick soled and heeled twice!'

We used to go to a venue in Liverpool called the Royal Tiger Club, and the Everton boys, including Alex Scott, also went there. It was a favourite haunt of the likes of Ian St John and while I wasn't a first-team player at Liverpool you were always welcome – and made to feel like one of the boys – as there was no demarcation on nights out. Everyone used to mix well. I remember seeing Billy Fury there and it was another fantastic club.

But the Cavern was obviously the focal point for the music scene in Liverpool at the time and it really was as cool as everyone made it out to be. It was definitely a special place in the Sixties and we would be there when the likes of Tarbuck, who was great pals with St John, was playing. I'll always remember taking my mum and dad, on one of their visits to the city, to see Ken Dodd, who was a massive star at the time. Footballers and showbiz celebrities mixed well then.

On one of my many trips to the Cavern, we were sitting watching The Beatles when they suddenly stopped playing and Paul McCartney shouted out, 'What time is it?' I shouted back the time and he said, 'Cheers fella!' We then went back to our digs and were listening to Radio Luxembourg and who was playing but The Beatles. I said to one of the lads, 'That's the group we just watched, imagine them being on the radio!' The rest, as they say, is history. We watched The Beatles play loads of times because they had a residency in there at one point and were very popular. It wasn't a bad way to spend the rest of your weekend after playing on a Saturday afternoon.

There was a really healthy contingent of Scots down at Liverpool, and Everton, at that time but we didn't tend to stick together. Everyone mixed well and I still see some of the lads I was on the ground staff with to this day. In fact, a few of us took driving lessons at the same time and one of the lads, George Scott, had the same instructor as me. I remember going out for a lesson one day and the instructor said, 'Oh, thank god it's you today and not Scotty. He took his test with me yesterday and I said to him, "Turn right here, Mr Scott," but he went straight on. I said, "I told you to turn right there," and he said, "Oh, I thought you said I was doing all right!"'

When I went for my test I made sure I had my Liverpool blazer on, but suddenly thought, 'I hope he's not an Everton supporter.' It was 1964 and I passed first time, so he must have been from the red half of the city. I was chuffed to bits and when I came home I got my first car – a Morris 1100. At the time it gave me more freedom because we only got up the road from Liverpool twice a year, which wasn't an awful lot. When the season finished, and the first-team players were all off on their holidays, the ground staff lads were still hard at work. We had to stay behind and give the stadium a fresh lick of paint. We painted walls, turnstiles, crush barriers, the lot. We were later getting up the road but still got a decent break in the summer and again at Christmas, so it wasn't too bad.

Before I could drive, I used to travel back up the road with a player called Tommy Leishman, who had won the Scottish Cup with St Mirren in 1959. He was our left-sided midfielder before Billy Stevenson arrived. He had a car and would take us up the road at Christmas. In fact, he lived in a house owned by the club in Liverpool and used to invite us down there now and again. He was a great guy and was driving an oil tanker up until recently from the works in Grangemouth, but he's retired now.

Shankly's star was rising when I went to Liverpool. He had previously managed at Carlisle and Huddersfield and arrived at Anfield in 1959. His remit was simple. He was brought to the club to ensure they got to the First Division. He was making a name for himself and when he got promotion in season 1961/62 he had no intention of letting it go. As he said himself, when he signed Ian St John and Ron Yeats, the club started going places. I recall him saying that he went to a board meeting and told the directors that he wanted to sign the two players. One director said to him, 'We can't afford to sign them', while another answered, 'We can't afford not to', and he got his way. I remember my dad taking me to Ibrox for a Rangers v Motherwell match and St John was different class. You could tell instantly that he was going to be a star. I'm sure Motherwell won 5-2 that night. They had a great team at the time but St John was the star, he was a wonderful player. He has to be one of the best centre-forwards of his generation. He wasn't the tallest but he was still brilliant in the air. His timing was superb and he would flick balls on for the likes of Roger Hunt, who was the perfect foil at Liverpool, and played in England's 1966 World Cup team. Being involved with guys like that at training was a wonderful experience and a great education.

Shankly was the type of man you would run through a brick wall for. He knew the game inside out and he had the knack of making every single player at the club feel a part of what he was trying to achieve. He also had a tremendous sense of humour, and I remember St John telling the story of when he first arrived at the club, and Shanks was showing him round Anfield. It was June and St John took one look at the bare. Anfield playing surface and said, 'Mr Shankly, there isn't a blade of grass on the ground,' to which Shankly replied, 'I brought you here to play football on the pitch, not graze on it.'

Tommy Smith was a real legend at Liverpool and played more than 500 games for the club, but he and I were on the ground staff together. We were the same age, and Shankly liked to take us away with the first team now and again. I remember Tommy and I went to see the team play at Highbury against Arsenal. It was 0-0 and this ball was played through the centre of our defence. Big Ron Yeats was just about to clear it when he got a shout to leave it from the keeper, Tommy Lawrence, but the ball went through his legs and into the net. As ground staff boys, we were down smartish after the game to get the towels out for the players, and there was Shanks waiting on Tommy to come into the dressing room. The big keeper came in first and looked really down in the dumps. He said to Shanks, 'I'm so sorry boss, I've let you, my team-mates, and everyone at the club down. I should never have opened my legs.' Quick as a flash, Shankly said, 'Tommy son, I don't blame you for opening your legs, I blame your mother for opening hers!'

I remember we were going to Iceland for a match and flew from Liverpool to Prestwick, where we were due to pick up a connecting flight to Reykjavik. We had five hours before the next flight so Shanks decided to take us all to Butlin's in Ayr to relax for a few hours by playing table tennis and snooker. We got off the bus outside the holiday camp and this big commissionaire opened the door and said, 'Welcome gentlemen.' Shanks said, 'Hello there, we are Liverpool, champions of England, and we're on our way to Iceland,' and the big guy said, 'Well, you're way off course, you need to go up to the top of the street...' It was hilarious and Shanks, who had a tremendous sense of humour, burst out laughing.

I remember he signed Tony Hateley, dad of the former Rangers player Mark, and paid £100,000 for him, which was a hell of a lot of money in those days. Anyway, after a month, Shanks dropped him, and big Tony walked into his office and said, 'Why am I not playing boss?' Shankly said, 'Why aren't you playing? You can't kick with your left foot, or your right foot, you can't trap a ball, need I go on?' And Tony said, 'But I'm good in the air boss,' to which Shanks replied, 'Douglas Bader, the World War II pilot, was good in the air but that wouldn't have guaranteed him a game here either son!'

Shankly was great. He was hard but very fair, an exceptional manager who proved he was one of the best of all time. He was the man that started Liverpool off and they managed to keep that success going for a few generations. He knew how to construct a team. He would start with the spine, by signing a strong goalkeeper, then a centre-half, midfielder and centre-forward. It sounds basic but all a manager can really do is sign good players and do his best to mould them into a team. Once the players go out on to the park there isn't much more the manager can do.

I speak to a lot of other managers and we all agree that on the gaffer's office door it should say 'mother, father, psychiatrist, psychologist etc' because you have to be all of these things and more as a manager. Players all have different natures and characters and you need to have a number of hats on to get the best out of them.

I was at Liverpool for three years and it was really difficult to break into the first team. You could be on the fringes for ages but if the guy in your position was doing his job, and he managed to steer clear of injury and suspension, then it was tough to get that jersey. Not only did Liverpool like continuity behind the scenes, they liked it on the park as well. The standing joke at Anfield was, 'What's the team today Mr Shankly?' He would say, 'Same as last year.' The team was winning and he was never going to change it.

When I first arrived at Liverpool, I played a lot of youth team games and 'A and B' league games as they were known. Then I progressed into the reserve team, which played in the Central League. The first team more or less picked itself but I was always ready to make the step up. Gerry Byrne was the right-back at the time, and he was playing with England, which severely handicapped my chances of getting first-team football. Gerry was a good player; steady as a rock, but I learned a lot from him because we trained together.

Talking about training, Shankly scrapped nets for a period at Melwood and replaced them with boards. He wanted high-intensity sessions. When the ball hit the net, it died. When it hit the board it came straight back out and the game re-started right away. Training under Shanks was really tough but we always felt incredibly fit.

When I signed for Liverpool I was under no illusions that I was going to be a first-team player. I had played for Scottish Schools and while I knew that I wouldn't walk straight into the team, I was a single-minded and determined individual and I was getting into that first team. That's why it was such a disappointment that I didn't manage to achieve that.

While I was at Anfield, John F. Kennedy was assassinated in Dallas, Texas. It was 1963 and I remember the players all talking about it in training. When I went home later that day, I was outside my digs and people were saying that it was a Russian that had shot him, and that there was going to be another world war. Years later, when I was sacked at St Johnstone, a supporter wrote in to the local paper and said, 'What do John F. Kennedy, John Lennon and Alex Totten have in common? I always remember where I was when I heard the tragic news!'

There was a time when I felt that Bob Paisley was never off my back in training and one day I pulled him up about it. I said to him, 'Why are you always getting on at me?' He replied, 'The day I stop getting on at you is the day you start worrying, because then I'm no longer interested in you.' I was delighted at that because it meant I was still in his plans, and it's a saying that I used with players during my own management career. All the coaches at Liverpool knew the game inside out and while Paisley was Shankly's right-hand man for first-team games, Joe Fagan took the reserves, but they would have regular meetings to update one another on the progress of all the players. The entire backroom team – including Shankly, Paisley and Fagan – were all good men and very fair. They earned their respect. They might have demanded discipline, but respect was a different animal.

From time to time I would knock the manager's door and ask if there was any hope of me getting into the first team. Shankly would sit you down and explain that the team was winning and playing well and that there was no way he could disrupt that. One day, though, he called me into his office and said the words that every young player fears. 'I'm going to release you, son.' He then added,

'It's not because you're a bad player but because your opportunities will be limited here. It would be better for your career to go and get a regular game elsewhere, because you're certainly good enough.' He handled it very well, but it was still a massive blow.

I would love to have made an impression at Liverpool, and play for the top team. As far as I was concerned, there was a big difference between the game down south and up here in Scotland. I think the game in England was a lot quicker and eventually, any good Scottish players, such as Alan Gilzean and Ian St John, would head to England to make their fortune. But I had a decision to make, and it looked certain that I would be heading in the opposite direction, from England to Scotland. For the first time in three years, I was without a club, although that wouldn't be the case for too long, not with a club like Liverpool on my CV.

3

Life After Liverpool

AS much as I'd enjoyed my time at Liverpool, it was in the past and I had to take everything I'd learned at Anfield and use it as a positive to find another club and make something of myself in the game. It was a cut-throat business and there were usually more players than team places, so I had to make myself stand out from the crowd. That wasn't too difficult when I arrived at Central Station, in Glasgow, after leaving Liverpool for the final time. There was no family fanfare, which was fantastic, but it couldn't have been any different from the fuss that had accompanied my departure to Liverpool three years previous. All the family had been there to wave me off and all that was missing were the flags and whistles. This time, though, it was just me and my mum. I remember stepping off the train and seeing mum with a big smile on her face. She was glad to see me. Sadly, though, the first emotion I felt was that I had let everyone down, and it wasn't a great feeling. I know she didn't see me as a failure, in fact she was probably just delighted to get me back up the road, but that didn't stop me feeling as though I had underachieved.

But thankfully there was little time for wallowing in self-pity as the phone started to ring. Eddie Turnbull, the Aberdeen manager, invited me up to Pittodrie for a chat. Aberdeen had finished mid-table in the First Division but had qualified for the final of the newly-installed Summer Cup, and Turnbull – a member of Hibs' legendary 'Famous Five' – was an ambitious man. He was keen on making me a Don, and it was a tempting offer.

I was also invited along to Dens Park, to meet Bill Shankly's brother Bob, who was manager of Dundee – and I'm glad I took up the offer. I had a good feeling about Dundee, and they had just been involved in a Scottish Cup Final with Rangers, which they lost, although it had been only two years since they won the Scottish First Division. I recall reading the papers the week before that cup final and being impressed by Bob Shankly's battle cry. Rangers had won the league, and would therefore qualify automatically for the European Cup, so Dundee were guaranteed a place in the Cup Winners' Cup, win or lose at Hampden, but Shankly was having none of it and was quick to dispel the myths that his side would be happy just to enjoy the big occasion safe in the knowledge that they were back in Europe.

I had a decision to make but I plumped for the Dark Blues, and moved into digs in the city, with a Mrs Couttie, in Elm Street. I enjoyed training and played three or four games in the reserves before being called up to the first team.

Bob and Bill Shankly were complete opposites. Bob, the elder brother, was an introvert, and a lot quieter, but knew the game inside out, no question about that. He was a former Falkirk player and had impressed me, just like his brother had, when we initially held talks about a possible move to Dens Park. The Shankly brothers were always on the phone to one another so when I was leaving Liverpool, I'm sure Bill tipped off his brother about me and had a hand in my move. One of Bob's greatest qualities was an ability to simplify what he was telling you. Nothing was complicated. During half-time of one game, the players were saying, 'We should play the ball inside the full-back more, because he's quite slow, and let Andy Penman run on to it,' and Shankly said, 'Don't complicate things,' which we all found quite amusing.

But while I had a feeling that I was going to enjoy my time in the Jute City, I couldn't have guessed just how incredible it would be. I made my first-team debut, along with keeper Ally Donaldson and Jocky Scott, against Motherwell on the Wednesday night and we beat them 6-0. It was an amazing start, but just 72 hours later we had Rangers at home. The *Dundee Courier* ran a feature that day on the young and the old. Willie Henderson and I were the young players, while the 'old' guys were Bobby Shearer and Alan Cousin. It set us up nicely for the game, but I'll always remember the great Jim Baxter coming into our dressing room before kick-off and saying to his Scotland colleague, and our captain, Alex Hamilton, 'Right, Hammy, 50 quid says we beat you.' Hammy refused to take him on, but I think the offer of a bet was then thrown open to the rest of us, although we all gave it a body swerve – not that we could afford to part with 50 quid anyway.

It was an incredible game and afterwards Hammy was perhaps just a little annoyed that he hadn't taken up Baxter's offer because we thumped Rangers 4-1 and played really well. Just short of 30,000 packed into Dens Park and witnessed a cracker of a game. Hugh Robertson scored a couple and while Jim Forrest had given Rangers the lead after just five minutes, it was merely a consolation. We were fantastic and felt we couldn't fail with the backing we received from the home fans inside Dens. It was like a cup final and every touch of the ball by a home player was greeted with a huge roar. It was something I hadn't experienced, as I had been playing for the second team at Liverpool. Mind you, Rangers showed how angry they were at the defeat by going out and scoring nine against Airdrie the following Saturday. They had some fantastic players at that time, including John Greig, Jimmy Millar and Davie Wilson – but we had a few good ones of our own.

We were up against Dundee United at Tannadice in our next match and it was another cracker. It was my first experience of the Tayside derby and I loved it. Of course, it helped that we beat them by three clear goals. The fans were ecstatic and so was I – especially after reading in a newspaper the following day, 'Dundee's merited win was in no small way due to the great defensive trio of Hamilton, Ryden and Totten.' That was nice to read. I had taken over from the great Bobby Cox, and while he would re-claim his place in the team later on, I was certainly enjoying myself. Shankly had wanted to shake things up a bit and it definitely worked. I was just delighted to get into the team and play my part, and so early in my Dundee career as well.

I loved life at Dundee and it wasn't long before I was thinking, 'This is why I came into football in the first place.' Regular first-team football was all I had ever dreamed of. While Liverpool was great, and it was a massive club, there was nothing to beat the feeling of running out that tunnel on a Saturday afternoon and playing in front of big crowds. I loved the buzz, the pressure, everything about it. It was exactly what I'd craved as a youngster.

After the match against United, a few of us went out for a couple of drinks and I was still on a high when I arrived back at my digs. I remember lying there, reading the evening sports paper and seeing the results on the front page. Dundee United 1 Dundee 4. A great result. I always looked for Liverpool's results as well, as my time there had fostered what would become a lifelong love of the club. They had lost at Sheffield Wednesday that day, and for a few moments I allowed my thoughts to drift back to my final few days at the club.

I loved Bill Shankly. He was a fantastic manager and a great man, and even though he had released me, it was something I never took personally. In the days leading up to my departure he had taken me into the office and said, 'Alex, we have the likes of Gerry Byrne and Bobby Thompson in front of you and reserve team football is no good for you at this stage of your career.' I was 18 years old and had been at Liverpool three years so I knew myself it was time to move on and challenge for a first-team position.

The move to Dundee was perfect for a number of reasons. First and foremost, I was enjoying my football, and playing in the first team, but I would also get down the road for the rest of the weekend after a match. It was only an hour and a half from Dundee to Dennyloanhead and I was almost home in time for tea! My time at Liverpool was a great learning process and just part of football, where more players don't make it than do, but there was a slight regret that I was in the first category and not the latter.

But I had moved to another big club and Dundee had won the league in 1962, beating the likes of Rangers and Celtic to the title. When I went there, just two years later, they were still a top team, and had players such as Alan Gilzean – definitely the best player I ever played with, both on the ground and in the air – although he eventually moved on to Tottenham Hotspur. He was such a massive player for Dundee, but he was also a really nice guy, and I would go up to his house in Coupar Angus a lot. We got on really well and he would try and help with aspects of my game. One of his best qualities was his never-ending supply of encouragement, which was music to the ears of young players like me. 'Gilly' and Hammy more or less ran the dressing room, and both played for Scotland at the time so they were the top boys. Hammy was also great and he would say, 'Do you fancy having a kick-about with my WB, sorry, my "Wembley Ball" or would you rather we played with my HB, my "Hampden Ball"?' He was a great laugh and a right good character and one of the main reasons we had a great dressing room at Dundee.

I just seemed to click with the two of them. Gilly was a wonderful player and proved that not only with Dundee but at Spurs as well, where he formed a lethal partnership with the great Jimmy Greaves. Hammy would come and collect me at my digs and we would go up to Montrose to see bands such as Herman's Hermits. We would also stay behind after training and practise lots of drills, such as passing, control, chipping it etc. He was a right-back and used to talk to his wingers all the time. He was great friends with the Rangers winger Davie Wilson and they played for Scotland together, but when they played against each other the banter was incredible. I remember one time he played the perfect ball down the wing to Andy Penman and turned round to the bench and said, 'Look at that, slack laces as well.'

I had run-of-the-mill Puma boots but Hammy always had the latest Adidas footwear and they were unbelievable. They were just coming on to the market. He always had the best.

The club usually supplied the boots at that time and there was a pecking order but as Hammy played for Scotland, his boots were sponsored by Adidas, and thankfully we took the same size, so he used to give me his old ones – which were still in great nick – and they were that comfortable you felt you were playing in your slippers.

He looked after me well. He had a white Jaguar and gave me a loan of it now and again. Jessie worked in a laboratory at Carrongrove Paper Mill and one time I went to pick her up in the Jaguar and I was sitting there like the Prince of Sheba. The folk coming out of work were just staring at it. There weren't many top-of-the-range Jags in Denny in those days. Hammy helped me a great deal in my career and we became really good friends. At that time, Dundee were a massive club and their top stars were known throughout the country.

We had a big boy named George Stewart, who was only 17, and I felt for him one day at training when he was violently sick after a running session. He was vomiting everywhere and Shankly shouted at him, 'Were you drinking last night?' and the lad said, 'Yes boss, I was, sorry.' 'What were you drinking?' asked the manager. 'black 'n tan,' said George. 'What the hell is a Black 'n tan?' shouted Shankly, because like his brother he was a teetotaller, so he didn't have a clue about alcohol.

By the turn of the year, Dundee were sitting mid-table in the Scottish First Division, while our neighbours United were deep in relegation trouble. For me, though, it was bittersweet, because Bobby Cox was back in the team, which meant I was surplus to requirements and languishing in the reserves – and that's not where any player wants to be.

In the February, we lost at Clyde, but bounced back to score seven at Tynecastle. It was an astonishing result, with Andy Penman scoring a hat-trick – and it kept our noses in front of our city neighbours, who had strung a few good results together and were starting to climb the table.

The following month we played Dunfermline at East End Park. The match finished 3-3 and Alex Ferguson scored for the Pars. Bobby Cox was sent off but our guys were furious after the match when it came out that the referee, Arthur Kidd, had allegedly been telling the Dunfermline players that Rangers were two goals down at Ibrox, thus spurring them on to try even harder in the second half, as both clubs were battling it out for a European place.

We were then involved in a crazy match at Firhill, where we scored FOUR times in the first 12 minutes against Partick Thistle – and could only draw 4-4. Keeping clean sheets was a real problem and we were losing an average of two goals per game.

The season ended with the Summer Cup, a sectional competition, but it wasn't a big success for either me, personally, or the club. Bobby Cox was temporarily out of the game because he had refused to pay a £50 fine imposed after a sending-off earlier in the season but the gaffer chose to replace him with someone else, so it was an inauspicious ending to a spell in my career that had started so gloriously – but I had known it was coming to an end.

Bob Shankly had moved on to manage Hibs and Bobby Ancell came in from Motherwell to take over the hot seat at Dens. His arrival didn't impact on me, though, because the telephone rang at home one night, and I was on the move – again!

4

The Par-fect Move

I HAD been at Dundee for a year, a mixture of enjoyable and frustrating times, when Willie Cunningham called one night. My prospects of regular first-team football at Dens Park were grim, and I knew it was time to leave. Willie wanted to take Hugh Robertson and I to Dunfermline and we were soon on our way to East End Park to sign a contract.

It was to prove the perfect move and I had a fantastic time at a fantastic club – with the 1960s being particularly good to Dunfermline, as they reached three Scottish Cup finals in that decade. Some of the crowds turning up at East End Park were incredible, and there were regular attendances of 20,000 on the Halbeath Road. Alex Ferguson was already at the club when I went there and I would later play with him at Falkirk as well. He was a smashing player and always aware of the best route to goal. He scored the biggest majority of his goals inside the 18-yard box and had a happy knack of being in the right place at exactly the right time.

On one occasion, though, we went down to Rugby Park for a Scottish Cup tie and Fergie had grabbed a double to put us two up. I was up against wee Tommy McLean and unfortunately he inspired them to a comeback. The tie went to a replay and Fergie scored a

25-yarder that went fizzing into the top corner past the Kilmarnock keeper Bobby Ferguson and we beat them 1-0. After the game the banter was flowing in the dressing room and we were winding Fergie up about scoring from further out than his customary couple of yards. We were a close-knit group and all got on well.

But I'll never forget the day I joined the Pars. I walked into the office to talk terms with the manager and he said to me, 'Okay, cards on the table, how much do you want for signing on?' Quite confidently, I said, '£500,' and Willie said, 'Okay then, it's a deal.' Immediately I thought that I'd sold myself short and should have asked for more. When Willie signed me for Falkirk a few years later I got £1,500, so I did okay for myself. No agents in those days.

I travelled every day with Fergie in the club minibus. There was this guy called Jim McLean – no, not that one – a big centre-half, and he was the designated driver. He lived in Motherwell and would pick Fergie up in Airdrie, before getting me in Dennyloanhead, and then on to Kincardine to collect a lad called George Peebles. It was a fantastic club to be at because there were no cliques and everyone got on with everyone else.

In 1968 we won the Scottish Cup and I had played my part in the earlier rounds. We beat Hearts in the final and then went to America along with Manchester City to try and promote 'soccer' in the States. We were away for five weeks and it was one of the most enjoyable experiences of my life. We were in a few 'States' on that trip, I'll tell you!

But one match that sticks in the memory was against West Brom in a European tie at East End Park. There was a crowd of 26,000 in and I was up against Scotland winger Bobby Hope, who was a smashing player, but one particular incident from that game sticks out more than most. Hope crossed in a ball and I heard the shout 'leave it' from behind me, but I was taking no chances and booted it straight into the stand. I looked round and there was big Jeff Astle grinning away. He scored the only goal of the FA Cup Final that year and was a smashing player, although a bit cheeky.

We drew the first leg 0-0 in Dunfermline but managed to beat them 1-0 down at The Hawthorns, with Pat Gardener scoring, so travelling back up the road after the match on the train was fantastic. The journey went by so quickly because we were all buzzing with excitement.

We had a lot of really good players in the squad and certainly didn't fear going to the likes of Ibrox and Celtic Park, probably a bit like Aberdeen and Dundee United, to a lesser extent, in the 1980s. I remember we played Celtic the year they won the European Cup and I was up against wee Jinky Johnstone. It was a cracking match and the only downside was that they beat us 5-4. We were 2-0 and 4-2 up but they pulled it back to 4-4 and Joe McBride got the winner in the last minute from the penalty spot. At that time, I was on £36 basic a week but we were on £100 a man to win that day, so when Celtic scored with a late penalty, that was given by the linesman, I was gutted. What a game it was, though. It was end-to-end stuff, and that was against the winners of the European Cup.

Jimmy Johnstone and Willie Henderson were two of the best wingers of their generation, but they were entirely different types. Once wee Willie was past, you didn't see him for dust, as his pace was electric. Jinky, on the other hand, would beat you, and then want to beat you again, but he was a fantastic entertainer. You always got a second bite at the cherry with Jinky, although it didn't always do much good! I've always loved wingers, as a supporter, player and manager. I was a hard, but fair, defender and never resorted to brutal tactics, or kicking lumps out of them, if you like. The last time wee Willie was through in Falkirk speaking at one of our hospitality events, he gave me a great mention, and said I should have played for Scotland, which was nice.

Big 'Tiny' Wharton was the referee in that nine-goal thriller against Celtic. He was a real character. If you played a nice pass he would say, 'Good ball Mr Totten.' We had a good rapport with referees then, whereas nowadays it seems to be a case of them and us.

I played for six senior clubs and while I could take something positive from them all, my time at Dunfermline was definitely the best. Probably being successful helped, but that wasn't the be all and end all. We had a great bunch of lads and that made everyone's life far easier. I still keep in touch with a lot of the guys, such as Roy Barry and Bert Paton. The last thing you want at a club is a few different cliques starting up – that's a recipe for disaster. It might be an old cliché but a happy dressing room has a greater chance of also being a successful one. When I became a manager and there were any bad apples in the dressing room, I got rid of them straight away. You all need to be pulling in the same direction. It's up to the manager to lead by example, which also means he can't be allowed to have any favourites.

Alex Ferguson was a real leader both in the dressing room and on the park. Sometimes you just look at a player and know that he has the right qualities to be a successful manager, and Fergie was one of these people. He was the 'shop steward' in the dressing room and had a really strong voice.

After training each day we would go to the Regal Restaurant in Dunfermline town centre for lunch. One of the lads, Paul Breslin, who had come from Queen's Park, had managed to talk Fergie into teaching him to drive. He had a big Ford Corsair with the 'L' plates up, so we all piled in one day and headed into town and when we got near the shops, big Jock, the local bobby, put his hand up and told Paul to stop, but he put his foot on the gas instead of the brakes and went crashing through the front window of Grafton's department store. We just sat there in amazement and I remember being in Fergie's company years later and saying to a few people, 'This man here is one of the greatest managers of all time – but don't ever ask him to teach you to drive!' Fergie turned to me and said, 'Alex, you'll never guess what Paul's doing now – he's a bloody pilot!' I said, 'But he couldn't even drive a car.' We had a right good laugh about it.

Going to Norway in August, 1966, was my first proper European adventure. We were up against FC Frigg in the old Inter-Cities Fairs Cup and I was in line to make my Euro debut. The Fairs Cup would eventually become the UEFA Cup, although even that has now been replaced by the Europa League, so there have been a few changes since my playing days.

It seemed as though Dunfermline were always in Europe in those days and just prior to the match in Norway all the focus was on Alex Ferguson. The season previous he had scored 43 goals for the Pars – a club record – but he had received a little criticism because he had still to score that season, even though it was only the end of August. And he couldn't have picked a harder team to try and break his duck against because the Norwegians were one of the most defensive-minded teams I ever came across in my entire career. We had all been telling Fergie that he was trying too hard to get his first goal of the season, and just to try and relax more and it would come.

Just before leaving Scotland, we were hit by the news that Jim McLean had asked for a transfer after a fall-out with Willie Cunningham. He wasn't only our big, strong centre-half, but also our captain, so it was a bit of a blow for everyone. He didn't travel to Norway as the manager was holding him in a 'serious breach of club discipline' as the papers put it.

But the home side had far more solemn things to worry about, as their coach, Jan Tangen, collapsed and died while playing in a bounce game the week before the match. He was only 43, which was absolutely tragic. The home players had vowed to put on a good performance in his memory. Frigg were second top of their league but we were reminded before the game that no Scottish team had ever lost on Scandinavian soil, despite the Danes, Swedes and Norwegians trying 13 times. No pressure then.

I did indeed make my European debut but it all turned sour after just nine minutes. Bert Paton slipped while trying to make a pass and the Norwegians broke upfield at lightning-quick pace. One cross into the box later and they were a goal up. We didn't lose our discipline or shape though and Tommy Callaghan headed the equaliser a few minutes before half-time.

Jim Fleming scored twice in as many minutes after the break to put us on easy street. That was the cue for our small band of supporters in the 6,000 crowd to go absolutely mental. But just a few minutes later, one of their players clattered me and I was lying flat out on the ground. I was hurting so much and was relieved to see our trainer Andy Stevenson run on to the park. However, I couldn't believe it when the referee ordered him straight back off again. I was in agony and it was only when big Tommy Callaghan remonstrated with the match official that he allowed Andy back on.

Thankfully I was able to play on and we were quite comfortable for the last half-hour of the game. It was a good result and not only had we managed to avoid being the first Scottish team to lose in Scandinavia, but we had given ourselves every opportunity of going through to the second round – even though Fergie, who was also injured during the match, had failed to break his duck. More serious than that though, it transpired that he had suffered a knee ligament injury, which was a real blow to both us and the player.

We also won 3-1 in the second leg, to progress to the second round, where we were drawn against Yugoslavian cracks, Dinamo Zagreb, and that would be a whole new ball game. Thankfully, Fergie was fit by the time the tie came round, and we needed his goals because it was 2-2 in the first leg at East End Park with just 15 minutes remaining. Enter Fergie, and he scored twice to give us a 4-2 lead. It was no more than we deserved because we had battered them relentlessly in the second half.

I always remember Fergie talking about the 'dark days' before he managed to fight his way back to full fitness. The leg was giving him real trouble and despite intensive treatment, he seemed to be taking one step forward and two back every time he attempted a comeback. Andy Stevenson had a special boot made for him and he was told to go home, sit in front of the telly and exercise using the specially-weighted boot for ten minutes every hour. It was a real slog for Fergie but he showed great resilience and mental spirit to do as he was told and came back as strong as ever.

When we travelled to Zagreb for the second leg, we were pretty confident we could finish off the job. Don't get me wrong, we knew it would be really tough, as Dinamo were a good side, but we also had good players. Sadly, though, it wasn't to be and we lost the game 2-0 – and fell victim to a brand new European rule, where away goals counted double. I must admit it was hard to take, especially as Zagreb's first goal was a mile offside, but that was what you got on the continent in those days. We could still hold our heads high because while we might have been out, we were certainly not disgraced.

We had all been really looking forward to an end-of-season trip to London since it had been announced a few weeks beforehand. We were to travel down on the Friday, play Arsenal at Highbury that night and then take in the England v Scotland match at Wembley the following day.

The 'Wembley weekend' as it was known was a massive favourite with football fans north of the border and I used to go down with my dad and some of his friends every second year. I recall seeing players such as Duncan Edwards and Stanley Matthews on some of the visits, and I would save up for months beforehand to ensure I had plenty of spending money. That year, though, it was to be an extra-special trip for me – until we lost to Dundee a few days beforehand. That seemed to put the tin lid on the 'jolly' because the following afternoon, the gaffer got us all into the boardroom at East End Park and said, 'Wembley's off, we're not going,' and that seemed to be that.

He said he had never been so disappointed with a defeat but then he warned us not to tell anyone at the newspapers, because Willie Callaghan and Alex Ferguson had a great chance of making it into the Scotland squad for a forthcoming tour of the Far East, and he thought it might scupper their chances. I couldn't believe it and headed home rather dejectedly. I had really been looking forward to playing at Highbury and then going to the international match. Anyway, I arrived home and my mum said to me, 'There's a telegram for you in the living room.' I picked it up, not having a clue who it was from, and it said, simply, 'Wembley back on!' The smile returned to my face instantly.

Playing against a top English team was a fantastic experience and there was a big crowd inside Highbury. The atmosphere was electric and I was up against a winger called Colin Addison. The Gunners won the match 2-1 and Fergie scored our goal. Afterwards, we were well looked after by Arsenal and that set us up nicely for the following day. England had won the World Cup the previous year but Scotland managed to win the game 3-2, so it was another great experience. We flew back to Edinburgh on the Sunday having enjoyed a great weekend. The trip was organised by our secretary, Tommy Walker, who was a lovely man. He had been a big star in his day for Hearts and Scotland, and latterly manager at Tynecastle, before working at Dunfermline. In fact, Tommy was so nice that some people reckoned he was a minister!

In April 1968, we took part in a game they said 'didn't matter'. In saying that, for those who took part, it was one of the most frightening experiences of our lives. It was the business end of the season, a Tuesday night and we were playing Celtic at East End Park. Days beforehand it had been billed as a league decider, but with Aberdeen beating Rangers at Ibrox, the title race was over. Celtic had won the championship and the match against Dunfermline was by the way.

Try telling that to the supporters, though, as more than 33,000 packed into the ground to see the match. The only trouble was the ground didn't hold that amount. More than 3,000 extra fans had forced their way into East End Park, which proved a recipe for disaster. Turnstiles were broken and walls scaled. At one point, we looked on as the cops drew their batons on the seemingly never-ending stream of fans trying – and succeeding – to get into the ground. Suddenly, the safety of those inside was severely compromised. Referee 'Tiny' Wharton, one of the top officials of that era, started the game, stopped it, re-started it and so on. It was almost impossible to concentrate on what was happening on the park.

By the end of the match, which Celtic won 2-1, more than 50 people had been injured, with many of them taken to hospital. One man was reported to be critically ill, while others had broken arms, legs and ribs due to the crushing. Trainers from both clubs were busy tending to the injured rather than focussing on the game. Supporters were on the terracing roofs, the pylons and even on the pitch. The previous crowd record at East End Park had been just over 24,000, for a visit of Rangers, but that didn't come close to the amount who had made their way, by hook or by crook, into the ground for this one. It was still a decent match but the spectre of serious injury, or even death, loomed large over the ground for the entire duration of the game.

Afterwards, the Procurator Fiscal called for a full report into the fiasco and Mr Wharton was asked to give a statement. I'll always remember him saying how he feared for the lives of supporters, especially when the first crush barrier burst. He stopped the game for almost ten minutes while stricken supporters received medical help. He ordered the players back into the dressing room but stayed on the park himself so that supporters would realise that the game would continue, which I thought was a masterstroke. Imagine the pandemonium that could've ensued had fans thought they had battled their way inside only to see the game called off early on.

Earlier that season, we had all become a little despondent when the draw for the first round of the Scottish Cup was made, and we were paired with Celtic. They had just won two titles in a row and were leading the race for a third. And with the match at Celtic Park, not many football folk gave us an earthly. The game was far from a classic but what we had was two teams going at each other hammer and tongs and Celtic just couldn't match our physical approach. It was 0-0 at half-time but goals from Hugh Robertson and Pat Gardner after the break saw us win, fairly comfortably, 2-0. However, we were a little dismayed to read the following day that our win was being called the 'greatest cup shock since Berwick beat Rangers the season before'. I thought that was unfair because we were a top four team in the First Division.

It didn't get much easier in the second round, when the draw pitted us against Aberdeen, but at least the tie was at East End

Park. It was played on a freezing Monday night and I was told to mark wee Jinky Smith, who would later move to Dunfermline. It took a last-gasp goal by Alex Edwards to get us through to the quarter-finals. That night, our victory was as much down to the fire in our bellies as the twinkle in our toes and I'm sure the Dons would have been disappointed to head back up the road with very little to show for their efforts.

For us, though, it was a case of onwards and upwards and we were drawn to meet the winners of the Partick Thistle v Clyde tie, which was postponed a couple of times before the Jags won through. In keeping with the other two ties, it was another tough 90 minutes and only a goal from one of my best mates, Bert Paton, ensured our path to the last four with a goal ten minutes from time.

Only St Johnstone stood between us and a Scottish Cup Final appearance. Dunfermline had already made it to two finals in the decade, and had won the cup once, but a third final in just seven years would have been a magnificent achievement. Mind you, we still had to get there, and we knew St Johnstone represented a tough obstacle. 'Tiny' Wharton was in charge and he held up the start of the match for six minutes. Not to allow the many thousands of supporters awaiting entry, or because supporters had decided to have a scrap with one another, but because one of our goal nets was frayed – and he ordered the groundsman to sort it out with his needle and thread!

It was St Johnstone who got off to the best possible start when they scored after just four minutes. It took a Pat Gardner equaliser in the second half to earn us a replay. Had we lost our chance of making it to Hampden? Not according to the bookies, who made us favourites of the four remaining teams. The others were Hearts and Morton. We were even-money to lift the cup, although we still had the replay at Tynecastle to negotiate, and that didn't start too well when Alex MacDonald, who would go on to play for Rangers in the European Cup Winners' Cup Final in Barcelona in 1972, scooped the ball over Bent Martin to give Saints the lead.

But our boys were made of stern stuff and Bert equalised before Ian Lister, who had come on as a sub, scored near the end of extra time to send us through to the final at Hampden. There might have been less than 10,000 at Tynecastle for the replay but the Pars fans in the crowd made one hell of a racket at the final whistle. It wasn't pretty, but we were through.

The build-up to the final was immense, although we still had to fight hard to finish as high up the league as we possibly could, especially as football beaks were dishing out £100 a point, and that was a lot of money for clubs in the 60s. But a row between the SFA and the Scottish League threatened to overshadow the occasion when the league deemed that we would be playing in opposition to a potential league decider at Ibrox, just a couple of miles from Hampden, between Rangers and Aberdeen – a game that had the potential to attract a crowd in excess of 70,000. When the war of words had subsided, the decision was that the two matches would be played on the same day. It wasn't ideal but as players we just had to get on with it and were determined that nothing would wreck our big day.

We limbered up for the cup tie by beating both Partick Thistle and Dundee United away from home, the latter in a 4-1 pasting. Bert was again in goalscoring mood and bagged a couple at Tannadice. Before the final, we picked up the papers to read that our manager was tipping us to 'skin Hearts alive'. He was convinced that Hearts didn't have an earthly of beating us. We could just imagine the Hearts lads pinning that story up on their dressing room wall.

Just over 45,000 turned up at Ibrox for the Rangers v Aberdeen match, but there were 11,000 more at Hampden for the showpiece match between ourselves and Hearts. I often thought it crazy to play both games on the same day because there were probably many thousands who would like to have watched both.

But for us it was all about winning the cup, and we did just that, with a bit to spare. It wasn't quite the 'skinning' forecast by George Farm but it was a victory nevertheless, and a pretty comprehensive one at that. The first half was instantly forgettable but things really livened up after the break. Pat Gardner scored first, before Ian Lister scored from the spot to double our advantage. Hearts got back into it thanks to an own goal but Pat scored a third to make sure the magnificent old trophy was heading east to Dunfermline.

There seemed to be no pleasing the gaffer though, because he was angry after the match, and no wonder. We were refused permission to take the cup out on to the field after the presentation ceremony. Roy Barry had the trophy in his hands and we walked down the tunnel, but were stopped from going on to the pitch by the police and told to return to the dressing room. It turned out that because of trouble involving the Old Firm in a previous final, everyone was now barred from taking a lap of honour, which really was a lot of nonsense. It was baffling to understand why on earth there would be trouble among the Dunfermline fans after their team had just won the cup. There were no Hearts fans left in the ground. The manager and several players accused the police of jostling them when they tried to go on a lap of honour, which left a sour taste in the mouth.

But we finally got our lap of honour – 48 hours later, at a deserted East End Park. A few of the lads thought it would be good fun to mock-up a lap of honour at our own ground, and thankfully a couple of cameramen were there to capture the moment. I suppose it was a sort of veiled assault on the killjoy authorities who had banned the traditional lap of honour after the match.

Anyway, nothing was going to spoil our cup heroics and when we arrived back in Dunfermline town centre, after the match, the scenes that met us were phenomenal. Thousands of happy Fifers had come out to greet us and we appreciated every one of them. It was a fantastic night and we were feted wherever we went in the town. The Scottish Cup was, and still is, our national trophy and means a great deal to an awful lot of people.

George Farm was a tough boss, but he had a great character, and I remember after winning the cup we were travelling through the town on an open-top bus and he was urging each and every one of us to drink in the moment. 'It doesn't happen that often,' I recall him saying. I think the whole of Fife had turned out and it was a magical day. We had the cup on the bus and everyone was in high spirits. Later, when I took Falkirk to the cup final in 1997, it was a big disappointment that I didn't bring the cup home for the people of our town. After the cup final of '68, we had also visited a swanky hotel in George Square for a meal before heading back up the road to Dunfermline.

George had replaced Willie Cunningham as manager, although I recall one occasion when we were in Switzerland, and I was rooming with Andy Stevenson, the physio. Willie came into the room and said, 'Is Totts sleeping?' Andy said I was and Willie mentioned that he was in the frame for the Rangers job. Scot Symon had just been sacked and the Rangers directors were seriously considering him. Sadly, it didn't work out for Willie and Davie White got the job.

Willie eventually moved on to Falkirk and when the time came for me to leave Dunfermline I was happy enough to make the switch to Falkirk, and join my old gaffer again. For me, signing for the team I had supported as a boy was a phenomenal feeling. Since then, of course, I've also managed the club, and been involved in the boardroom, which completed the set.

5

Heading Stateside

W E were taken on a tour of the United States and Canada as a reward for bringing the Scottish Cup to East End Park – and what an experience it was. We were away for around five weeks and visited just about every corner of that vast continent. The adventure began when 16 players, manager George Farm and his backroom team, and five directors flew out from Prestwick Airport to New York.

We had originally been scheduled to start the tour in Bermuda but that was cancelled in favour of a match in Boston, Massachusetts against Fall River Astros – and what a terrible decision that turned out to be. But we departed Scotland on a high, with the management team delighted that Roy Barry, Bent Martin and Alex Edwards had signed new contracts just before we left – so it was a great start to the tour.

We played around a dozen games, four of them against Manchester City, who had the likes of Franny Lee and Mike Summerbee in their ranks. They had been involved in a titanic struggle with bitter rivals Manchester United for the English First Division title and had won it on the last day of the season. The tour organisers had billed our matches as the 'unofficial British Championship' and we were more than happy to go along with the hype. For once, it wasn't the Old Firm grabbing all the headlines abroad!

But the tour stalled the moment we got to US immigration at Kennedy Airport when stuffy officials decided they weren't letting Willie Callaghan into the country. It was a nervous wait for players and manager alike as they checked and double-checked his visa. It turned out that the last time Willie had been in the States, on a family holiday, he had forgotten to hand back a portion of an immigration form, and the Yankee authorities had 'blacklisted' him from ever entering their country again. Thankfully, he was eventually allowed through and we were able to enjoy the first day of our trip in sunny New York.

One thing we didn't enjoy, though, was our match against Fall River. What a disgraceful start to our US tour. I reckon every single player who played in that match was left with cuts, lumps or bruises – although it didn't start out that way. We were all excited at the prospect of playing our first match on Yankee soil, but poor old John Lunn was soon wishing he hadn't bothered as he was punched full in the face by a supporter of the opposing team. And I believe it wasn't the first time that lot had been involved in stuff like that. We were later informed that a few Scottish teams, including Rangers, as far back as the 1920s, had received a real going over in Fall River. Makes you wonder why they were allowed to continue playing against touring sides.

We only managed to play half the game, on a field that can only be described as 'ploughed' and with the poorest floodlighting I have ever seen, and I still perish the thought of what might have been had that game been allowed to continue. The catalyst for the abandonment arrived when a crazed supporter ran on to the pitch and caught John with a right hook. There was just a few seconds to go to the break and sadly the half-time team talk didn't revolve around tactics or anything as basic as that, but more about how we could get the hell out of that place in one piece. We managed it, but only just, and with the help of an armed police escort and wailing sirens.

After the fan had punched John, George Farm spoke to a couple of our directors, local officials and the police – and all parties agreed that the game should be called off. It was quite clear that the problems would only escalate after the break. We were in the dressing room when the decision was made – and thank god for that. The dressing room was directly below the stand so we could hear a lot of angry voices, and when the announcer told the 3,000 fans of the decision, all hell broke loose. During the match, the home fans had cheered every time a Dunfermline player went down under a heavy boot, so we knew that the biggest majority of them were crazy, although we didn't realise just how crazy. In their fury at the game being abandoned, they tore down turnstile gates and smashed windows – then they tried to storm our dressing room, and that's when the armed guard came in handy. In fact, I'm sure we also heard a gun going off in the crowd, that's how scary it was. They weren't happy because they had paid to see 90 minutes and only saw half that.

The riot lasted an incredible two hours, and all the time we were shaking like leaves in the tiny dressing room. These people were out of control and even the cop admitted he was terrified – and he had a gun! Eventually, reinforcements, pistols drawn, arrived to form a corridor, through which we were able to 'escape' this living hell. We ran for the coach like our very lives depended on it, but still they hurled abuse and threatened all kinds of violence. It was only when we got back to our hotel that we felt safe, and I'll always remember George Farm saying, 'I think we will need to recruit Elliot Ness [a legendary FBI boss] if this sort of behaviour continues.'

It was the greatest feeling in the world getting on that bus, especially after three hours of mental torture. It remains to this day the craziest place I have ever been in my life – and the whole thing kicked off because of an incident in which one of their fans felt the need to assault my team-mate.

The thing is, their team, which was composed mainly of Brazilians and Portuguese, had actually looked quite good to start with, but began to turn nasty when we had two goals ruled out for offside. Realising we were the better side, and that it was only a matter of time until one of our goals stood, they started to kick everything and everybody that moved, and their fans revelled in that sort of behaviour. It was never going to end in anything other than carnage. When we eventually got out of the dressing room we had to run a gauntlet of hate and were never so relieved when the bus pulled away from the ground. I remember looking back and seeing all these people still going crazy, faces contorted with rage. It was just a mad experience.

It was a little friendlier when we met the owner of one of the biggest teams in America, Al Kazamak, I think his name was, a massive big guy, and we were talking to him after one of the games. Alex Edwards, one of my team-mates, was a great player, and he asked the big guy how much the Yanks got for wages and signing-on fees, and big Al replied, 'Now that depends Sonny, some guys get nothing, and others get three times that.' And wee Alex said, 'Oh, that'll dae me!' We were all killing ourselves laughing.

We also bumped into a guy called Ernie Winchester, a former Hearts and Aberdeen player, who was playing for Kansas City Spurs, and he told us that he was living the American dream. He said it wasn't only the climate that was fantastic, but the wages and the lifestyle as well. The proof was right there in front of us, in the shape of a fancy big car – and his flashy pad complete with swimming pool. The downside though, as far as Ernie was concerned, was the lack of atmosphere at games.

I was only 21 at the time and for me, I was another one living the dream. Over in the USA, staying in top hotels and spending money. It was all fantastic and I enjoyed every single minute. Both ourselves and Manchester City were hailed as heroes. City had won the English First Division and we had the Scottish Cup, so it was a tour of champions, if you like. We had also finished fourth in the First Division table, which was commendable for a team like Dunfermline. We had a player called Jimmy Thompson who was writing a diary for the *Sunday Mail*, and I'll always remember he wrote how I was the life and soul of the party. I know I'm perhaps a bit more conservative these days, but I really did enjoy a laugh and a joke back then. As a young player I used to be up to all the dodges, but as a manager you have to be a wee bit more serious.

I wasn't a manager then, though, and I'll always remember Jimmy writing that I was 'the biggest discovery of the tour'. I liked firing off a load of one-line gags but it backfired when we visited a club in New York and the lads 'persuaded' me to get up on stage and do my party piece – and my wisecracks fair brought the house down. They were all saying that when my time in football came to an end, I should consider stand-up comedy as a new career. In fact, some of them said, 'Why wait?'

We saw some amazing places on our travels. We were in New York, Kansas, Los Angeles, San Francisco and all over Canada. In fact, while we were in Toronto, we were pleasantly surprised one day when we walked into our hotel and heard that the English FA Cup Final between Everton and West Bromwich Albion was to be beamed live straight into our TV lounge. It was quite a thrill to be able to watch the whole of the game by way of something called the Early Bird Satellite. Ironically, folks back home in Dunfermline weren't able to see it but we were thousands of miles away and it wasn't a problem for us! I must admit it was a bit strange settling down for breakfast and watching a live football match. It might be commonplace now, with games kicking off on any day of the week at any time, but not back in 1968. While in Toronto we were staying in the Royal York Hotel which, we were told, was the biggest in the Commonwealth, and I could believe it. It was huge.

By the time we reached Toronto, we had already covered a heck of a lot of miles. Mind you, we were all just mighty relieved to touch down safely in Canada as the journey from New York was pretty hairy to say the least. After that, we would all have been quite happy to spend the rest of the trip on the ground. We did receive a really nice surprise in Boston when a gentleman by the name of Tom McMillan came into our dressing room before the game and told us he had played left-back for the Pars in 1921. That was quite something.

While in America we were caught up in a welcome home parade for the Vietnam War disabled. It was very emotional and there were brass bands playing, while thousands of people had turned out to welcome their soldiers back from the conflict in south-east Asia.

We travelled back to New York from Toronto and were treated to a night out at the legendary Madison Square Garden, where we watched the Dick Tiger–Bob Foster world title fight. The venue was just 150 yards from our hotel. We were accompanied by a number of Celtic players, who were staying in the same hotel as us.

Our match against New Jersey All Stars was cancelled, which gave a few of the players a chance to visit family or friends, if they had any in that part of the world. Others, such as Bent Martin and Hugh Robertson, decided to take in some of the wonderful sights of a fantastic city. Bent and Hugh took a stroll through Times Square, before going into a restaurant for a meal – and if they had arrived just a few minutes earlier, they would have witnessed a terrifying shooting. Just before they walked in, a customer had shot both his girlfriend and the restaurant manager. I remember the lads saying the food wasn't all that bad!

While in New York, we lost a game 2-0 and our manager, George Farm wasn't in the slightest amused. When we got back to the hotel he said to everyone in the foyer, 'Right, sit on your arses. That was an absolute disgrace. Getting beat by a bunch of old men was embarrassing and you should all be ashamed of yourselves. Right, it's 7pm now, I want everyone back in this hotel by 10pm – and not a minute later.' Of course, we weren't too happy. I mean, who comes home by 10pm in New York? Roy Barry was our captain and he told everyone to go up to his room. Sixteen of us piled in and he said, 'I'm not happy about this. We've just won the Scottish Cup and we're only getting out until 10pm. It's not on. If I stay out later they will send me home, but if we all go out and stay out late then they can't send everyone home.'

We had a great night and, as you can imagine, missed our 10pm curfew by quite a bit. Next morning, we had a meeting with the chairman, Leonard Jack, who was a lawyer. Farm wasn't there and Leonard said, 'Listen lads, the manager told you all to be in by 10pm and you disobeyed that, so now I'm left with a dilemma and I don't quite know what to do.' Wee Alex Edwards, who was really comical, piped up and said, 'Sack the bugger.' Everyone started chuckling and Leonard said, 'Sack who?' And wee Alex said, 'The manager!' That was that, and we all got off scot-free.

After New York it was on to Kansas and despite our very best efforts, we never did find the Wizard of Oz! One thing I did manage to do, though, was make a complete ass of myself – again. We were presented with a television film of my efforts at attempting to ride a donkey, which was one of the mascots at the local club. It was hilarious at the time, and then again when we all gathered round to watch the film. As I said, we had a wonderful team spirit at East End Park and I felt totally at ease with my team-mates. From Kansas, we headed up into the sky again and a 12-hour flight to Vancouver. Everyone was pretty much exhausted when we touched down in Canada. When we got to our hotel we discovered that there was a 'kitchen' in every room, so if you didn't fancy going down for breakfast, you just made it yourself.

We had enough memories from that trip to last a lifetime but there was something special about seeing the White House while we were in Washington. Bert Paton and I had accompanied Willie Duff, a goalkeeper, who had relations in the city, and a short detour allowed us to see the Presidential building, which was really something. We also saw President Kennedy's grave. It was quite funny because beforehand, Willie had asked George Farm if he could take Bert and I to visit his relatives, as we had a couple of days off, and the manager said, 'As far as I'm concerned, you can take the whole bloody lot of them.' I'm sure he loved us really.

While in Los Angeles, we were sitting having a drink one night when all hell broke loose. Suddenly there was the wailing of sirens all around and highway patrol cars were buzzing past the bar we were in. When we went back to the hotel, we discovered that Senator Bobby Kennedy, John F. Kennedy's brother, had been assassinated in the Ambassador Hotel while we were in the city. Senator Kennedy was a big hero to a lot of people in the US, so it was massive news. Martin Luther King had also been killed just a couple of months before that, so there was an awful lot of unrest in America at that time.

It was against that backdrop that we played our fourth match against Manchester City and we certainly did ourselves justice by drawing 0-0 with the English champions. A local team had put up a trophy for the winners so the match was decided by penalty kicks – although this time it was a shoot-out with a difference. Each side nominated one player to take six kicks. We went with Ian Lister, who scored five out of six, and City chose Tony Coleman, who scored all six, so they got their hands on the handsome trophy. During the match, Alex Edwards missed a sitter from just three yards out, so you can imagine the ribbing he took over that.

San Francisco was a beautiful city, and another tick box in our list of venues. We virtually had a whole day before we played against a local side and we were all told, once again, that we had to be in by 10pm. We enjoyed a great day out but Roy Barry, Hugh Robertson, wee Alex Edwards and myself ended up at a club with the likes of Franny Lee and Mike Summerbee, from City, who weren't on a curfew as they had a clear schedule the following day and, as you can imagine, we again missed our deadline by quite a bit.

So, next morning we were lined up against the wall, like some sort of firing squad, and the manager read the riot act. 'As punishment,' he growled, 'you're all playing today and if you get beat you're getting sent home.' And he turned round to Alex and said, 'And as for you, my contacts tell me you didn't get in until 2am,' and the wee man butted in and said, 'Well, they're wrong, I didn't get in until 5am.' Anyway, we played St Louis off the park and beat them 3-1, so we were off the hook. I'm still convinced to this day, mind you, that the manager would have had no hesitation in sending us home.

The game itself had been a worry to us, though. We were part of a double header and had watched Man City lose 3-0 in the game just before ours. The referee for their game was shocking, and the match awfully rough, but we needn't have had any fears because our ref was just fine and we played some good stuff to win with a bit to spare. Bert Paton scored a wonderful scissor kick in that match and I often thought that had the great Pele scored that goal, then it would have been beamed all over the television.

After that match we had a few drinks, and even the manager couldn't have denied us that. We had a double celebration as both Bent Martin and Willie Callaghan received word that their wives had just given birth. It was fantastic, and even though we were almost at the end of the tour, and were exhausted, and full of bumps and bruises, we really let our hair down that night.

Everyone was in good spirits and in our penultimate match, we thumped Rochester Lancers 8-1 thanks to an electrifying display of football – and in temperatures well into the 80s. The next morning, we boarded a flight for New York, and it shouldn't even have stuck in my memory – but I will never forget it. The flight should have taken just 45 minutes but it took double that, and they were easily the worst flying conditions I have ever encountered. We had thunder, we had lightning and then, when we were close to La Guardia Airport, we had to circle for around 40 minutes because of fog and lightning in the worst thunderstorm ever recorded – of that I'm sure. Think the scary scenario at Fall River – and multiply it by ten. There is just something so vulnerable about being in the air in circumstances like that.

Our last match, against the Ukrainian Nationals, was played in atrocious conditions. Torrential rain and thunder kept the crowd down, but we played some delightful football and won 7-0, which meant we had drawn five, won three and lost just one of our nine matches. I had never been to America before, so to experience that at the age of 21, and get paid for doing so, was just amazing. It really was the trip of a lifetime. We knew we weren't a Rangers or a Celtic, but we were still a big team, and that showed because the reception we got in America was second to none. In saying that, Dunfermline were always a top four side while I was there so they were one of the Scottish big guns at the time. Jock Stein had moulded the side before moving on and Willie Cunningham and then George Farm had taken over and kept up the success rate. We had shown the Yanks that we could play football, but it was a collection of battered and bruised players who touched back down at Prestwick Airport, just glad to be home for a well-earned break.

6

The Bairn Identity

WILLIE Cunningham had left Dunfermline to manage Falkirk and they were battling relegation from the First Division at the tail-end of the 1968/69 season. A 2-2 draw at home to Partick Thistle saw them take the dreaded drop into the division below despite, according to Willie, having enough chances to win half-a-dozen games.

Meanwhile, over at East End Park, my own time at the Pars was grinding to a stuttering halt. I looked on as we lost out in the semi-finals of the European Cup Winners' Cup in Czechoslovakia. Slovan Bratislava beat us 1-0 after a 1-1 draw in Dunfermline, and that was that. The referee in the away leg, a 6ft 4in Yugoslav, had been terribly weak and allowed so many cynical fouls by the home side to go unpunished. It was a ridiculous way to exit any tournament – but particularly at such an important stage. Dunfermline had another great season and had finished third in the league but I knew my time was up.

It was quite funny, though, because most mornings when I was leaving Falkirk to head for training at East End Park, I would see Willie Cunningham coming in the opposite direction. We always gave each other a wave, although one morning he was flailing his arms around in the car as though he was drowning, so I stopped and pulled into a nearby petrol station. I was worried that something serious was wrong, but when I jumped out the car, he had this big smile on his face. I asked why he was waving like a madman, and he said, 'I'm asking if you would like to sign for Falkirk, that's all.' I couldn't stop laughing but when he told me he was serious, I was sorely tempted. It was out of my hands though as Dunfermline were still in Europe at that point and George Farm wasn't letting me or anyone else go anywhere.

But I continued to 'meet' Willie near the petrol station in Falkirk most mornings and on one occasion it was *me* who was waving *him* down. We stopped at the petrol station again and had a long chat. Within a week or two I was a Falkirk player. We had formal talks at Brockville and I signed on the dotted line. It was a sort of homecoming for me, if you like – and I'll always remember capping the move with my first ever senior goal, which was a special – and unique – moment. I instantly connected with the Falkirk fans and we had a great relationship. Not only that, but this was the team I had supported as a boy, and the Class of 1957 had been idols of mine, but more than that this was my grandfather's team, so it was special for me to finally be playing for Falkirk.

I made my competitive debut for the Bairns in August 1969, at home to Forfar Athletic in a League Cup tie. Sadly my grandfather never got to see it, but I know he would've been so proud of me. It might not sound much, but it was a big deal for me. We won the match 3-1 and I'll always remember picking up the paper the next day and being astounded by what I read. In fact, I'll never forget the opening line, 'Falkirk seem certain to clinch promotion this season.' It was only day one of the League Cup and already we had the league title in the bag. This was one journalist who wasn't mincing his words. But we did win our League Cup section and started our league campaign with a comprehensive 3-0 home win over East Stirling – with future Scotland manager Andy Roxburgh getting us off the mark early on.

We had been motoring along quite nicely until a 3-0 home loss to rivals Stirling Albion stopped us in our tracks. We bounced back though – and then the unthinkable happened. We were 3-0 up at Cliftonhill against Albion Rovers when I found myself just outside the box – the opposition box that is! The ball came my way and I hit it first time. It flew into the back of the net and while it might not have been the most important goal scored that afternoon, it certainly was to me, as it was my first senior goal. In fact, if you will indulge me, I'll read out the paragraph that goal earned in the next day's papers. I've kept cuttings of all my senior goals and, needless to say, the pile isn't that tall! Anyway, the report read, 'Left-back Alex Totten scored his first goal for the Brockville side when he pounced on a rebound and whipped a good shot through a ruck of players and past the unsighted Brown.'

Seven days later, we were involved in the most incredible game at Brockville against Queen of the South. We were 3-0 down after just 24 minutes, thanks to their centre-forward, McIntyre, who scored a hat-trick – and then we scored seven! It was 3-3 at half-time and we hit another four in the first 20 minutes of the second period. Just to ensure a really wacky afternoon, Queens scored twice near the end to make the final score 7-5. Somehow I don't think defences were on top that day!

But if things were hot on defenders that afternoon, the heat was cranked up when we played Dundee United Reserves at Brockville close to Christmas in the Second XI Cup. The team lost 4-1 and there were astonishing shouts of 'Cunningham must go' from the terracing. Apparently the supporters blamed the manager for selling Johnny Graham to Hibs, although thankfully the chairman came out and backed the gaffer, saying 'These people did not know what they were shouting about. They were just a few hot-heads – some of them the worse for drink – who wanted to cause a bit of bother because their team lost.'

But the club bounced back in tremendous style – and I was reunited with an old mate. The gaffer shelled out £20,000 to sign Alex Ferguson from Rangers and he was pitched straight into our top-of-the-table clash with Cowdenbeath. Fergie had knocked back the chance to join Nottingham Forest, and that gave everyone at Brockville a massive lift. I believe the fee was a record for a Scottish Second Division side.

I was delighted, but surprised, that Fergie moved to Falkirk. I remember him and Willie Cunningham had a massive bust-up after a European match in Zagreb with the Pars, and Roy Barry had separated them, but obviously that was forgotten about, and I knew that Willie had always admired Fergie as a player, and he turned out to be a smashing buy for Falkirk. The season we won the league at Brockville we scored 96 goals and Fergie was in among them more often than not.

Fergie's debut was put on hold as our match with the Fifers was called off due to bad weather, but that only left him chomping at the bit to get started and Berwick Rangers suffered seven days later when he scored twice in a 3-1 victory. He was off the mark, but not to be outdone, Andy Roxburgh grabbed all three the following week as we beat Queen's Park 3-0 at Hampden, a ground Andy would later become synonymous with as Scotland boss. There was no stopping him and when we banged in half-a-dozen seven days later, Andy again claimed a treble. We had a great dressing room and the introduction of Fergie had sparked off a real chain reaction.

Sadly I don't think we managed to play a league game in the whole of January 1970, and we slipped back in the table. We had five or six games in hand on leaders Cowdenbeath but any manager will tell you that it's better having points on the board. We had progressed in the Scottish Cup, though, and after seeing off Tarff Rovers, we were drawn against First Division St Mirren at Brockville. We didn't fear anyone at our place and we beat Saints 2-1, with Fergie getting the clincher. Close on 10,000 roared us on to victory that afternoon.

We had far more than that in when we faced Aberdeen at home in the quarter-finals. We lost 1-0, but had enough chances to win a couple of games. Our Scottish Cup dream was over, which at least left us an opportunity to focus on promotion, although it was the beginning of March and we were a staggering seven games – and

13 points – behind Cowdenbeath. It was going to take one hell of an effort to overhaul them.

Queen of the South were second and we shook off our Scottish Cup hangover by heading for Palmerston and beating them comfortably. Our fans obviously believed in us and we had more than 1,000 at Dumfries with us. But with the Blue Brazil continuing to win, our remit was simple: Win every remaining game and we would be champions – but we had 14 left! We continued to believe, and when we went to Dumbarton and won – thanks to goals from Andy and Fergie – we really did start to believe. We had moved up into second place, seven points behind Cowdenbeath, but with four games in hand.

The title race was heating up and when we beat Arbroath at the end of March, we were right on the shirt-tails of Cowdenbeath – and were due to meet them at Central Park on the Tuesday. Fergie was taken off in the Arbroath game when he was involved in a collision that saw him lose a tooth, but we knew it would take more than that to keep him out of the big game. The kick-off was held up for around ten minutes as a crowd of 10,000 packed into Central Park, something that's so hard to imagine these days. Sadly, the visiting fans would be left disappointed as Cowden won 2-1, which left them strong favourites for the title.

Our game was cancelled on the Saturday, but we were still cheering when Brechin held Cowdenbeath to a 1-1 draw in Fife. The point was enough to clinch promotion for them, but could it be the lost point that would help us win the title?

We beat Alloa 1-0 in a midweek derby match at Brockville but could only draw with Brechin on the Saturday at Glebe Park – although the destination of the title was still in our hands. We won 3-0 in another midweek clash, this time at Forfar, and that was enough to ensure promotion – but we wanted the big prize, and knew that a win over Cowdenbeath would all but give us that. We owed them for that earlier defeat. There was no messing around this time and a 2-0 victory at our place put us within touching distance of the league flag.

We went into a home match against Stranraer needing just a point for the title, but what a scare we got. Almost 5,000 were present and we could feel their nerves. In the second half, we were under the cosh and it was *our* fans calling for the full-time whistle near the end. Thankfully the match finished goalless and we were champions for the first time since 1936. It was a great feeling to win the league with the team I had supported passionately as a lad and, of course, it was my first league medal. We had goals in that side and it was a special title for me.

On our return to the First Division, we sailed through the League Cup section with five wins and a draw. We then took a point off Clyde in our opening game. It felt good playing in the top flight again and we knew that sometimes you have to take a step back to go forward.

Then it was back to reality with a bump. We headed for Ibrox the following weekend, had Fergie sent off for a 'coming together' with John Greig, and lost the game 2-0. I still managed to enjoy the match and the praise which followed. We were under the cosh for large parts of the game but still received a pat on the back in print in the following day's papers.

We had our League Cup quarter-final tie in the midweek, and Cowdenbeath exacted some revenge by winning 1-0 at our place, although we still had the second leg to rectify matters.

Back to the league and we really came of age at East End Park when, courtesy of Andy Roxburgh and Fergie doubles, we won 4-2. But a tough spell was looming and we exited the League Cup after a real bruising second leg at Central Park ended goalless.

After a dodgy start to the season, we started to string a few wins together and by November, we had moved up into the top five. A 0-0 draw against league leaders Celtic at Brockville saw us jump up to joint third, and a few of the critics who had tipped us to go straight back down were conspicuous by their silence. But although the team was performing well, it was another bittersweet moment for me, as I was on the periphery, with the gaffer preferring Gregor Abel and John 'Tiger' McLaughlan – who eventually signed for

Everton for £70,000 – in the full-back roles. It was frustrating, because with just a single substitute allowed in those days, a player's chances of being involved were limited. But the team was winning so it was difficult to complain, and when we drew 1-1 with Dundee United in the middle of December, it was 11 games unbeaten.

The day of 2 January 1971 is one that not many people involved in Scottish football will ever forget. Rangers played Celtic at Ibrox in a league match and 66 people lost their lives in a crush at the end of the game. It was so tragic and the disaster affected everyone. For people to go to a football match and not come home was just awful. That night, so many dads, uncles, sons and brothers failed to make it home. It touched everyone in the country. Fans and players of every club in Scotland felt it really hard, and it remains one of the most horrendous things I have ever encountered in football.

The following week we beat Dunfermline 3-2 in an absolute cracker at Brockville. I think everyone inside the ground – including yours truly – had settled for a draw when our captain George Miller popped up late on to score the winner. It was a fantastic victory, considering we lost Fergie after just 20 minutes to injury. We were joint third with Rangers and it was a good feeling.

No one expected us to remain where we were but we had gone ten games unbeaten at home before losing to Hearts, and with that went our previously excellent home record. We then lost at home to bottom-of-the-table Cowdenbeath and many thought we were on a slippery slope back into the Second Division, and that view was merely compounded the following weekend when we lost 4-0 at Celtic Park. It was a tough time for everyone at the club.

We stopped the rot with an excellent 3-1 win at Easter Road against a battling Hibs side before edging St Mirren at Brockville. We weren't going anywhere without a fight. Far from being a side in danger of slipping down the table, we had arrested the mini-slide and were pushing hard for a place in Europe – something that would've been unthinkable at the start of the season.

Meanwhile, I managed to score my first goal at Ibrox, from a penalty kick in a reserve league match. We were 2-0 down – to a double from Andy Penman – but Bobby Ford got on the end of one of my crosses to knock it home, and I then scored from the spot after Graham Fyfe had handled. Playing against guys like Penman and Derek Johnstone kept me sharp and ready if the call came from the first team, who were sitting sixth – with the fifth-placed team qualifying for the Inter-Cities Fairs Cup – a competition I knew well from my spell at East End Park. In the middle of April, though, we lost 3-1 at Dundee United – who had Walter Smith in their side – and that set us back somewhat as United were our main rivals for Europe.

Our next match was against Aberdeen, who were top of the table, and we proved we were a good side by beating them 1-0. Dundee United lost at St Mirren and our faint hopes of Europe had been temporarily rejuvenated. We had to win at Airdrie in one of our final matches of the season – but it turned into an unmitigated disaster. I'll always recall the Diamonds needing to score at least six goals to pip Rangers to the final Drybrough Cup place, but who on earth would have thought they would have got them against one of the best defences in the division, something I know only too well, as it was keeping me out of the team most weeks. By the end of the game there were a few red faces in the away dressing room at Broomfield as Airdrie scored seven. It was embarrassing but we had to take it on the chin.

My time at Falkirk came to an end with another trip to the Old Firm, this time Parkhead, for a match against Celtic Reserves in the first leg of the Second XI Cup Final. They thumped us 4-0 but it was little wonder when you consider they were able to include players such as Kenny Dalglish, Danny McGrain, Bobby Murdoch, Tommy Gemmell and Stevie Chalmers. It seemed as though half their team had a European Cup winner's medal in their back pocket. In the second leg at Brockville, we gave a better account of ourselves but still lost 2-1, and that was that for me.

I'd had a decent time at Brockville, and while all players want to play every week, we know that isn't possible, but it's no consolation when you're sitting warming the bench or playing for the second string most weeks. It was an experience, though, and it was great hooking up with Fergie again, and Andy Roxburgh. We won a title with a free-scoring team and a great continuity in personnel selection that first season. It was a tremendous feeling for a local boy to actually play for the team he had supported as a boy.

My dad had followed me and been there for me throughout my career and he came along every week to watch me play for Falkirk. It was fantastic for me to know that both my parents were right behind me. They were always very supportive.

I knew my time was up at the end of my second season and when Willie released me, he said, 'I'm sorry Alex, but I can't let sentiment come into it,' and I never forgot that. Later on, when we built the new stadium at Falkirk, Willie was a guest of mine and I always got on really well with him. He was a gentleman and when he passed away I was at his funeral. I remember his wife, Maureen, coming up to me and telling me that Willie had always been fond of me, and that feeling was definitely mutual. We always got on well and I appreciated him being honest with me when he was letting me go. When I became a manager I always tried to be fair and honest with players. When I played at Alloa, the gaffer, Dan McAlinden, didn't tell players if they were released. They got a letter sent to their house and that was how they found out. I always vowed that if I ever became a manager I would speak to players face-to-face if I had any difficult decisions to make. It's not a nice job but it comes with the territory.

So I was a free agent and had interest from a couple of teams during the close-season. One offer that interested me came from Queen of the South. I agreed to meet their chairman Willie Harkness at Abington Services and after a chat I signed a contract and met the players the following Saturday.

It was a strange set-up because we didn't train in Dumfries. The players were scattered to the wind during the week and trained at a variety of places before meeting up on a Saturday for the football. We were part-time so I trained with Stenhousemuir. Alex Smith was the manager at Ochilview and he was kind enough to let me use the facilities there. When we were at home, I would get the train down to Dumfries on a Saturday morning and we would all meet up at the Cairndale Hotel for a pre-match meal. When we were away from home, we got picked up all over the place. Jim Easton was the manager and we would also work on our set pieces on the Saturday morning. I knew Jim quite well as I'd played with him at Dundee when I came back up the road from Liverpool.

Willie McLean took over as manager the following season and couldn't believe the rush to get out of Palmerston after the game on a Saturday. It wasn't like we didn't enjoy his company but if we didn't get the 5.15pm London to Glasgow train, we were stuck in Dumfries until around 10pm. It was a lovely town, but... Now, the game didn't finish until around 4.45pm so you can imagine the stampede. It was a quick shower, and the taxi was waiting to take us straight to the station. We had a great dressing room, and the team spirit was second to none, but anyone who wasn't ready was left behind. No questions asked.

It was a good experience and I was friendly with all the guys and we would have a bit of banter and a game of cards on the way back up to Glasgow, and then a wee drink when we got off the train. Queens were a great club – and I loved the name, Queen of the South. Even now, I enjoy going down to Dumfries to see everyone. Big Alan Ball was the goalkeeper back then and he's still involved to this day. It was a good club and a great playing surface.

The downside was the fact that we didn't see each other until a Saturday, so it was difficult to strike up understandings and partnerships on the park, but at that particular time we used to attract really good crowds of around 5,000. The local derby was against Stranraer – even though they were 80 miles away! Carlisle United were probably the nearest but they were in the English league. I was the regular penalty taker while I was at Palmerston and that was a responsibility I thrived on.

I had a good first season at Queens. We were in the Second Division but were up there challenging some decent teams. We had the likes of St Mirren, Dumbarton, Arbroath and Cowdenbeath all fighting for the two promotion places, so it was a big ask for a group of players who only met up on a Saturday morning. We were on the fringes of promotion most of the season but a last-day 1-1 draw with champions Arbroath meant we finished seventh in the 19-team league.

The following season was one long struggle. I don't think we were ever out the bottom half of the league, although our effort was never in question. It might have been a logistical nightmare but the lads all loved playing for Queens. For me, though, the end of the season brought another move, although this time it would be a heck of a lot closer to home.

7

Stepping Into The Dug-Out

I WAS sitting chilling at home one night when there was a knock at the door. It was Dan McAlinden and Frank Connor – the Alloa Athletic management team. They'd heard I'd left Queen of the South and wanted to sign me. It was a move that interested me and, as it was close to home, it didn't take too long to consider. I thought, 'Why not?' and quite happily agreed a deal, but not before big Dan had given me the ultimate 'line'. He said, 'You will love it at Alloa. It's a beautiful place, and we have the Ochil Hills as a spectacular backdrop. It's lovely.' I said to him, 'What about the team?' He answered, 'Hopeless, but you're gonna change that!'

They were a couple of real characters, especially Frank, whom I really liked, although that didn't stop me homing in on a weakness of his a couple of years later. I'd just taken over as manager of the Wasps, and we were playing Cowdenbeath one Saturday. Frank had moved there as a coach but I couldn't believe it when I saw he was in goals because the first-team keeper was injured. The thing is, I knew Frank had a bad shoulder and while I loved him to bits, I said to the lads, 'As soon as a corner comes in, hit him hard!'

They did just that and Frank was carried off and we went on to win the game. I suppose it shows just how much winning meant to me. Frank was a really fit guy but we were friends before and after the game – although not during it. It doesn't matter if it's your brother or your granny, you want to win. For me it has always been about getting the points.

I always had a great respect for Frank and later discovered that when he was assistant to Jock Wallace at Motherwell, Jock asked him about me. He was going to Rangers as manager and was on the lookout for an assistant. I was in the frame and Frank later told me that he put a good word in for me.

When I signed for Alloa, I was more than happy to be with a club just 20 minutes from the house. I made my debut in a pre-season friendly against South Shields and we battled out an uninspiring 1-1 draw, but it was all about the league campaign for Dan and Frank. The season previous, the Wasps had finished in the bottom half of the table and the management team were desperate to push up the league in the 1973/74 campaign.

We finished bottom of our League Cup section, which included decent teams like Airdrie and Clyde, but got our league campaign off to a winning start with a 3-2 success at East Stirling, although it was tough. We followed that up with a 2-0 win over another of our local rivals, Stenhousemuir, and then went up to Brechin during the week and won 4-0. The following Saturday we maintained our 100 per cent record with a 3-1 win at Stranraer, but were still third in the table. Hamilton had won their first five, and Airdrie their opening four games. You know, it's funny how you can remember certain games more than 40 years on, but that's usually the way of it when you're winning.

There was a full midweek card late in September and after 90 minutes of football up and down the country we were the only team with a 100 per cent record. Airdrie and Hamilton drew their games and we somehow scrambled a 2-1 win at home to Brechin. We were at home to Stirling Albion a few days later and kept our remarkable run going – and suddenly we were top of the table.

It got a bit tousy at times, as local derbies invariably are, but we held our nerve and big Willie McCulloch scored the only goal of the game.

But nothing lasts forever and we drew our next two matches, before losing a couple on the trot. It was now time to see what the players were made of, and it was pretty stern stuff as we dusted ourselves down and won three or four games in a row to remain in the top three. We also came through a tough Scottish Cup tie against league leaders Hamilton to 'earn' a trip to Stranraer in the second round! It was a long, hard season and we eventually lost our grasp on the promotion places and Airdrie went on to win the league, with Kilmarnock also promoted.

My final season as a player at Recreation Park was an interesting one. We hadn't enjoyed the best of fortunes on the field and were locked in a three-way battle with my old team Queen of the South, and Stranraer, to avoid the unwanted mantle of the 'worst team in Scotland'. But February 1980 was a decent month for us and we achieved back-to-back victories over Cowdenbeath and East Stirling, which moved us up to the dizzy heights of third bottom.

Queen of the South had hauled themselves out of the bottom three and were replaced by Meadowbank Thistle. But with just a few weeks of the season remaining it couldn't have been tighter. Ourselves, Queens and Stranraer were locked on 28 points, and Meadowbank had just a point more. There might not have been silverware up for grabs but it couldn't have been any more exciting for the supporters. Then, all of a sudden, we were bottom without kicking a ball. Stranraer and Queens won midweek matches to leave us languishing in the basement, where no team wanted to be. It was disastrous – and we had just one game left to save our season. Sadly, we failed to take advantage of a home game against Queen's Park, lost 1-0 – against ten men – and that was that. We were labelled the worst team in the country, and that was a tag that hurt badly.

The summer of 1980 was an interesting one. Hugh Wilson had been manager at the club but left the post to take over at

Cowdenbeath and the board of directors decided they wanted Falkirk coach John Binnie to replace him. I had a great relationship with Hugh and was sad to see him go. He was a gentleman, maybe too much of a gent, because sometimes you need to be a bit of a so-and-so in football. Our chairman, George Ormiston, interviewed John at his newsagent's shop but he decided to turn down the post, which opened the door for yours truly.

I was 34 and, despite keeping myself fit, and happy to keep playing, I was heading towards a career in the dug-out. The Alloa board were well aware that I was keen to become my own man and offered me the job. Ironically, when I later became manager of Falkirk, I took Gregor Abel as my assistant and got rid of John Binnie, but that's the way football works – and Hugh Wilson did a bit of scouting for me. It's a funny old game!

Gregor and I played together at Falkirk, and often battled for the same place in the team, but I had no hesitation in making him my number two because we worked very well together. You can't beat continuity in a team and, later, when I left Falkirk, Gregor took over at Brockville. If I'm being honest, I was probably a better manager than I was a player. I was steady enough but my career spanned from the ages of 15 to 34 so it was a good career and one that had far more highs than lows.

One of the first things I did when I took over at Alloa was to phone Alex Ferguson. We had always been good friends and he was manager of Aberdeen at the time – and doing very well. We arranged to meet up at a hotel in Dunblane and enjoyed a good natter and, yes, he did pass on a few wee tips!

Alloa was a good club with good directors and they gave me my first chance in management, and for that I will always be grateful. One of the first people I spoke to after getting the job was big Dan McAlinden, and I was a bit surprised by something he said. 'Oh, Alloa will always be Alloa,' because they were the worst team in Scottish football at that time, according to league positions, but I don't always believe things like that and worked really hard to turn things around at The Recs (Recreation Park).

It was quite clear that major surgery was required, but as we couldn't afford to buy players, Gregor and I set about scouring the free transfer lists and picked up loads of players that way. In fact, I think we brought in about 11 free transfers and arranged a friendly against crack junior side Bo'ness United, which was the ideal opportunity to assess whether or not some of them were good enough. In pre-season, we had other boys in on trial. Players aren't always given a free because they aren't any good, there can quite often be mitigating circumstances. I had heard reports about a lad called Willie Temperley from Bo'ness United and he was a cracking player. He had already worked under the likes of Jock Stein at Celtic, and with Hibs boss Eddie Turnbull, but he had a bit of a reputation. A few people advised me to sign him but my thoughts were that if Jock and Eddie couldn't handle him, then what chance did I, as a rookie manager, have. I decided to leave it. I didn't think it was the right time to be taking chances like that. The Alloa ship needed steadying and I played it cagey.

But one thing I was forced to change when I became manager of Alloa was my relationship with the players. I needed to keep them at arm's length, a distance if you like. That was the case when I was at both Alloa and Falkirk, although it changed again when I went to Rangers. At Ibrox, Jock Wallace was the bad guy and I was the assistant who would put an arm round the players. As an assistant you need to be closer.

Our first big test came in my first official match in charge of the club – a friendly at home to Glasgow Rangers. The Ibrox side put out a young team but they still proved too strong for my free transfer squad – although we put up one hell of a fight, and that was when I realised that I had a bunch of players who wanted to play for me. We lost the game 2-1 and Gordon Dalziel was among the Rangers scorers but I was more interested in seeing Colin McIntosh give us the lead.

But we let ourselves down badly in our next pre-season match, a 5-1 loss against Highland League side Elgin City, and it was clear to Gregor and I that there was a lot of work to be done. Mind you,

I wasn't complaining much when we went to Edinburgh for our first league match and trounced Meadowbank Thistle 3-0. We then played a couple of League Cup ties against Hibs and while we lost the home leg 2-0, we redeemed ourselves by holding them to a 1-1 draw at Easter Road, which reclaimed some lost pride.

One of the first things I wanted to install at the club was a decent defence, which we managed, and we were proving a hard team to beat, but if only we could have turned some of our draws into wins, we might just have achieved something special that first season. Mind you, we were top of the table at the start of October, and had lost just one match in ten. By the end of the month we were still top, despite having drawn half our 14 matches. At least the treasurer was happy as we had managed to stick a couple of hundred punters on to our average home gates.

Back-to-back away wins at Clyde and Stranraer had us three points clear at the top in November and we were enjoying an incredible turnaround in fortunes – although there was no way anyone was becoming complacent. Mind you, I allowed myself to think back to what big Dan had said about 'Alloa always being Alloa' and enjoyed a wry smile…then we lost 4-0 at home to Montrose, and 3-1 at Albion Rovers. What was that Jimmy Greaves said about football being a funny old game? There was definitely nothing funny about it, though, and it was Peter Houston, who would become a good friend – and manager of Falkirk – who started the rout that day at Cliftonhill.

Queen's Park had deposed us as league leaders, and the two sides met at The Recs the week after our defeat in Coatbridge. That midweek at training was more about re-establishing a winning mentality among the players, because Gregor and I knew that a third defeat on the trot would be disastrous, and would almost certainly kick-start a slippery descent back down the table and, who knows, perhaps a return to the fortunes of the previous campaign – but we weren't about to let that happen. The guys were fired up for the visit of Queen's and we had more than 1,000 in when the players kicked off. We fair rattled into them from the start and Arthur Grant had us two up after just six minutes. Back came Queen's, though, and were level by the half-hour mark. Thankfully we showed real character for the remainder of the game and scored another three – with Arthur claiming a hat-trick – and entered December back on top of the pile.

I'll never forget the following Saturday, an away day at Brechin. I'm told it was a decent match, and that we drew 1-1, but don't recall seeing much of it due to one of the fiercest blizzards I had ever witnessed. The snow was so thick that at times I couldn't tell what was happening. How the referee knew either was beyond me, but we drew 1-1 and maintained our place at the top.

I remember sitting down for Christmas dinner with Jessie that year, taking a sip of my brandy and thinking, 'What a year.' We had finished up the previous season as the worst team in the country, I had been given my first job in management, and we had ended the year top of the Second Division. But while it had taken a lot of hard work to get us to where we were, everyone at the club knew it would be twice as hard to maintain our standards in the second half of the campaign, as our part-time status kicked in – but we were ready for the challenge.

We were top until near enough the end of March, but defeats against Queen's Park and Cowdenbeath – when we lost five goals – set us back quite a bit. Two more losses saw us slip to mid-table, the position we finished in at the end of the term. It had been a gruelling first season in management, but I had learned an awful lot both about the game and myself, and we would be back all the stronger for it a few months later.

Gregor and I worked hard in the close-season but on day one of the League Cup campaign we lost 4-1 at Forfar. It was such a disappointment, but Arthur Grant ensured we got our first win the following Saturday by scoring all four goals against local rivals Stirling Albion – and we needed all four to ensure we got the points! He then scored twice in our final group game against Stirling to help us avoid the sectional wooden spoon. It was hardly the start we had envisaged.

Our first league match was against Forfar – who had beaten us home and away in the League Cup section – and they did it again, winning 2-1 at The Recs. I was furious, not only at the defeat, but at the attitude of one of my players that day. I put Colin McIntosh on up front as a sub and he was obviously in a mood because he hadn't started the game, so he just wandered about at half-pace. The steam was still coming out my ears when we got into the dressing room after the game and I snarled at him, 'Let me tell you something son, you've had a free from Dunfermline, a free from Partick Thistle, and you've just made it a hat-trick.'

He turned up for training on the Tuesday night and Gregor said to me, 'Colin wants to see you.' I told Gregor that I had said everything I needed to after the game against Forfar. What annoyed me was that I, and every other player, had endured bad games throughout their career, but no manager could ever complain if you had given your all, but that was nowhere near the case that day.

We won a few and lost a few and, generally, made an unspectacular start to the league campaign, but one match in particular – which drew a crowd of just 200 – stands out from the rest. We played Meadowbank Thistle in Edinburgh and drew 1-1 but when I got home I heard the news that Bill Shankly had suffered a heart attack, and I was distraught. It may have been 20 years since he had been my mentor, but I still thought the world of him, and my thoughts were definitely with Shanks and his family that night.

For me, the turning point in our season was a 1-0 win over Berwick Rangers at home. They were second top at the time but the narrowest of wins pushed us up to joint second and, more importantly, gave my players the belief that they were good enough to live with those at the top. We had served our apprenticeship the previous season, and glory was there for the taking.

Scott Murray became the second Alloa player to score four times in one match when he managed the feat at Albion Rovers, but as the year petered out, football was at a premium due to the icy conditions and we ended 1981 sixth in the table. We knew we needed a better 1982 if we were to achieve our goal of promotion.

We finally saw some action at the end of January and romped past Hawick in the Scottish Cup – but only after a first-half scare when the minnows had led 1-0. Four second-half goals took us through. We were rewarded with a home tie against Ayr United in the second round. We knew it would be tough as Ayr were sitting third top of the first division, but we pulled off a real shock by winning 2-1 in front of more than 1,000 at The Recs. It was a brilliant day and Alan Holt got the winner. Next up was a trip to Hampden – although it was Queen's Park in the third round, not the final!

We took that form into the league and thumped league leaders Brechin 4-0 on their own patch, but lost 2-0 to Queen's the following Saturday to exit the cup. They played in the league above but we genuinely felt we had a chance of reaching the quarter-finals so it was disappointing, especially as Queen of the South's reward was a home tie against Forfar.

At the start of April we gunned down East Fife at their place and the win put us second top of the table. It was the perfect time to make our push for promotion, especially with most of our rivals dropping points. Clyde looked favourites for the title but we were certainly bent on grabbing the second promotion place. We kept winning, and so did the Bully Wee, ably led by winger Pat Nevin.

We were in pole position, and within touching distance of the First Division. We could almost reach out and smell it, but a disastrous five-day spell all but put the tin lid on our ambitions. We lost 3-0 at home to Clyde on the Wednesday night and then suffered a shock 3-2 loss at rivals Stirling Albion. It was a disaster. We had a great chance to regain the initiative at home to bottom side Stranraer the following Saturday but could only draw. Thank god our rivals also dropped points.

On the penultimate Saturday we drew again, this time with mid-table Cowdenbeath. Arbroath won to join us in second place on 48 points, and it would go right down to the wire. Our last game was away to our bogey team, Forfar Athletic, while the Red Lichties were due to travel to struggling Stranraer. We had by far the better goal difference but spoke to the players that midweek about going to Station Park and winning – and thinking about nothing else. This would be the most important game of my fledgling managerial career and I wanted it so badly. Berwick Rangers were also in the hunt and if ourselves and Arbroath slipped up, a win for the Wee Gers at Stirling would see them promoted. It was to be an interesting final day.

Berwick could only draw at Stirling but Arbroath won 3-1 at Stranraer. That mattered not a jot though because we were popping the Irn Bru corks at Forfar after an early goal by Ian Smith won us the game. It was in keeping with what was at stake as Ian showed remarkable bravery to put his head in where it hurts to nod past one-time Rangers keeper Stewart Kennedy. We celebrated long into the night and the feeling that I had achieved something notable was a great one.

I remember getting a call from Willie Ormond, who was manager of Hearts at the time. He wanted me to come to Tynecastle as his assistant. It was certainly an attractive job because Hearts were a big draw at the time. I went through for a chat and was seriously considering it. I asked about my contract and couldn't believe his answer. He said to me, 'Well, I've got a contract, but you would just be working on a...' and his answer seemed to drift off somewhere. I thought about it for a few days, because he had been Scotland manager and I liked the thought of working with him, but the fact that he had been so vague about a contract filled me with dread and I decided not to take the chance.

If the previous close-season was a busy one, then this topped the lot. I was desperate to consolidate in the First Division and the chairman backed me by releasing cash for players. I signed Stuart Munro from St Mirren, and he would go on to make a bit of a name for himself in the game. First, though, he was set to make his name at The Recs. I also signed Kenny Thomson, from Dunfermline, and Clydebank's David Houston. Then the draw for the League

Cup was made and we were in with Dunfermline, Arbroath and league champions Celtic. There was much to look forward to.

We got off to the perfect start by winning at Arbroath but the gulf between ourselves and Celtic was evident and we lost 5-0 at The Recs. The treasurer was the only happy 'Wasp' that night. We lost 4-1 at Parkhead, but certainly didn't disgrace ourselves, and the players soon realised what it would take to get to the top of their profession – we knew there was a long and arduous road ahead. Mind you, one unwanted legacy of the match against Celtic was a sickening clash of heads which saw our player Drew Paterson suffer a depressed fracture of the skull, which almost finished him off. He later sustained a broken leg against Albion Rovers, which was a great shame as he had bags of potential. A 3-0 win over Dunfermline in our last League Cup match ensured we didn't finish bottom of the section.

I managed to sign big Willie Garner on loan from Celtic and he did a great job for me. He helped us shake off our League Cup hangover and by the end of September we were third in the First Division table thanks, in the main, to a terrific home record. In one match, at the end of October, though, a win over Dumbarton was slightly overshadowed by the curious incident of 'the flying pie'. I thought the referee David Murdoch had a shocking game and when the door to the match officials' dressing room opened, after the match, someone threw a pie at him. For ages, it was a big mystery – a bit like the case of the flying pizza at Old Trafford that left Alex Ferguson covered in tomato sauce and Arsene Wenger chief suspect.

The celebrated sports journalist David Francey included 'pie-gate' in a book he wrote and it was a mystery for a while, with many people under suspicion. At last I can now own up and clear my conscience. I threw it but my aim was pretty bad so I probably missed him. I shut the door right away so I don't know if it actually hit him and I've never been told otherwise so it will forever remain a mystery in that respect. It was thrown in a mix of anger and jest. I wanted him to enjoy the pie, even though I hadn't enjoyed the game. The referee didn't know who threw it although I suppose that's it out in the open now.

On another occasion, we headed down to Darlington for a friendly match, and there was quite a crowd in the Darlington end. When our goalkeeper was injured, the physio ran on to treat him and suddenly this roar went up. When he came back to the bench, I said to him, 'What happened there?' He answered, coyly, 'My teeth fell out!'

We were comfortable at The Recs and crowds were hovering around the 700 mark, almost double the average of my first season in charge, but I still felt there was so much more we could achieve.

Meanwhile, over at Brockville, John Hagart was sacked after a string of poor results that saw the Bairns languishing at the foot of the First Division. The club were struggling financially and chairman Alex Hardie said the decision was based purely on finance, as they could no longer afford a full-time manager. However, he did also allude, slightly, to the club's perilous position at the foot of the table. A few days later I read in one of the papers that I was on the shortlist for the vacant manager's job, along with Willie Ormond and Jim Shirra, a former Falkirk player. It was business as usual for me, though, and I tried to remain focussed on my own job at The Recs.

However, Saturday 27 November would be the last time I took charge of Alloa, although what a way to go out. We travelled across to Stark's Park to face promotion-chasing Raith Rovers and beat them 1-0. It was a victory that consolidated our place in the top half of the table and it was a win worth celebrating. I took training a couple of nights later, and that was that. I was off to Falkirk and it was time to say goodbye to the many friends I had made at Recreation Park, because a new chapter in my life was just starting, and one that would see me continue a love affair with my hometown club.

Recreation Park might not have been the most glamorous ground in Scottish football but it had been my base for almost ten years and I was proud to call it home. Morale was very low when I took over but we all pulled together and the team spirit we developed was second to none. Throughout my time as gaffer, I often harked back to the words of Dan McAlinden that 'Alloa would always be Alloa'. Well, I showed that wasn't true, because I left the club in far better shape than I found it, but that wasn't just down to me. It was a collective effort and the players and backroom staff deserved a big pat on the back for everything we achieved.

The day I left Recreation Park was very sad, because I had been there a few years as player, coach and manager. There were tears in the boardroom when I told the directors I was leaving. The club were great to me and it was an experience that I thoroughly enjoyed. They gave me a chance in management and I will never forget that. It was a difficult decision to leave in many ways but in others it was easy, because I wanted to progress and realised I could only take Alloa so far – because of fan base and budget etc. Falkirk were a bigger club with a bigger support but they were also MY club, and that had a big bearing on my decision. I was ambitious and wanted to keep progressing in the game and, due to a lot of hard work, I think I realised those ambitions.

8

Home Is Where
The Heart Is

IN November 1982 I was all set to embark on my latest
adventure. Falkirk were bottom of the First Division and the
new chairman, Eddie Moffat, offered me the job the day after
he took over at Brockville. Did they see me as the salvage expert,
after the manner in which I'd taken Alloa from the depths of
despair to respectability in the First Division?

I was 36, and hardly what you would call an experienced
manager, but the Bairns obviously saw something they liked and,
of course, there was no way I could knock back the club I had
supported as a boy. It was my dream job. Both Gregor and I were
former players and loved Falkirk to bits. But still, I knew it was a
gamble to leave Alloa, where I had built up the club, only to have
to start all over again at Falkirk – but it was a gamble I knew I had
to take, and Gregor was with me all the way. Falkirk was a sleeping
giant and it was our job to awaken it.

On my very first night at training, I said to Gregor, 'You take
the session, I'm nicking over to The Recs to thank the Alloa
players for all their efforts.' I introduced myself to the Falkirk
lads and then left the ground. Now, the Falkirk players always got

paid after training on a Thursday night, which was something I wanted to change, so I took the wages with me and didn't see the players again until the Saturday afternoon. Apparently they were all asking for their wages after training but Gregor told them I would speak to them on the Saturday. They weren't too happy, but I was comfortable with that. We were all in the dressing room before the match at Brockville and I produced this big satchel which held all the wages. I put it down on the treatment table and said, 'You know, what a day this is, you play football and then you get paid – after the game today.'

I was keen to change things because the previous manager had been paying them on a Thursday night, naming the team on a Saturday and those who weren't in it were leaving before kick-off, which I felt was both unprofessional and disrespectful to everyone else at the club. I wanted all players there for the game so I decided to pay them after the final whistle, and that way those who weren't stripped stayed to cheer on their mates.

It wasn't so bad at home games, where we had the safe to keep the cash in, but when we were off on our travels I would be stuck with this big satchel full of money until after the game, but right away I had made my mark. They might not have liked it but they had no say in the matter.

We didn't have the greatest of starts but by the turn of the year we had managed to haul ourselves off the foot of the table and after clocking up a fourth win in a row, against Queen's Park, we drew Rangers in the third round of the Scottish Cup at home. The cops set a limit of 15,000, but I still reckoned it would make the club a few bob, so I asked for £10,000 to sign Peter Houston from Albion Rovers. Chairman Eddie Moffat and Malcolm Allan, the vice-chairman, promptly dipped into their own pockets to come up with the cash, which I thought showed real commitment to the club.

I felt it was a really exciting time to be manager of Falkirk. The club might not have been on its uppers but for someone who had missed few Falkirk games as a youngster, and who could still rhyme off the names of all the players of that era, it was the best of times. Not everyone gets the chance to manage the team he supported. In my young days, teams were very wary of coming to play Falkirk, and I wanted to make them afraid again.

When Rangers arrived for the cup match, the ground was packed. The atmosphere was electric and our game plan was to get in among them from the word go. We did that. We upset their rhythm and didn't give their creative players such as Davie Cooper and Jim Bett any time to settle. It was goalless at half-time, but we had played really well and been first to every ball – and then came the cruel twist of fate that sent us spinning out of the cup. Allan Oliver tried to clear a Kenny Black cross and succeeded only in sending it into his own net. The heads went down and the tie was over when young Andy Kennedy scored a second. We were certainly down, and perhaps out, but morale was still high.

Hearts were top of the league at the beginning of March but it was a confident bunch of players who left Tynecastle with a 2-1 win, thanks to an injury-time winner by our centre-half Alan Mackin. The first goal had been a cunning effort from Bobby McCullie. He waited until Hearts lined up their wall, moved the ball slightly to the right and stuck it in the corner of the net! We showed we could last the distance against the better sides and were climbing the table steadily as a result. Another win the following week took us up to joint fifth in the table, and we were growing in confidence as a result.

At the end of April we faced my old side, Alloa, at Brockville, and a 2-1 win took us to within a point of them in the table. We had been behind them all season but enjoyed an incredible run of results to get up alongside them, although on the last day of the season, Alloa won 1-0 at Airdrie and we lost 2-1 to Dumbarton at home, which meant we finished the season in eighth place, two behind the Wasps. When I had taken over the club, our only goal had been First Division survival, and we achieved that, but I wanted to know where we would be in a year's time. I was building for the future and to help make the Bairns a force again.

To that end, we organised a glamour friendly against Leeds United to open the new season, and I had a new player in my ranks. I had just signed Kevin McAllister and not only would he make a real impact in the match against the Yorkshire side, but he would go on to become one of Falkirk's greatest ever players. But it was a team performance that got us a 2-2 draw against Leeds, and we took that form into the first game of the season, a 1-0 win at Alloa – which gave me a good feeling for the campaign ahead. It was a classic derby with no quarter asked, nor given, and there were a sprinkling of bookings as both sets of players showed their determination to start off with a win. But the Wasps gained instant revenge when they knocked us out of the new-look League Cup with a 6-4 aggregate win, which included a 4-2 victory at our place.

We had a decent start to our league campaign but after six matches everyone was chasing Partick Thistle. Inspired by youngster Mo Johnston, they had won all their matches and even though we were fourth in the table, we were four points behind. By the first week in October we had chipped away at Partick's lead and were just a point behind, and Kevin was proving a real match-winner. When we beat Meadowbank at home he was outstanding. I had high hopes for wee 'Crunchie'. Alan Irvine was another class player, but when we beat Ayr 1-0 at Somerset Park the following week, it was Arthur Grant who stole the show with the only goal. Thistle lost at Meadowbank, so we were top of the league. It was a remarkable transformation in just under a year, when we'd been bottom of the First Division. Suddenly, looking at the league table in the papers the day after a match became enjoyable again.

At the time I took little interest in events at Ibrox. Rangers fans weren't happy with a poor run of results and protested outside the ground after their latest reverse, at home to Motherwell, who were managed by former Gers boss Jock Wallace. The defeat left current manager John Greig under real pressure and I could sympathise with him because it was such a pressure job at Ibrox. But I had my own problems to iron out and we relinquished top spot in the league when we lost 1-0 at Brechin.

We had a chance to regain our position at the summit the following week when league leaders Partick visited Brockville. Just over 5,000 turned up and they were treated to a cracking game. Wee Crunchie had us two up at the break but the Jags scored twice late on to earn a draw. Kevin's first goal was almost unique, a rare headed goal from probably the smallest man on the park, although his second was trademark Crunchie, as he rounded a couple of defenders before firing home. He definitely deserved to be on the winning side that day.

Over at Ibrox, there had been change and Jock Wallace was named as the new manager – and the bookies were tipping yours truly to replace him at Fir Park, which was something of a compliment. Mind you, St Johnstone boss Alex Rennie was also in the frame. For me, though, it was business as usual and I was just determined to get the Bairns back on top of the table, although Partick were making it very difficult. Things were going well and our gates had improved dramatically, rising from something like 800 to 2,500. It helped that we were winning regularly but I also like to think that our supporters were encouraged by the brand of football we were playing.

Obviously someone noticed, and all of a sudden I was in demand. I had only ever met Jock Wallace once, when I was after a player he had at Fir Park. I quite fancied the big boy Bruce Clelland and Jock invited me through to Fir Park and I was ten minutes in his company.

Then, on 11 November 1983, at 8am, the phone rang at home and my wife answered it. She didn't recognise the voice. I took the receiver, 'Jock Wallace here son, how would you like to come to Rangers and be my assistant?' The call came right out of the blue. He told me he was going to Aberdeen the following day for his first game and that he would call me on the Monday. I was told to keep it quiet – which, as you can imagine, was tough. Mind you, that didn't stop me telling my dad – and it was one of the best feelings I'd ever had, as he was a big Rangers man. When I told him, his face lit up and that made me so happy. In fact, to this day, every time I pass my mum and dad's house, I always think back to the moment I walked through the front door to tell him I had been offered the job. That moment will never leave me.

We were playing Clyde and went to the Dutch Inn for our usual pre-match meal. We were all sitting there tucking in, and I simply couldn't believe the secret I was keeping, and then who comes on the television, on the football preview show *Saint and Greavsie*, but big Jock, and I'm thinking, no one knows that he phoned me yesterday.

After the game against Clyde, our chairman asked me up to the office and I started thinking, 'What does he know?' But he said, 'Motherwell have been on the phone, they want to interview you about the vacant gaffer's job.' I thought it was only manners so I went through to a Coatbridge hotel on the Monday night and met Mr Livingstone, the chairman, and about six other people, and he said, 'Alex, we want to offer you a five-year contract. We've had so many managers here recently, between Jock Wallace, Davie Hay, Roger Hynd and Ally McLeod, that we're now looking for a bit of stability.'

It was a great contract and so different from anything I had known before in football. There was a five-year deal on the table and magnificent money and, of course, the chance to manage a full-time Premier League outfit. It was very tempting. I'd had other offers before that. Dunfermline had tried to persuade me to go back, twice, in fact, and I was tempted, because of the good memories I had of the place, but when the call came from Jock, even the Motherwell offer, good as it was, had to be pushed aside. I told them I would call them on Wednesday, and when I phoned them back, I said, 'I really appreciate the offer but I have to turn it down and you'll find out why in the next couple of days.'

I had decided to take the job at Ibrox, but before I left Falkirk there was one last function I had to perform. I didn't have a contract with the Bairns, and because of the tremendous feelings I had for the club, I didn't want to see them miss out on compensation from Rangers, so I asked the chairman to draw one up, which meant they would get a few quid for me. I thought it was the right thing to do. I told Mr Moffat that if I didn't go to either club, and decided to stay at Falkirk, then I would rip up the contract and continue as normal, and he seemed happy with that. Mr Moffat was speaking to Campbell Ogilvie and Rae Simpson at Rangers to try and get as much money as possible so it dragged on for quite a while. It got resolved eventually but I still don't know to this day how much they got. Mind you, there was a point when I said to the chairman, 'Surely, you can't stop me going to Ibrox, it's a great opportunity,' but he assured me he wasn't, and that he just wanted to make sure Falkirk were properly compensated.

Going to Rangers was weird, and people definitely reacted differently around me. Just after I moved to Ibrox, Jessie and I went out for a meal with a few friends, one of whom was a big Rangers man. I'll never forget being in the restaurant that night and the guy in question just staring at me all night. It was strange, but Rangers definitely does have an incredible effect on people.

My time as manager of Falkirk had been short-lived, but very successful, and I left the club on a sound footing, which gave me a lot of pleasure. Falkirk were still 'my team' but I was now an employee of Rangers Football Club – and that felt very good indeed.

9

Ibrox-Bound

AS per the initial arrangement, Jock called on the Monday and asked me to be at Ibrox at 4pm on the Friday and I went there with a whole range of emotions: joy, trepidation, pride etc. The first person I met was Stan the commissionaire, and he said to me, 'Mr Wallace is waiting for you at the top of the marble staircase, Mr Totten.'

I walked up the stairs, taking my time and enjoying the moment. There at the top of the staircase was Alan Morton, the Wee Blue Devil, staring down at me from the famous portrait. Like an expectant schoolboy I walked into the Blue Room, where Jock said to me, 'Great to see you son, you're now a Ranger. Come and meet the directors,' and there was Willie Waddell, Rae Simpson and more, so that's when and how it all started. Walking through the front door and up the marble staircase was a nerve-wracking experience. It wasn't like working at any other football ground. In fact, it wasn't really like working at a football club at all. The entrance and staircase at Ibrox just screams history and tradition, and makes the hairs on the back of your neck stand to attention.

On one occasion Jock and I were in Switzerland, and we'd had a wee drink and I asked him, 'Why did you come in for me, there must have been dozens of other candidates?' He told me, 'Ten minutes was enough,' and that was that day in his office at Motherwell. He also said, 'I liked the way you acted, and your passion for the game. Something just clicked for me and I immediately shelved plans to call the others on my list.'

In Switzerland, we visited the same wee restaurant a couple of times. It was run by a lady called Lisa and she really looked after Jock and I, and the players. When we were back at Ibrox, a mystery parcel arrived at the stadium one day. It was postmarked 'Switzerland' and it turned out to be two beautiful handkerchiefs, addressed to 'Mr Jock' and 'Mr Alex'. It said, 'Thank you for your manners and kindness while you were in my country, Lisa.' It was a lovely gesture. Switzerland was a beautiful country, although not every player in the squad appreciated its natural appeal. We were in a coach heading for Sion one day and a lot of the lads were playing cards. I was admiring the beauty of the snow-covered Alps and I turned to Bobby Russell and said, 'Look at that Bobby, isn't it magnificent?' He didn't even look up from his deck of cards and replied, 'Alex, when you've seen one hill, you've seen them all!'

At the end of the tour, we were heading back to the airport on the coach, and it was scorching hot. A lot of the players had taken their shirts off, and we hid big Davie McPherson's. He was only 17 at the time, and when we arrived at the terminal, he went to put it back on – but it had 'vanished'. In his squeaky voice, he said, 'Okay guys, school's out, now where's my shirt?' Quick as a flash, big Jock turned to him and said, 'When your voice breaks, you'll be some player son,' and that was the cue for uproar on the bus.

I'll never forget my 'debut', against Dundee United, and the moment Jock and I walked out the tunnel together. I was quite shy, the complete opposite of the big man. He led the way, punching the air and lapping up the applause. I was walking behind him and didn't know what to do, so I just sort of applauded him, which later seemed a bit odd.

I met all the players for the first time before the match, Davie Cooper, Ally McCoist etc and I think we went 20-odd games with just one defeat, and we beat Celtic 3-2 in the League Cup Final, when Ally got a hat-trick. We also went a world tour to Australia, New Zealand, America and Canada, which was an incredible experience.

I left a part-time job at Falkirk to go to Rangers and Jock attempted to sum up the differences between the clubs to me on my first day in the job. He said, 'When you lose with Falkirk the whole of Stirlingshire knows, but when you lose with Rangers, the whole WORLD knows.' He had a great way with words and it was usually the case that when big Jock spoke, people listened.

When he told me to take the first training session I simply couldn't believe what I was seeing with Davie Cooper. He was just so talented. You would have thought the ball was tied to his boots. I was dealing with international players but Coop was just different class. Later on, when I got the sack at St Johnstone, I received a call from a friend called Jim Docherty. He owned a garage in Auchterarder and said to me, 'Come up and get a car, I've got plenty.' I knew he'd always admired Davie Cooper so I phoned up Coop and he was up for the visit. I hadn't told Jim we were coming and when we parked in the driveway, he couldn't believe it when Davie Cooper stepped out the car. The camera was out and he took loads of photographs.

I always got on well with Coop and the same with all the other boys. I remember when we beat Celtic to win the League Cup, Coop gave me his shirt for my son, Bruce, and he still has it up on his wall to this day. As well as being a brilliant player, Coop was also an absolute gem of a person.

It was a whole new way of life for me at Ibrox and to go full-time with a big club like Rangers was pretty incredible. One of the things I had to get used to was dealing with the media. It was something I had done before, but never on a par with anything I experienced at Rangers. After one particular game, against Morton, I was speaking to the press, and they preferred to talk about speculation linking Davie Cooper with a move to Aberdeen. I made it clear that we intended keeping Coop at Ibrox, and said, 'Davie's contract is up at the end of the season so there is bound to be speculation. Last week it was Liverpool, this week it's Aberdeen, but as far as I'm concerned, Davie is a Rangers player and that's that. I'm also confident he will remain so after this season.'

One of my proudest moments in the game arrived after a league match at Ibrox. My dad was a big Rangers fan and Jock invited him up to the office after the match. We were sitting there, chatting about the game, when suddenly Jock said to dad, 'You know, one day this will be Alex's office, because I'll step up to be general manager and he will take over as manager.' The idea was to keep the continuity going, just like Liverpool, with Shankly, Paisley, Fagan and then Kenny Dalglish. That was Jock's way of thinking, but obviously it didn't quite work out like that, which was a great shame, because I would love to have managed the great Glasgow Rangers. It would have been such an honour and I suppose I came the closest you can ever get without actually getting the job.

In saying that, I did get to manage the team on one occasion. Okay, so it was just the Tennent's Sixes, but I was manager and that's all that counts. Oh, and we won the competition, so I have a 100 per cent record as boss! It was the first tournament of its kind in Scotland and was staged at Coasters Arena, in Falkirk. We had the likes of John McClelland, Robert Prytz, Jimmy Nicholl and Derek Ferguson in the line-up, so is it really any wonder we won the trophy? We beat Dundee 4-2 in the final, which was great, because we had three-quarters of the arena that night and the fans were buzzing. We also had a great bunch of boys and it was a pleasure to manage them.

After a few weeks at the club I could still scarcely believe I was a Ranger. I milked my time for all it was worth. As a club employee, I was entitled to park my car under the stand, but I would walk back out on to the street and in the front door. Just the feeling of walking through the front door off Edmiston Drive was unlike any other. It was the tradition and it was just that type of club that you wanted to do everything right.

I was an area sales manager with Goodyear while I was manager of Falkirk so it meant giving that up, but it didn't take me too long to make up my mind when Rangers came in for me. I always remember Ian Durrant calling me when he had his testimonial dinner at the Thistle Hotel in Glasgow and inviting me to sit at the top table. There were 1,000 people there, and I was at the top table with John Greig, Andy Cameron and Dougie Donnelly. You simply can't buy that. When Durranty got the bad injury I went to see him in hospital because I really liked him, and I still remember the first time I saw the wee man playing. It was in a reserve match up at Tannadice and Jock wasn't there that night. I reported back about what a wee gem this kid was and he soon blossomed into a real player. We went to Stamford Bridge to play Chelsea in a benefit match for the Bradford Disaster Fund, and the game had gone about ten minutes when John Hollins, the Chelsea manager, said, 'Who's your number ten, he's a great player,' and it was wee Durranty.

That trip to London is up there with the best memories of my time at Ibrox. We were so well looked after by the Blues and they couldn't have done enough for us. After the game, we were taken to a hotel near the ground for a champagne reception and it was fantastic – and it was also the first time I had been 'treated' to Ally McCoist and his famous rap, which was something else, and I'm still not sure if London was prepared for it! But we were staying in a nice hotel in Brighton – close to the one that was bombed at the Tory Party conference – and Chelsea gave us the use of their team bus to take us to and from the hotel. The coach was packed full of every little luxury you could think of. There was the obligatory bar on board and we decided that the players should let their hair down after the match. The lads gave us the whole songbook on the two-hour journey from London to Brighton and big Derek Johnstone knew all the words of every song in that book! It was a memorable trip.

When I went to Rangers at first, I told Jock there were a number of good players in the First Division, lads such as Kevin McAllister, Bobby Connor, Alan McInally and Bobby Williamson. So we sent Willie Thornton to see Williamson and we got him for £100,000.

Bobby was fantastic and when we signed him he was a brickie. I also recommended Stuart Munro. I'd signed him while I was at Alloa and told Jock about him. We went to see him against Hamilton at Douglas Park and he was the best man on the park by a mile.

After the game, Jock told me to go down and offer my former chairman £15,000, and Stuart ended up at Rangers for six years. It was a great piece of business. Kevin McAllister was also a great player. I was a manager for 22 years and he is the best player I ever signed, and I signed a lot of players in my time. Alan Gilzean was the best I ever played with and Davie Cooper was probably the best player I coached, although he was a natural.

Five months after moving to Ibrox, we played Ajax in a friendly at home. Our League Cup Final win over Celtic had guaranteed a slot in the following season's UEFA Cup so Jock thought it would be good to meet European opposition to give us an idea of where we were at. It was a move that could have backfired spectacularly, but the opposite happened. We thumped them 4-0, and the sad thing was that only 12,000 turned up to witness it. Ajax had a cracking team at that time and included players such as Frank Rijkaard, Ronald Koeman and Marco van Basten that night.

We had a player at Rangers called Siggi Jonsson, an Icelandic lad. He had been with us since he was 13 or 14 and we knew he was a real star of the future. He played in all the youth tournaments abroad with the likes of Ian Durrant, but as soon as he was 16 he left in a hurry and signed for Sheffield Wednesday, which was a real kick in the teeth for Jock and I. He got £100,000 signing-on fee and big Jock was raging. Later on, he was badly injured after coming up against Graeme Souness in an international match.

Siggi roomed with Durranty and there was one occasion when Ian wasn't feeling too well and the lad sat there feeding him crisps! He was a nice lad but we would have thought a lot more of him had he come and told us that Sheffield Wednesday had approached him, but he didn't and Jock and I thought that very sneaky.

On one occasion, Jock and I went down to Liverpool to have a look at Gary Gillespie and as we approached the city he was starting to feel a bit peckish, so I hit on the idea of going to my old digs. Mrs Carroll didn't know we were coming and when she opened the door you could have knocked her over with a feather. She couldn't believe it. We went in and she made us a lovely meal and we had a great natter about the old days – and Jock left her a few quid to cover the meal. We were only 200 yards from the ground so it was in the perfect location.

Another trip south of the border wasn't as pleasant, though. I had gone to see Manchester United and Dundee United at Old Trafford and it finished 3-3. It was a great game so I decided to go and see the second leg at Tannadice, but big Jock wanted to go down to Old Trafford to see Celtic play Rapid Vienna, which was being played at a neutral venue after some carry-on at Celtic Park. We stopped at a service station on the way down and Jock was out filling up with petrol and was taking some real stick from groups of Celtic fans, but it was all good fun. The banter was flowing and the Celtic fans were saying things like, 'Aw it's bad news for you Jock, Mrs McStay's expecting again,' which was a reference to how well her son Paul was playing at the time.

We then headed to the ground and were invited into the lounge at Old Trafford. Kenny Dalglish and Alan Hansen were there, and we were standing talking to them, but could hear the murmurs from the Celtic supporters, and also caught some of the stares. 'What's two Rangers men doing down here?' was one of the comments. We felt really uncomfortable.

Celtic lost a goal with about ten minutes to go and Jock said, 'Come on Totts, let's get out of here,' but a lot of Celtic fans were also leaving and he told me to walk behind him when we got out of the stadium. The abuse we took was unbelievable. Some of the things said to us were right out of order.

We had gone down in his Jaguar XJ6 and as he didn't like driving, I usually took the wheel. The Celtic fans were banging on the car roof, and rocking it back and forward, and Jock said, 'Just put your foot down Totts.' I did, and they all scattered, shouting and bawling at us. Normally when we were down in England we would stop at a service station for a cup of coffee, but we just headed straight up the road. In the car, he turned to me and said, 'You know Totts, I've been in a lot of scary situations in my life, including the Malayan jungles, but that's the most frightened I've ever been – I thought we were for it there.'

All it would have taken for some serious trouble to kick off would've been one person to throw a punch and all hell would've broken loose. There were thousands of them so we wouldn't have stood a chance. What started off as banter soon turned poisonous and Jock wasn't the only one who was scared. We had parked a couple of hundred yards away from the main entrance so we had quite a walk to the car, but it felt like an eternity.

One of the things I enjoyed most about my time at Rangers was that Jock always gave me my place, which was great. We would sit in the office and talk about what we would do at training the following day. We worked as a team, and I always appreciated that. I would stick in my tuppence worth and Jock soon knew my feelings on wingers, and how I felt they were vital to the entertainment side of the game.

I enjoyed working with the big man and he was great with the players in the gym – although I don't quite know if they would concur with that view. Jock believed that your power came from your stomach, so did quite a bit of work with medicine balls – and both he and I always took part in these exercises. He would always be on at the players to work on their stomach and, from time to time, he would say to the young players, 'Are you doing your stomachs?' 'Aye,' would come back the reply and 'boof', he would punch them one in the stomach to see if they flinched – and they invariably did!

We used to go to Gullane Sands, which was incredibly tough – Murder Hill they called it, and after the session was over the players would throw us in the water. After drying off, we'd go up to a hotel in Gullane for lunch and then back to Ibrox.

The coaches were all positioned at different parts of the hill to encourage the players to keep going. Jock was very hands-on and took most of the training. He was always that way. I remember the late, great Sandy Jardine talking about Jock's first spell at Ibrox, and he said to me, 'People can say what they want about our training methods but we were the fittest team in Scotland.'

We started off training in the dressing room, where the players did their stomach exercises, and then they would run to the Albion training ground, and he would go crazy if one of the players had his socks at his ankles. That was a policy of his – no socks at the ankles. And that is the way it should be. I would say to players, 'We start at 10am, if you're late you're fined, and don't turn up in jeans. You come smart but casual.' That was my policy and if the players didn't like it they were free to go elsewhere. It was also Jock's policy.

We also did pre-season at Bellahouston Park, and would mark out a small running course, with coaches stationed at strategic points, but Robert Prytz, who would always be last, would run past you muttering, 'Alex, this is not football.' He absolutely hated running, but I'm sure he realised the value of fitness.

I was at Liverpool as a player, and also with Dundee, who were a big club at the time and had won the league, but Rangers was a different proposition altogether. They were just such a special club. I remember we played Inter Milan in a big European tie and the journalist Gerry McNee came with us. Before the game he interviewed Franz Beckenbauer, the German manager, who was there to see the big lad Hans-Peter Briegel. After the game, Gerry spoke to Liam Brady, and then we went to a restaurant for a meal and he managed to get a chat with Karl-Heinz Rummenigge, and he said, 'I'm hanging out with you guys more often, I've got a month's work in one day!'

Before that tie, I had been over to Italy to watch them play at Juventus. It was the second time I'd watched Inter, and managed to build up quite a dossier on them. That was Jock's thing, he was very thorough in his preparation. Before we played home European ties, Turnberry was our hideout and we were treated like kings. Everything was the best. We would train on the Tuesday and Jock and I would have a game of golf. The players weren't allowed to play, mind you, because they were playing the next night, but we always enjoyed a round or two!

When we played Osasuna, we decided to go to Dunblane for a change and played the Queen's Course at Gleneagles. It was great, and I'd go through to his house and we'd play golf at Bothwell. His wife Daphne was also a really good player. Jock was great to me. He took me to Ibrox when he could have taken a lot of other people and that's something I will always appreciate. He gave me the opportunity and was definitely lining me up as his successor. In fact, I'd been there six months when John Paton took over as chairman and I remember reading an interview with him in the *Sunday Express* which said, 'When Jock steps up to general manager, Alex Totten will take over as team manager'. It was quite something to read.

But one Monday morning, Jock came up to me – gloomy expression etched all over his face – and he said, 'Totts, that's me away, they're bringing [Graeme] Souness in.' I was shattered, completely shattered. Jock collected his things and he was gone. I know nothing is forever but I still felt we had unfinished business and that it shouldn't have ended like that.

David Holmes, the Rangers chief executive, called me up and said he wanted me to meet Souness. I went up to his office and he introduced us. Souness shook my hand and looked away, which made me feel really uncomfortable. Holmes said, 'Graeme wants to go down and meet the players.' I took him round the dressing room, 'This is Peter McCloy, Derek Johnstone, Davie Cooper.' Just as he started to give them all a talk, the door burst open and it was Ally McCoist, late again! I said to him, 'What a morning to be late.' Souness then went back to Sampdoria and I was in charge for a week, which included a match at Clydebank.

There were many similarities between both Jock and Bill Shankly. Both men knew the game inside out and wanted their teams to play football. I learned from each person I worked with. Each manager has something different to offer. I was very fortunate to have worked under both Shankly brothers, but I learned an awful lot from Jock. He was big in stature and always liked his players to be fit. That was his number one thing because if you're fit, you're halfway there.

When I went to Ibrox there were four international players at the club – Robert Prytz, John McClelland, Jimmy Nicholl and Davie Cooper. By the time I left, there was just the one – Coop. Big Jock spent £600,000 in three years. Souness came and spent £16m, and his first two signings were Terry Butcher and Chris Woods. Terry later told me that he had no intention of going to Rangers. He was apparently set to sign for Tottenham but Souness called and asked for a meeting. Terry said to him, 'If I'm going to come to Scotland I want this, that and the next thing...' And Souness said, 'Okay.'

The whole ball game changed overnight with the arrival of Souness. I mean, his first two signings were the England captain and goalkeeper. When Jock and I were in charge, the players were all on the same basic wage and that was our policy, but it frustrated Jock at times because there were a lot of players he wanted to go out and sign but felt the money just wasn't there, and all of a sudden they found pots of cash for the new manager, although I suppose that was the carrot to lure Souness to Ibrox in the first place. But I just wish Jock had been given that money because I'm convinced he would have done really well with it. He had been at Leicester and knew the English scene very well and was well respected down there so he could also have tempted some big names north of the border had the budget been there.

I remember we played a game at Falkirk between Rangers and a Falkirk select side and Dougie Bell was playing. I said to him, 'I always remember big Jock paid £120,000 for you and your first game was at Easter Road.' We won 3-1 and Dougie was the best man on the park and after the game Jock and John Paton were sitting at the front of the bus, and Mr Paton said, 'Any more like him Jock and we'll give you the money.'

The first game after Jock left was against Clydebank, and it was a match that didn't so much dent my professional pride, as completely knock it for six. We lost 2-1 at Kilbowie, which was something of a shock. After the match, I said, 'Managers and coaches are the people in football who get the sack, but players can't escape responsibility either. I feel sorry for our fans. As far as I'm concerned, I was looking for a lot more from a Rangers team than I got. Players should have pride in their own display, but no one else can give them that other than themselves. If Graeme Souness had someone watching then they should have wanted to show how much it meant to play for Rangers.'

There's no doubt it had been a difficult week with players affected by Jock's sudden departure. Some of them, such as Nicky Walker, were in tears. He had signed Nicky three times for various clubs, so he took it particularly hard.

A couple of days after the defeat against Clydebank, David Holmes called for me, John Hagart and Stan Anderson. We went round to his office, which was in the Broomloan Stand, and Davie, who was a Falkirk man, said, 'I know you from our Falkirk days Alex, but Graeme wants to bring in his own men,' which was absolutely fine. It was Chick Young who told me that Walter Smith was the favourite to be Souness's assistant, so the last thing I did before leaving was to leave a note on Walter's desk wishing him all the best. Walter and I are good friends so there were absolutely no hard feelings.

I then knocked Souness's door and wished him all the best too. He only opened the door a wee bit – perhaps he thought I was going to thump him! But he told me he appreciated my words and that was that – I walked out the front door for the last time as a Rangers man. I felt a bit sorry for John Hagart, because he was from Edinburgh and knew Souness, and I felt he had a chance of being kept on, but it was a new broom and a complete clear-out. Souness started from scratch but these things happen.

The whole Rangers experience was fantastic, and I would never say a bad word against them. Everything about the club was bigger and the media interest every day was incredible, but I enjoyed it. In general I didn't get any grief from Celtic fans in the street. I think you try and treat people the way you want to be treated yourself. The supporters of both clubs have a real rivalry going on but both management teams and players by and large have a healthy respect for one another.

I always remember Jessie being interviewed by the media when I left Rangers, and she said, 'We have always been a quiet couple – our life is our family. We've never been ones for the high life. When Alex got the Rangers job, people told me to give up my part-time job and buy a big house, but I never did because I know how football works. It can be so precarious. One minute you're up, next you're down. In football, nothing is ever certain. This situation has certainly proved that. I'm as proud as punch of Alex and the job he's done at Ibrox. I was thrilled when he got the job, and neither of us are sorry he made the move.'

I spoke to Souness just before we played Rangers in the Scottish Cup the season before last. We have a mutual friend, Graham Gillespie, and his phone went while we were chatting. I heard Graham tell Souness he was with me and he asked to speak to me. He asked what I was up to and I told him about the Rangers match, and that I was going down to see Liverpool the following week. He told me I'd enjoy it as Brendan Rodgers had them playing well. We chatted for a while and he said, 'It was great to speak to you again', and he definitely seemed far more humble, probably because he insisted he wasn't interested in football management anymore!

10

Taking On The World

THE summer of 1984 has to be up there with my greatest times in the game. At the end of May, we jetted off on the first leg of our world tour – destination Australia. Also on the itinerary were stop-offs in New Zealand, the USA and Canada. It was full of promise from the word go, and it delivered. Mind you, it could also have been termed 'the tour from hell', given the amount of injuries we suffered, but more of that later.

As we were leaving Glasgow Airport, Bobby Williamson, who we had just signed from Clydebank, turned up with this enormous suitcase. I took one look at it and said, 'What have you got in there Bobby?' It turned out he had 14 pairs of trousers with him – and then we found out he had never been abroad before! It was hilarious, but Bobby was someone I got on great with.

We received our first big shock shortly after touching down in Melbourne when we were told that our first match, against the Aussie national 'B' side had been moved to the Melbourne Cricket Ground, because demand for tickets had far outweighed supply – and organisers were expecting a crowd of around 50,000. In fact, when we arrived at the airport, there was an exiled Gers fan there to meet us and he had flown in especially from Papua New Guinea. That's when you realise how massive Rangers Football

Club actually is, and the appeal it has. The jet lag was horrendous but the welcome we received down under helped us get over it.

Ally McCoist was a real character and was in trouble with big Jock before we had even left. Coisty was looking around the shop at the airport and when he came out, the rest of us had left for the departure gate. When he finally caught up with us, Jock grabbed him and told him he was on his last warning! He then got lost at Heathrow, and Jock's patience was wearing thin. We arrived in Melbourne at 5am and Jock said, 'Right, everyone get to bed for a few hours, and be downstairs no later than 8am for a team meeting and breakfast.' I didn't get down for breakfast until after eight, and when I walked in, I noticed Coisty mouthing 'thank you Totts'. It turned out he had just made it down in front of me, but after eight, although Jock couldn't collar him as I was even later.

Then we encountered the first storm of the tour – and it might have been easier had it come from the skies. It seemed like the Aussie public were far from happy about playing a 'soccer' match on the hallowed turf of the MCG, although big Jock defused the situation slightly when he said at a press conference, 'I know all about hallowed grounds, I've just come from Ibrox!'

We organised our first training session for the day after we arrived in the country, and Jock and I had a real surprise in store for the players. We sourced a local hill – just like Gullane – and I'll always remember the big man trying it first and admitting he was knackered! It would have been quite funny had it been a private session but there were more than 200 Rangers fans there watching us, and most were kitted out in Gers tops and scarves. That night, we were invited to a function which had been organised in our honour by the Altona Rangers Supporters' Club, and the club went all out to ensure we had a fantastic night.

The first match was an enjoyable encounter, although Sandy Clark was unavailable for selection after injuring an ankle in training. Bobby Russell was then a victim of a freak accident when the ball ricocheted off the back of an opponent and hit him square in the face. He suffered a nasty eye injury and was taken straight to hospital. There was a lot of bruising on his face but initial reports suggested there was no damage to the retina, which was a big relief. Mind you, Bobby's injury didn't prevent us heading straight to Surfer's Paradise after the game! Jock thought the fresh sea breeze and warm surf would do far more good than another tough training session, so we enjoyed our break in the beautiful little holiday town.

But no sooner had we enjoyed Surfer's Paradise than our dream tour had turned into a nightmare. The players went out for a few drinks – and Bobby Williamson ended up with a broken leg. There were all sorts of rumours flying about the Aussie papers so Jock held a press conference and described the players' behaviour as 'horseplay'. Nevertheless, as a result of his injury, it looked like Bobby, who had cost a lot of money, was set to miss around six months of action, which was a big blow to both club and player. He was in hospital for a fortnight before being flown home. I really did feel for him because he had just returned to the side – in Melbourne – after recovering from a groin injury. We all went up to see him and he was trying to put a brave face on it, but he must have been gutted. As a consequence, we made arrangements for young Eric Ferguson to fly out immediately as cover.

We were also boosted by the arrival of Davie Cooper and John McClelland, who were joining up with the squad after turning out for Scotland and Northern Ireland respectively. We had only played one game but were already glad to see the cavalry turn up! In fact, it was quite uncanny because just as Coop and John were joining up, so too was Bobby Russell, who had just been released from hospital after the facial injury.

The next match was another clash with the Australian 'B' side, and we moved to Brisbane to prepare for the game, but even though we won 2-1, Jock was absolutely furious with the players for the way they played in the first half. The Aussies scored first but Sandy Clark equalised just before half-time, although his goal didn't save the players from one of the big man's infamous half-time roastings. Mind you, it seemed to work as we were much better after the break, and Iain Ferguson got the winner – his first goal for the club.

Jock and I spoke at length about our third match, against the Aussie 'A' team in Sydney. We knew they liked to play defensive football, and the big man tagged the encounter the 'Blue machine against the Aussie robots!' He was happy about the different type of challenge though, as he reckoned it would stand us in good stead for our European matches, where we would come up against some really defensive-minded teams. Now, I wish that's all we had to talk about after the game – but we ended up with another player laid up in hospital with a broken leg. Colin McAdam was the unlucky guy and we were all devastated for him.

We lost the match 3-2, and the player we had put out on loan, Aussie striker Davie Mitchell, was the chief architect of our downfall. Davie scored one, made another and was sadly the innocent party in the incident that led to Colin's injury. It was another devastating night for us but we simply limped on to the next match, although Jock was all but forced to hold a press conference the following day and deny that our tour was cursed.

But if we thought our run of injuries was over, we were sadly mistaken. In our next game against an Aussie select, Sandy Clark had stitches inserted in a nasty head wound after a sickening clash with an opponent. In saying that, Ally McCoist – as usual – came up with an answer to the crisis – he would sleep on his own. It transpired that all four casualties – Bobby Russell, Bobby Williamson, Colin McAdam and Sandy Clark – had all been rooming with Coisty prior to their injuries. It led him to say, 'No one even wants to sit with me at breakfast, never mind sleep in my room!' He also promised Jock and I that he wasn't sticking pins in voodoo dolls when he went to bed at night!

From Adelaide, it was a six-hour flight to our next location, Newcastle, where we were once again scheduled to meet the Australian 'B' side. One young Ranger who had really come of age in Australia was Hugh Burns. When we left Scotland, he was a reserve team player, but his displays definitely pushed him on to the fringes of the top side, and it was merited. One man who didn't make the journey to Newcastle was chairman John Paton, who stayed behind with Colin McAdam, and accompanied him back to Glasgow as soon as the big man was released from hospital.

And we were glad to sign off from the Aussie leg of the tour with a sparkling 4-2 victory, in which we gave our supporters plenty to cheer. In fact, I recall big Jock saying that it was the best we had played since he returned to the club. So, it was on to New Zealand, although we were all sad to be leaving Bobby Williamson behind. He was still in hospital, and looked like being so for around another month, such was the severity of the break.

The journey to Auckland could've been better. Bad weather meant we were diverted and it took around 13 hours to get to our destination. We were weary when we arrived in New Zealand – and discovered we were kicking off in just 14 hours! We were set to face the President's Select at the Mount Smart Stadium and despite our pre-match woes, we won the game 3-0. The whole point of the visit was to weld together a first-team squad and, despite a catalogue of injuries, we were well on our way to achieving that. Now, though, we were off to the USA, and the first stop was Minneapolis.

But even I was forced to accept that the tour was perhaps jinxed when the club doctor revealed that our goalkeeper, Peter McCloy, had suffered a broken finger during the match in New Zealand. It was put in plaster, which meant we had a goalkeeping crisis ahead of the match against Minnesota Kicks, especially as Nicky Walker was nursing a niggling knee injury. Big 'gas meter' was ruled out for five weeks as a result of his injury and, for a time, we thought that big Jock might have to come out of retirement and play between the sticks – but he soon knocked that one on the head and 'convinced' Nicky that he was fit to play!

And that particular match turned out to be a little farcical – for all sorts of reasons. We only had 12 fit players, as Bobby Russell was suffering from blisters picked up on the rock-hard Aussie surfaces and Ian Redford required an op to remove a cyst from his back, but just before the game we discovered that we weren't playing the

Kicks, but the Minnesota Strikers. It transpired that the Kicks had gone bust, and the Fort Lauderdale Strikers had taken over their franchise and changed their name.

It was all a bit confusing but it mattered not a jot when striker John MacDonald had to go off injured with a cracked bone in his foot. It meant that Sandy Clark, who we had already substituted, had to go back on. We lost the game 5-2, although it wasn't a big surprise given the jet lag and injuries. Oh, and there was also the small matter of the organisers thinking we were arriving the day after we did – which meant they hadn't booked our hotel rooms! When we did eventually find a place to bed down for the night, our exhausted party couldn't sleep because of violent thunderstorms.

We moved on to Canada, and although we were given yet another fantastic welcome, we lost our first game 2-0 to Toronto Blizzard, who had the one and only Jimmy Nicholl in their side. It was then time to wind up the tour with a challenge match against German side Stuttgart. It was an entertaining game and the crowd seemed pleased. We drew 1-1, with Eric Ferguson scoring our goal – and getting the man of the match award. It would have been nice to end with a win but the Germans equalised midway through the second half.

Earlier that day, big Jock had said to me, 'Right Totts, the boys have been through the mill on this tour, there's a bundle of dollars, get them a good drink.' But I went to a local T-shirt store and bought all the players individual shirts with messages on them, although unfortunately the messages aren't for public consumption. I presented them all that night and we had a great laugh, with even Willie Waddell sniggering, which didn't happen that often. Seriously though, it was the perfect way to end what had been a gruelling, but enjoyable, world tour – and I don't think anyone who was with us could have denied that it was certainly eventful.

11

Jock's Boy

IF big Jock reckons it took him just ten minutes to decide I was the number two he wanted for his second spell at Ibrox, I can tell you it took me even less to realise that I was going to enjoy working with him – and that we would be lifelong friends as a result. He was a great man, and if we ever disagreed, or had a cross word, it was sorted out just as quickly as we had fallen out.

He was an incredibly loyal man and when you got to know him he wasn't this big gruff guy who just shouted all the time, there was far more to him than that. Don't get me wrong, he *did* shout a lot, but he was a man of substance, and there was usually a damned good reason why he was bawling his head off. He always treated me very well, but he got on great with everyone and talked to everybody. He was a big man in many ways, not just in stature, but he was also very kind.

I remember we went over to Dublin to play Bohemians and everyone seemed to take to him. He was that kind of guy, very likeable. It was a European match, in 1984, and it came close to my earlier experience as a player at Fall River. The game was played amid one of the most poisonous atmospheres I had ever encountered. There was trouble throughout the evening and at one point Jock went out on to the pitch to appeal for calm – and got a mouthful of abuse for his troubles. And even when we got on the team bus after the game, it was a case of heads down and let's get to the airport in one piece. It was a frightening experience, although it was different in the lead-up to the match while we were staying at the Fitzpatrick Castle Hotel – although we did have 24-hour security.

On the evening before the match, the Bohemians directors took our backroom staff to the Berni Inn for a meal, but I couldn't concentrate on my food because one of their guys was sitting tucking into his steak and his tie was floating around in a pint of Guinness. It was hilarious, and I was going to tell him several times, but just couldn't find the right moment. When he eventually noticed, I had to turn away. Bohemians' secretary, wee Phil, had been at the club for years and lamented the passing of old-style tactics at dinner that night, culminating in his famous line, 'It's changed so much, Alex, it used to be about wingers and wide men, nowadays, though, it's all bloody sweepers and cleaners!'

When they came over to our place for the second leg we took them to the Grosvenor, which was a bit different from the Berni Inn, but it was still a good laugh. I remember going over to Dublin to 'spy' on them and I was really well looked after – they were lovely people. Later on, as manager of Kilmarnock, St Johnstone and Falkirk, I took all three teams to Dublin and the people were fantastic.

Jock commanded terrific respect wherever he went and this was never more in evidence than on a visit to a Rangers supporters' club in Glasgow one night. We were sitting at the top table and one of the club officials was trying to get a bit of hush, but not managing too well. Suddenly, Jock stood up, bellowed 'quiet' at the top of his voice, the place fell deathly silent, and he started singing, 'May the streets be broad and narrow...' Next minute the place erupted, and everyone was up on the tables singing 'Follow Follow'.

And every time we went to away games, he would say to Sam the driver, 'Right, that's us getting near their ground, get the tapes on and open the window..."Follow Follow, we will follow Rangers".'

Jock was a staunch Rangers man but he certainly wasn't a bigot and saw it all as harmless fun. He liked to feel the atmosphere as we were approaching the ground and, of course, the supporters loved to hear the songs coming from the team bus as it pitched up at the front door of the stadium.

I was in his office one day when there was a knock at the door. It was Colin Stein, who was in charge of the under-14s. Colin had been a fantastic player for Rangers, and knew a striker when he saw one. He said, 'Gaffer I've got a player for you, but there might be a wee problem. His father's a Catholic and the mother's a Protestant. Big Jock said, 'Is he good enough?' and Colin said, 'Aye, he is,' and big Jock said immediately, 'Sign him.' He was only 14 and Colin said, 'His name is John Spencer and I think he has a real chance.' The next thing, we had a few letters of complaint from places like Larkhall, but Spenny was a right good player.

The whole Rangers–Celtic thing is absolutely fine as long as you can see the lighter side of it. On one occasion, I was down at Largs for a coaching seminar and everyone had a theme to work on. Mine was, 'This player had scored all the goals to get us to the cup final, but you have to drop him for the final, how do you go about it?' I was at Rangers at the time and the player I had to tell in the role play was big Tony Higgins, who was quite a clever boy. I'm trying to explain my decision but Tony keeps butting in and saying things like, 'Oh boss, all my pals and family are coming from Canada to see me, and I scored all the goals to get us to the final.' I said, 'I know you did, but I'm dropping you for the final,' and quick as a flash, he said, 'Is it because I'm a Catholic?' and the whole place erupted.

The Old Firm games were something else, and Jock would say to me, 'Alex you haven't lived until you've beat Celtic in a cup final' – and we did. We beat them 3-2 in the League Cup with Ally McCoist the star of the show. It was just the most incredible day – from start to finish – and it was the best feeling in the world knowing that I had won my first trophy as a coach at Rangers. We went back to Ibrox for a celebration after the game and then on to Panama Jax in Glasgow city centre. I didn't make it home that night and stayed in the Albany Hotel. Halfway through the evening, Jock said to me, 'There's a medal Totts,' which was a great gesture, because the assistant manager didn't get a gong in those days.

And we beat Dundee United the following season, when Iain Ferguson, the blond one, got the goal, so I got two winners' medals. And yet, when I took Falkirk to the cup final in 1997 there were only 14 medals and the manager didn't get one. It was the team plus three subs and that was the lot, which I didn't think was right.

I was 22 years in management but learned an awful lot from Jock, although he never, ever ceased to amaze me. Training at Rangers was first class and there was a tremendous amount of banter at the Albion, which was just across the road from Ibrox. We had some great players there and watching them even on the training field was something special. I recall one day in particular, when we had a bounce game between the first team and the reserves. Jimmy Nicholl flicked it forward to Robert Prytz, who collected the ball on his chest and volleyed it past Peter McCloy, right into the top corner.

I was a great one for players showing off their skills and was applauding the move. I was standing there clapping when big Jock raced past me and ran on to the park. He ran straight past Davie Cooper, past Ally McCoist, and I thought he was going to pat wee Prytzy, who was 5ft 6in, on the back for such a cracking effort, but he lifted him clean off the ground and roared, 'Oi you, stop making a fool of the goalkeeper!' All the boys started laughing but Jock was the unofficial 'chairman' of the goalkeepers' union and hated to see them humiliated. Prytz was astounded but I thought it was really funny. Jock took most of the training, because he really enjoyed being in amongst the boys, but I was also given my fair share of sessions because he knew how much I loved working on the training ground.

But there was no messing about with the big man. He liked everyone to be smart, with a collar and tie, and that was his policy. Respect has to be earned, but discipline was mandatory and I think it stood us in good stead, because Rangers was that kind of club. The tradition and history of Rangers Football Club is unrivalled throughout the world – despite the problems they've encountered in the last few years. But where discipline was concerned, Jock was preaching to the converted, because I'd grown up with that as my mantra, and it all started at Liverpool under Shanks.

I always remember we were going over to Majorca for a week's training as it was snowing heavily in Scotland. Celtic were also at Glasgow Airport, although I can't remember where they were going. Anyway, as usual big Jock had his collar and tie on, while Celtic manager Davie Hay was casually dressed, with an open neck shirt. Jock shouted to a photographer to take a photo of the pair, and he turned round and said, 'That's one for me Totts!' He was always thinking!

When I was at St Johnstone we took the players to Fuengirola, and Terry Butcher, who was manager of Coventry City at the time, was there with his players. I phoned Jock and we all went out for a meal. His photo was up on the wall in the restaurant and the owner said, 'Oh I know Mr John very well.' His star had never dimmed. We went up to his apartment afterwards and chatted about 'the good old days', then it was a case of on to the balcony for a few drinks. He had a great view and I knew he was happy there. He loved it in Spain and I think the heat helped him cope with his illness.

Jock and Daphne also came through to my house a few times and we went out for a meal on several occasions. I got to know Jock away from the football and he was a great man. He was a genuine big bloke and just loved football. One night he came through to my house and said to my daughter, who was 12 at the time, 'What are you doing at school?' She said, 'Maths, English and Latin.' He said, 'Latin, you'll be becoming a Celtic supporter next.'

But he used to laugh about these kind of things and after the Celtic games, Davie Hay would come in and have a cup of tea. There was a great rapport between them. The playing and management staff at both clubs had a healthy respect for one another. Most people had a healthy respect for Jock. He was just that type of guy. I mean the whole religion thing didn't bother me one iota, I signed Protestants and Catholics all my days in management, but it was obviously a big deal in Glasgow, although I adapted to the situation quite quickly. Jock loved Rangers. He was a staunch Rangers man and loved all the traditions of the club, but he also had tremendous respect for Celtic, and that feeling was mutual.

When I was manager at Kilmarnock, after Tommy Burns left, big Jock called and said, 'Totts, can I come down for a game?' I said to him, 'Gaffer, that would be great.' We were playing Hearts that day and he travelled to the game with Jim Jefferies. I took him into the dressing room and he met all the players, and they were saying, 'Wow, it's Jock Wallace.' He then asked if he could take training on the Tuesday. I agreed, thinking it would be great for the players to have a wee change. Jock knew his stuff and the players would really have benefitted from it. He called me on the Monday and said, 'Sorry Totts, I cannae make it, I'm at Gleneagles playing golf, but you know I think the sun shines oot yer erse,' and that was the last I ever spoke to him. The next I knew, I was at his funeral. When I heard that Jock had died, I was so low. I loved that man to bits and he is someone I will never, ever forget.

12

Son Of The Rock

NO one wants to lose a good job but life goes on. I had thoroughly enjoyed my time at Ibrox but the reality was I was back on the list of out-of-work managers (or assistants) and looking for a new challenge. I had absolutely no regrets about knocking back Motherwell and going to Rangers. Not once did I think 'what if'. I still remember vividly the moment I was given the job at Ibrox and couldn't wait to tell my dad. There was no one prouder, but he knew I'd given it my all, and when I left Ibrox he told me that the phone would ring – and, of course, he was right.

In the meantime, thankfully I managed to get my old job back as an area sales manager with Goodyear. With being full-time at Rangers, I had given it up, but they were happy enough to take me back, probably as I'd been salesman of the year before I left.

In June 1986 I was down south at a conference in Wolverhampton, just after Christmas, when the phone rang. It was Alex Wright, the Dumbarton chief executive, and he wanted to see me at the weekend.

I went along for a chat, he offered me the manager's job at Boghead – and I accepted. It was a part-time position, which tied in perfectly with my job. I was able to do both, and that suited me down to the ground, and once again I had Bert Paton by my side.

At Dumbarton, we trained Tuesday and Thursday and our physio, Bob McCallum said to me right at the start, 'I know we're not going to be able to keep you here, but that's football,' which I thought was nice. We hadn't even kicked a ball, so that proved to me that I was highly regarded in the game, and that's always music to the ears. I don't care what anyone says, but people like to be respected for the work they do.

I was there for one season when St Johnstone came in for me. Geoff Brown spoke to Sir Hugh Fraser, who was chairman at Sons, and I met him at Cumbernauld. I left Dumbarton second top of the First Division and went to Perth, where Saints were the third worst team in Scotland, and I always remember picking up the paper one morning and reading, 'I can't believe that Alex Totten is leaving a team in that position to go to the third worst team in the country.' But I just felt that I could never get a crowd at Dumbarton, because they were all heading across the Erskine Bridge to Ibrox and Parkhead. Secretly, I knew I had Perth all to myself.

While at Dumbarton, we went on a short pre-season tour of the Highlands, and took 16 players with us. We enjoyed games on the Friday and Saturday, and were due to leave on the Sunday lunchtime. I said to the players on the Sunday morning, 'We will all meet up at about 10.30am and go for a walk before getting the bus down the road.' There were a few murmurs before one of the guys said, 'Eh, boss, we can't go for a walk at that time, because most of us will be at Mass.' It turned out that 12 of the 16 players were Catholic, and I said to them, 'You know lads, I didn't have this problem at Rangers!' We all had a good laugh about it and it turned out that only a couple of us went for a walk!

While at Dumbarton, I sold Allan Moore to Hearts and Harry Curran to Dundee United, and I would later be reunited with both. Owen Coyle and his brother Tommy were also at Boghead and when I moved to St Johnstone I signed Tommy, although I should also have snapped up Owen. He was just 16 but was one of the most infectious kids I'd ever worked with. He was only a skelf at the time, but he later phoned and told me he had a chance to go to Clydebank, and was asking for a bit of advice. He wanted to know if he should go and what he should ask for as a signing-on fee. I picked up the paper one morning and saw that the Bankies had signed him for £22,500, and later sold him to Airdrie for £175,000. I made a mistake there. I should definitely have taken him to Perth.

We were approaching the festive season and the lads mentioned that they always got a hamper and a turkey from Sir Hugh Fraser at Christmas, so when it was just a week before the big day, and we were asked to stop training and go and see the chairman, we were rubbing our hands in anticipation. He was standing at the front door and up he came and said, 'Merry Christmas everyone', and walked straight out the door. We were all shell-shocked and thought it was a wind-up, and that he would soon turn round and come back in. We watched, and waited, but he just got into his big car and drove off. We stood there open-mouthed just looking, although we all had a good laugh about it afterwards.

I was only at Dumbarton for a year, but I thoroughly enjoyed my time there. It was a slightly longer drive to work than I was used to but it was a nice part of the world and I used to enjoy seeing the River Clyde on my way into the club. Dumbarton is a really historical town and, of course, the castle sits proudly on top of the imposing Dumbarton Rock.

There was a real homely spirit at Boghead and everyone, from the chairman down to the tea ladies, got on like a house on fire. In fact, on one occasion, not long after I'd joined, the chief executive said to me after a game, 'Come on Totts, let's jump into the bath with the players,' but I left him to it because I liked to keep a wee bit of distance between myself and the players. It was a philosophy I maintained throughout my managerial career and I think it stood me in good stead. I'm still good friends with many players I managed, so it shows it wasn't frowned upon by them too much.

At the start of 1987, our results were consistently good and when we beat Queen of the South 1-0 at Palmerston, in mid-February, we moved up to third in the table, tucked in behind leaders Morton and Dunfermline, who were on 41 points each. We were four adrift but had games in hand. A 1-0 win over Partick Thistle at the beginning of March consolidated third spot and set up a promotion tussle with leaders Dunfermline – one of my old clubs – the following week at East End Park. It was a really frustrating afternoon though, as we put everything we had into the game, only to lose out to a Steve Morrison goal in the tenth minute.

I was furious with the referee after he sent off Steve McCahill, unfairly in my book, and we had a blazing row although, as usual, I didn't get anywhere. The game had everything. It was exciting and the big crowd created a cracking atmosphere. But it was a bitter blow for everyone connected with the team. In reality, we hadn't really expected to be involved in the promotion race, but we were and wanted to see the job through. Our promotion plans were finally dashed the following week when we could only draw 2-2 with Airdrie at home, despite goals by brothers Owen and Tommy Coyle. We remained third but were seven points behind the Pars.

We had a chat about things on the Monday after the Airdrie game and the players were determined not to give in. We won 3-2 in a hard-fought encounter with Kilmarnock, which put us four points behind Morton and five adrift of Dunfermline with four games left to play. But it was agony the following week when both Dunfermline and Morton lost – and we lost 2-0 at bottom-of-the-table Montrose. That was that. We'd blown our big chance, which was so frustrating and hard to accept. We won our last two matches to finish third in the table, just three points behind Dunfermline and four short of Morton. It was a valiant effort but the reality was we had come up just short.

That would be my one and only season at Dumbarton but when the call came from St Johnstone, and I decided to accept the job, friends and family thought I was mad. I had decided to leave a team who weren't too far off being a Premier League outfit – to take up a position at the third worst team in the country. I was never one to shy away from a challenge though, as I think I've proved throughout my career – and another one was just about to start in Perth. Was I mad? Only time would tell.

13

Off To Perth

WHEN I was offered the St Johnstone job it's probably an understatement to say that the team was struggling. They were in the bottom division and hovering around in the basement. Still, it was an easy enough decision. The move merited a single paragraph in the nationals and that suited me fine – the last thing I wanted was a fanfare following me up the A9. That only builds up the pressure, and the need to succeed intensifies. Don't get me wrong, I put enough pressure on myself to succeed, but external pressure was an unwanted extra.

My first game in charge was against Raith Rovers, and it was the last game of the season. A draw was probably a fair result, although it was just good to get the first match out of the way. Quite often, the first one can be a mere sideshow to the arrival of a new manager but I was only interested in getting settled into the club and working extremely hard to get Saints moving in an upward direction.

One glance at the league table was all that was required to see the amount of work that needed to be done – and there wasn't much leeway in moving down by the way! Prior to moving from Dumbarton, all I could see was a club with masses of potential. Planning permission had just been granted for a new stadium and there was a real buzz of excitement around both the club and town.

I always liked to play open, attractive football, and that was what I took to Perth. The chairman, Geoff Brown, acknowledged that and said it was one of the qualities that had attracted him to me in the first place. The attraction for me was simple. I was in love with football and saw a great opportunity to rebuild a once-great club and try to take it back up to where it had been not too long before. For me, the very mention of St Johnstone evoked tremendous memories of attacking football, European nights and players such as Henry Hall and John Connolly. It was game on.

When I was named as the 13th St Johnstone manager, superstition was the last thing on my mind. This was the dawning of a new era, with new directors, a new management team and a new stadium on the horizon. It was exciting and I was determined not to let anyone down. Many people might think that it was all downhill after a couple of years at a club like Rangers, but that is certainly not the way I was thinking. Dumbarton had been a new beginning for me, and a chance to be my own man again. When I took over at Muirton, my football career was moving in the right direction. At Boghead, I don't think we ever managed a gate above 1,000, but the potential was definitely there to get the crowds turning up at Muirton again. I was excited about my new challenge.

There weren't too many fixtures left in the campaign when I moved to Saints so I organised a couple of trial matches to see exactly what I had in the dressing room. The upshot was that I decided ten or 11 players had to go. Had these players been top performers, I would never have been offered the job in the first place, but you have to give guys a chance, and that's one thing I always did throughout my managerial career.

But I soon realised that the job was perhaps a bit bigger than even I had recognised initially. As a player, the close-season could sometimes be a bit too long, but on this occasion, there weren't enough days in the week, or weeks in the month for the task that lay ahead.

I held a 'Meet the Manager' session at the club and told supporters I couldn't promise them anything in terms of on-field success, but what I could promise was lots of effort from the players during the forthcoming season, and I think they appreciated that. I meant every word.

One of the first things I did was to appoint Bert Paton as my assistant. Bert had been a smashing player in his own right, and had managed Cowdenbeath and Raith Rovers. He had also worked under Willie Ormond, so he had all the relevant credentials. We had worked well at Dumbarton so I had no hesitation in asking him to join me in Perth. I would trust Bert with my life, and that's important when it comes to finding the right number two.

The board made money available to me and the first player I signed was Steve Maskrey, from Queen of the South. Steve was a proven goalscorer and went on to score quite a few for Saints. I had worked with Steve before and knew exactly what I was getting – goals and a great shift for 90 minutes. Others arrived and, piece by piece, the squad was coming together.

But if that was the players coming in, what about the full team of guys heading in the other direction? One of those was club skipper Andy Millen. When I arrived, and spoke to Andy, he told me he normally received £500 for signing on. I had never really seen him play so I was reluctant to simply hand over £500 of the club's money on a whim. I told him so, and added, 'Give me six games, I'll see you in action and then decide if I want to hand over the money. That's fair, isn't it?' He didn't agree, and again asked for his £500. I told him the terms and he left for Alloa soon after in a straight swap for Kenny Thomson. I thought my suggestion had been a fair compromise, but Andy obviously didn't see it that way.

I made Don McVicar captain of the team and it was one of the best decisions I ever made. He was a real leader, both on and off the park. Another player I inherited was Sammy Johnston, and he was special. I signed other players as and when money became available but was always aware of club finances and appreciated that the board couldn't give me what they didn't have. I shelled out

£5,000 on striker Willie Watters, from Clyde, and he repaid me by scoring 16 goals in his first season at the club. I like to think that what I was giving the players was leadership and my full respect, and I got the latter in return.

We managed to get promotion in my first season and a lot of that was down to the consistency I was able to have in team selection. I had a load of players who clocked up 30-plus appearances that term. It was also important that the players gelled not just as players but also as people. You can't make people like each other – but you can have a good try. We had gone up to the Highlands to play in a pre-season tournament at Rothes, and I decided to 'room' players according to their positions in the team, and I think it might have helped foster understanding within the squad.

Something definitely happened because we got off to a flying start and beat Premier League St Mirren in the Skol Cup, just months after they had won the Scottish Cup by beating Dundee United. It was a welcome scalp. We also went to Pittodrie in the Scottish and were unfortunate to lose 1-0. The green shoots of recovery were definitely there and by Christmas we were locked in a title battle with Ayr United. They had some great players, such as Henry Templeton and John Sludden, and I think the Honest Men scored almost 100 goals that season.

Just a few weeks before Christmas, we went to play Stirling Albion – managed by former Dunfermline star George Peebles – on their new artificial pitch. We thumped them 6-0 and after that game I felt that we had truly arrived. It wasn't just the scoreline that pleased me but the manner of the victory. We played really well and the feelgood factor around the place at that time was up there with the best I've ever known. Mind you, I had to put up with a bit of stick from the Albion fans that day, as they were really frustrated by their team's performance, and that game heralded the worst line I'd ever heard when it comes to abusing opposition players or managers. Just as the sixth goal flew in, this wee guy on the terracing, well dressed, with a trilby hat, shouts, 'Hey Totten,

I'll tell you something else – your shoes don't match your suit!' I was in hysterics, as was the rest of the bench.

But when the championship race moved into the final furlong, and it was still a two-horse race, it appeared as if Ayr were just getting their noses in front. However, there was still the carrot of promotion and we clinched a return to the second tier by beating Arbroath 4-0, with Willie Watters getting a hat-trick. It was a great feeling and I remember the players agreeing to requests for souvenirs from our supporters, and giving up their shirts, socks, shorts and even shin guards. It was the most amazing sight. We might have taken five points from Ayr United but it was Ally MacLeod who had the last laugh as his side won the title. We only lost five games all season and as far as I can recall, the 59 points we racked up was a new record for St Johnstone. It was a proud day for everyone at the club.

We were in the First Division but a decision had already been taken to reduce the numbers in the top flight by two. It was now a ten-team league, which meant it would be twice as hard to get into the Premier League, especially with Morton, Dunfermline and Falkirk all dropping out. We had made a small profit from the promotion season and the board were good enough to hand over the cash to sign Paul Cherry and Roddy Grant from Cowdenbeath and Stuart Sorbie from Alloa. One glance at the teams in the league suggested the Pars and Bairns – who had both retained their full-time status – would be favourites for the single promotion spot. To be honest, it wasn't something I thought all that much about. Any manager will tell you that the job of building up a club is a marathon rather than a sprint. You do your job on a day-to-day basis and while you're always striving for success, any silverware you pick up is a bonus.

I recall going to Brechin to see a lad called Danny Powell. Glebe Park is a tight pitch, and Danny showed up well. He looked a good striker with an eye for goal. We went on our pre-season up north, played the likes of Huntly on wee tight parks and again Danny did very well. We then played a pre-season tournament on our home ground of Muirton, the biggest playing surface in Scotland, and had the likes of Dundee and Aston Villa competing. After the first game, Danny came in knackered, and said, 'I didn't realise that park was so big.' Straight away. alarm bells started ringing in my head. I had paid £5,000 for him but within four months he was gone, on a free transfer. He wasn't for me.

Last year, I got a phone call from a pal of mine, who was at an Arbroath game, and he said, 'Alex, I have someone here who wants a word with you.' It was Danny, and he said to me, 'Hello boss, it's great to speak to you again. I just want to tell you that I loved playing under you, but it was my fault that I didn't make it at Saints. I let you down.' It was amazing to hear Danny's voice after so long, but his revelation shocked me.

Anyway, we didn't have the greatest start to the campaign, and lost five in a Skol Cup match at Tynecastle before coming off second best to Dunfermline in our opening league match. We also had a couple of early injuries to contend with, including a bad one for Alan McKillop, so it was a difficult period for us. But we had just come up from the bottom tier of Scottish football so maybe this was the way it was going to be. As a person, first and foremost, and as a manager, I wasn't prepared to accept being an also-ran as my lot. We worked doubly hard on the training ground and started to get our rewards.

By Christmas we were hovering around in the top three but even the mention of the word 'promotion' would've had you certified as a total dreamer. But we hung on in there and it was only losses against Partick Thistle and Dunfermline – the eventual champions – that left us needing 'snookers'. For a short period, perhaps we had dared to believe, but for me, consolidation in the First Division was always the aim, and we certainly achieved that.

I first met a man called Harry Goodwin when I was manager of Saints. He'd been up at Pittodrie and wanted to come down to our place to take some photographs of the team and stadium. We really looked after him and, before he headed off to Easter Road to see his friend Murdo MacLeod, he remarked on how much he had enjoyed the visit. We then became great friends and he told me of how he had been the only photographer on *Top of the Pops* for seven years, so you can imagine the collection of photographs he amassed during that time. He took pics of The Beatles and Jimi Hendrix. In fact, you name it, Harry snapped them.

All of a sudden, he became the most wanted photographer around, and he invited me down to the Victoria and Albert Museum, in London, where he had an exhibition on. Jessie and I were also asked down to one of his shows at Liverpool's John Lennon Airport, along with Murdo and his wife. We were down at Preston for an exhibition, at which the likes of Ken Dodd, Tommy Docherty and Martin Buchan were present. Harry would phone about once a fortnight for a chat, and he was a lovely man. He was also pals with Alex Ferguson, and had taken pics of Fergie at his house. In fact, I gave him a Falkirk tie and he wore it everywhere he went. When Jessie and I went to all his exhibitions, one thing was a constant – his Bairns tie.

When he died I was invited to be one of his pall bearers, and helped carry his coffin in and out of the church, which was quite an honour. His funeral was in his home city of Manchester and it was attended by lots of big names. He was such a lovely guy and the only tipple he had throughout his life had been a cup of tea. He was a big loss.

Back to the football, and in the Scottish Cup, we knocked out Stenhousemuir and Forfar Athletic, and after the tie against the Loons, there was speculation in the press that I was the man to fill the hot seat at Dens Park. The job at Dundee was a big one, but I wasn't interested and knocked the story on the head. The St Johnstone chairman offered me a new contract but I was far too busy to sign it, although it remained on the table. We were drawn away to Morton in the quarter-finals of the cup and a potential semi-final tie against either Rangers or Dundee United was the carrot for the winner.

We allowed a 2-1 lead to slip at Cappielow which meant a replay at our place. A massive crowd turned out, so big, in fact, that the kick-off was held up for 15 minutes to let supporters in. I'll always remember sitting there in the dressing room before the match. My team talk had long finished and you could sense the tension in the air. All of a sudden, Paul Cherry started singing 'Bonnie Wee Jeannie McColl', and it remains to this day one of my funniest memories in the game.

And I'll tell you something, that moment of comic genius was worth a thousand team talks. The players went out there so relaxed, although my nerves were frayed by the end of a pulsating encounter, which finished 3-2 in our favour. Word then filtered through that an Ally McCoist goal against Dundee United had set up a semi-final against the Light Blues. It was certainly a moment to savour and I recall rushing on to the pitch at the end of the game like a man possessed and saluting our fans – all 10,000 of them. We had been hanging on by our fingernails at the end and it was a clear release of pent-up emotions.

We had met Rangers in a testimonial match for our long-serving player Doug Barron and I had been delighted when Graeme Souness sent a full-strength Gers side up for the match, but there would be far more at stake in the semi-finals of the national competition. The bookies made us something like 14/1 to win the tie, and many said that we would just be delighted to grab a big pay day. The treasurer, perhaps, but I wanted more than just to share the same patch of grass with Rangers – I wanted to beat them and get to the Scottish Cup Final.

It was a great occasion for the club, there was no doubt about that, but there was something sinister at work and I had to make sure that the match wasn't turned into a game of revenge – the manager against the club who had sacked him just a couple of years beforehand. This game wasn't about revenge. It was St Johnstone v Rangers and an opportunity for my club to reach their first Scottish Cup Final. Perth was buzzing and everyone wanted to talk about the game, about how to get tickets, and the rest, so the directors decided we should relocate to the Dunkeld House Hotel, which once again showed the professionalism at our club.

We were dealt a major blow when we lost Steve Maskrey to a shocking tackle at Raith Rovers. His knee was a mess and he missed out on the game. It was a real pity because he had scored doubles against Stenny and Forfar. But we won the first psychological battle – the right to wear blue shirts – and almost 50,000 supporters filed into Celtic Park for the big match. The tension had started to build as our team bus was heading along London Road. While the Rangers fans were enjoying a pre-match drink, the players were treating them to a rousing rendition of – you guessed it – 'Bonnie Wee Jeannie McColl'!

To be honest, I hardly slept the night before. I knew we were capable of beating Rangers but my one big concern was how my players would handle the biggest game of their lives. It was different for Rangers, because they had been over the course so many times and were used to playing in semi-finals, but I wanted to see my team do themselves justice – and they did just that.

Before the match, the players were out walking the pitch and I was standing between the dug-outs, at the entrance to the tunnel. Next thing, the Rangers chairman Sir David Murray was behind me and he said, 'You have done a wonderful job with St Johnstone, Alex,' which was something I really appreciated. We had a brief chat and his parting words were, 'You know, that could have been Ayr United out there instead of Rangers,' and with that we both went our separate ways. He was referring to an approach he had made to take over the Somerset Park club before he had gone to Rangers. An offer, I believe, which was knocked back.

I had one more 'duty' to perform before the match, and that was to accept a beautiful silver salver from the Woodvale Rangers Supporters' Club, from Northern Ireland. It was a fantastic gesture, and showed that I was still highly thought of by Gers fans.

But it was soon time for my team talk, and it is probably the best I ever gave in my career – even if I say so myself. We were in the home dressing room, which I'm sure Rangers were quite happy with, but I asked my youth team coach, Tommy Campbell, to give me the nod when big Terry Butcher started to lead his team out

– and then every single one of us burst into song. We wanted to let Rangers know that we were a proud side and that we weren't about to roll over like some two-bit lower-league team. There was a wee Celtic steward conducting our choir and big Terry later told me that the plan had worked to a tee.

During the match, Rangers fans were 'giving it laldy', and one particular song they traditionally reserved for anyone who came from anywhere north of Glasgow got a good airing. Then, all of a sudden, this Rangers supporter behind the dug-out shouted to me, 'It's okay, Alex, we're no' singin' about you – you're a good bluenose!' It was priceless and even in a game with so much at stake there was still room for a wee laugh.

Rangers had a lot of good players, including the likes of Ray Wilkins, Mark Walters, Richard Gough and, of course, Coisty, but, we had our own stars and players such as Paul Cherry, Doug Barron, Grant Jenkins and Kenny Thomson stuck to the game plan for 90 pulsating minutes. They didn't give Rangers a sniff at times.

The game ended goalless but I thought we deserved more than another crack at Rangers and, of course, an extra pay day for the treasurer. Every one of my players was a credit to themselves and St Johnstone. It was an excellent and professional performance and I was proud of them all. We had thousands of fans at Parkhead and the sight of my exhausted players taking their post-match bow in front of our supporters will live long in the memory.

The replay was played at the same venue on the Tuesday night and we had a few knocks to contend with, so I was forced to go with a less-than-fit Steve Maskrey. Our players were part-time so I knew in my heart that we had probably lost our chance of knocking out the team who would go on to win the Premier League a couple of weeks later. Sadly I was proved right and we lost 4-0. Perhaps a combination of weary limbs and an upturn in the performance levels of Rangers was the reason for the drubbing. Rangers fully deserved the victory but our appearance in the last four had moved us up a notch in the standings, and making almost £100,000 from the ties helped us invest in our future.

We had five league games left after the semi-final and picked up just a solitary point from the ten available – and as far as I was concerned that was unacceptable. The players had obviously struggled to pick up their motivation levels after the Rangers match and after a woeful performance in the final match of the season against Clyde at Firhill, I let rip. I gave them something to think about over the summer months.

It might have been the end of the season for the players but it was also the end of an era for the club – we were on the move to pastures new, and our very own 'mini Ibrox'.

Throughout the campaign – and my five-and-a-half years at Saints – I had been well supported by family, and my dad, and brother-in-law, Tom Smith, never missed a game in all that time and, more often than not, my son Bruce was also at our games. It was incredible backing and they followed me all over Scotland.

14

Pastures New For Saints

MUIRTON Park, home to St Johnstone since 1924, was about to head to that great stadia graveyard in the sky. In the final home match of the season, against Ayr United, almost 7,000 had turned up to pay their last respects and John Sludden, fittingly a former Perth Saint, scored the last goal at the old ground. As soon as the final whistle blew, that was the cue for our supporters to invade the pitch and 'extract' their own little piece of club history.

To this day I still have a little piece of the Muirton playing surface in my garden, but don't tell anyone!

After the game, there was one last duty to perform at the old ground, and that was to have my final bath in the home dressing room – and there to share it was our chairman, Geoff Brown, and former Rangers star Derek Johnstone, who was on duty for the BBC. What a day that was. It was emotional and, to be honest, it was just good to get it out of the way.

But we needed somewhere else to play our football and Muirton was sold and eventually a supermarket popped up on the site. The multi-million pound deal allowed us to build McDiarmid Park,

Scotland's first ever custom-built, all-seater football stadium, and it was also thanks to the generosity of Perthshire farmer Bruce McDiarmid, who had originally owned the land. In return for his patch of land, Mr McDiarmid was given shares in the football club. There was little of the old ground at the new, apart from the floodlights which, I believe, had been purchased when Saints sold Ally McCoist to Sunderland.

I watched just about every brick being added and the new stadium was officially opened in August, 1989, with a visit from Clydebank for a First Division match. More than 7,000 filed in to the new ground and saw St Johnstone get off to a winning start at our new home, which was important, because we had lost the final game at Muirton and we didn't want to go down in the records books as losers on the opening day at McDiarmid.

We had been looking around for a big-name club to play at the official gala opening of our new stadium – and they don't come much bigger than Manchester United. With having known Alex Ferguson from my playing days I gave him a call at Old Trafford to see if he would be interested in bringing United up to Perth. There wasn't even the slightest hesitation in his voice when he said yes, and the only thing we had to find was a suitable date. We did that, and Tuesday 18 October was marked down in bold in diaries throughout Perth as the day the Red Devils were coming to town. All you had to do was look around the streets of any housing scheme in Scotland and you would be sure to see a kid wearing a United or Liverpool top, so we were delighted when Alex agreed to our request.

I was thrilled when United brought a team full of stars, including the likes of Bryan Robson and new boy Gary Pallister, the record domestic signing at £2.3m, to McDiarmid Park. It was also great to see Bobby Charlton and Sir Matt Busby travel north with the official party. It was a fantastic gesture by Fergie, and we couldn't thank him enough. The place was packed out that night and a Brian McClair goal proved the winner, but I don't think anyone was too bothered about the result.

However, there was a shock in store when the floodlights decided to conk out on the half-hour. Mind you, it wasn't too long before the emergency lighting kicked in and once the fault was found, we were able to continue with the game. I suppose it proved that the stadium could cope with the unexpected. United's star names were again left to wait in the team bus for an extra 20 minutes after the game had ended. Fergie took the coach on a short detour, to visit a lady who had worked with the club when he was a player there. Mrs Gibson was the tea lady and Fergie decided to share one last cuppa with a lovely woman. I'm sure the players and directors didn't mind too much.

Now, though, it was time to get started on the big push to the top flight. In planning for the new season, I raided Hearts for winger Allan Moore. He was a player I'd first come across at Dumbarton and I knew he would do a good job for me. He had been forced to play second fiddle to John Colquhoun at Tynecastle and had a decision to make. First-team football at Saints or stay and battle for his place at Hearts. I used a little bit of psychology in my own battle to sign him and took Allan straight to our new ground. I wanted to sell the club to him and prove we were on the up. I knew that Allan had a wife and family to support and that stepping back into part-time football perhaps wasn't in his best interests but while it wasn't an easy decision to make, I was well aware that players also want to play every week. I knew I could use my contacts to get him a job and told him it was like taking a little step back to move his career forward again. Thankfully he agreed and I splashed out a club record fee of £85,000 to get him.

To be honest, Allan later admitted that the new ground had swayed his decision and that he realised the club must have been ambitious to be in a new ground like McDiarmid Park. He also happened to mention that Muirton had been a bit of a dump! Allan had two characteristics that I loved. He had real pace and he was a crowd pleaser. That would do me and I knew it was money well spent. I also brought in Harry Curran from Dundee United. But while I liked to look after the players, I was overjoyed personally when I was offered a contract extension that would take me through to June 1992, and I wasted little time in signing my autograph on the sheet of paper.

After a shaky start, we got our shooting boots on and started to string a few results together. We were soon top of the table but it was a long campaign and I knew there would be a lot of twists and turns. With only one team being promoted to the Premier League we knew it was going to be tough, but our cup performance against Rangers the previous season had given us tremendous belief, and the fans backed us to the hilt.

At the start of September 1989, I once again locked horns with an old pal – Frank Connor. We went back a long way. In 1982 we were working our hardest for Alloa – and after parting company we ended up at the other end of the soccer spectrum – as assistant managers at the Old Firm. But we were back as rivals in a game billed as Scotland's match of the day – the First Division crunch between Raith Rovers and St Johnstone at Stark's Park. Raith led the table on goal difference after a 100 per cent start. We both cranked up the heat in the press on the day before the game and they seized on the fact that Frank and I always seemed to be involved in ding-dong battles.

Harry Curran and Allan Moore were big-time players and I knew we were in good shape. Both were also better players for having been at clubs such as Dundee United and Hearts and I was confident we could get a result. All I needed was our top scorer from the previous season, Steve Maskrey, to end his re-signing dispute. It was something that was hanging over our heads like a dark cloud and I wanted it sorted out – and fast. But the game against Raith was a cracker and we won 2-0 – although I still felt the need to apologise to our fans for what I thought was a pretty poor display. I locked the players in the dressing room for 20 minutes after the game and we had a 'chat' about how we might be able to improve things! It had been billed as the match of the day and almost 5,000 turned out to see it. I still felt we let our fans down and reminded the players that their job lasted 90 minutes.

We then beat Falkirk 2-0 at McDiarmid Park, and I praised the supporters for the part they played in the win. There were more than 7,000 in that day – the fourth biggest crowd in Scotland – and I was just delighted with the way they responded and came out to back the team and create such a good atmosphere for the players. They were definitely our secret weapon. From our first eight games, we had won seven and drawn the other. It was a decent start.

That was stretched to 15 games and the run was halted only by a narrow defeat to Airdrie in November. I couldn't have asked for more. But the match that caught the attention of the public – as well as the players and I – was the game against Partick Thistle, Chic Charnley and all, and they were on a superb 25-match unbeaten run. They sold out every single one of their 10,169 seats. An all-ticket match in the First Division, so rare a phenomenon that the BBC even turned up to cover the action. It was a great match, and one that I still recall so clearly. There was something approaching ten yellow cards and a red, but the vital statistics showed that we won 2-1 with goals by Moore and Maskrey who, thankfully, was back in the fold. I wasn't the only one delighted with the victory as there were 13 envelopes each containing £25 waiting for the players at reception on the Monday morning, from a mystery donor.

We were motoring along nicely and undefeated on our travels – until the day before Hogmanay. A 4-0 drubbing by an Owen Coyle-inspired Clydebank brought our promotion charge to a shuddering halt. It was the heaviest defeat we had suffered under my management. We stuttered a little and suddenly another trip to Firhill became not so much a 'must-win' match but a 'must not lose'. As you can imagine, it was a close encounter of the fiery kind and all that separated the sides at the end of the game was a Mark Treanor penalty. The same player had suffered an early bath after clashing with Charnley, but we left with the points, and that was the most important thing. Heading into the second half of the campaign, it looked like a straight shoot-out between ourselves and Airdrie, who were managed by Jimmy Bone.

We were drawn to play Rangers again in the Scottish Cup – this time at Ibrox – and we lost 3-0, but our share of the gate receipts from a 39,000 crowd provided a welcome cash injection, and I suppose the defeat allowed us to concentrate fully on the league.

And I made sure the players wouldn't get too down after the Rangers game by announcing a surprise signing, which shocked everyone at the club. I brought in Paul Hegarty from Dundee United because I felt he had the kind of experience to help us over the line. He instantly became the most decorated player at the club and even though he was 35, he was as fit as a fiddle. He was in his testimonial year at Dundee United but they allowed him to come to us on a free transfer – and he continued to train full-time at Tannadice. His arrival at McDiarmid gave us the right boost at just the right time.

It wasn't too long before I smashed through the £100,000 transfer barrier when I signed Gary McGinnis from United. He had been nine years at Tannadice and he was brought in to stiffen up the back four. Once again, though, the directors had given me their full backing and I was desperate to repay their faith by leading the club to the promised land of the Premier League – but there was still one heck of a struggle in front of us. And in one final boost to the morale of the playing squad, if another was required, we were told that were we to win promotion, then the squad would turn full-time.

We were all set for the final 14 games of the campaign. There was a potentially explosive match against leaders Airdrie looming, but first we had to see off Albion Rovers, and that was when our season almost imploded. We went two goals down and suddenly all that hard work off the park looked like being for nothing – until we rallied and scored four times to run out winners.

On the last day of March 1990, Airdrie arrived at McDiarmid Park for what everyone was calling the 'title showdown'. They were a point in front of us and hadn't lost in just under 20 games. Once again, the 'sold-out' signs went up and the 9,556 attendance was a new stadium record. Four years after I had arrived in Perth, finally a place in the Premier League was on the line – and I couldn't wait. We started brightly and hit the woodwork three times in the opening exchanges. We were playing well and only an opening goal had eluded us, and then, disaster. Stevie Gray scored for the Diamonds and their stand erupted. It was a real sucker punch and it would have been so easy for the players to fall apart, but we had installed a true fighting spirit within the squad and they simply never gave up.

But time was going on and when Steve Maskrey was tripped in the box, all eyes shifted to the referee. It seemed to take an age but he pointed to the spot and Mark Treanor slammed home from 12 yards. There were just 14 minutes left and we had to win, a draw was no good to us. And then big Roddy Grant headed home his 17th of the season, and we celebrated like all our Christmases had come at once. But I had to remind the players that we had won nothing. A late Kenny Ward goal had clinched the win, but all we got was two points and there were still five games to play. Mind you, it was a huge psychological boost.

The next round of games gave us a cushion. We beat Partick at Firhill and Airdrie lost at Clydebank. We were three points to the good – and then the nerves kicked in. We were so near, yet so far, and when Clydebank won 3-1 at our place, and Clyde left with a draw, it was squeaky bum time. Thankfully, we had destroyed the psyche of Airdrie in our table-topping clash at Perth and the wheels completely fell off their challenge.

I took the team down to Somerset Park for a vital match against Ayr United and we stopped off at the Towans Hotel, in Prestwick, for a pre-match snack. It was owned by former Rangers goalkeeper Norrie Martin and was a favourite haunt for Saints whenever we were in that part of Ayrshire. I had a lengthy chat with the players at the hotel and told them it was time to be positive. To my mind we had been the best team in the league all season so the ability and desire wasn't in question – but I needed it one last time.

There was a fantastic crowd inside the ground, the bulk of which had travelled down from Perth, and we were determined to reward their loyalty with a title. Paul Cherry scored for us and then John Balavage saved a penalty. Surely it was written in the stars that we were going to the Premier League. Steve Maskrey made sure of it and when the final whistle sounded we were in dreamland. Our fans were ecstatic and I walked round the perimeter wall shaking hands with as many supporters as possible. We then partied long into the night – although Bert Paton and I almost missed the celebrations, due to third degree burns. The players decided they would throw us into the communal bath, although I wish they'd tested the temperature of the water first. It was roasting hot and I don't think either Bert or I touched the water before we were both back out.

Emotions soon got the better of me and I broke down in tears in the dressing room. I told the players that the highlight of my career up to that point had been walking up the marble staircase at Ibrox to become assistant manager of Rangers, but it didn't match the feeling of winning the First Division title. Taking a team of my own to the Premier League was something completely special and the greatest moment of all. I was proud of every single person at that football club.

We went back to the Towans to celebrate in style and the adrenaline, as well as the champagne, was still flowing. In fact, there was a wedding on at the hotel that night so it was a double celebration. Willie Thornton once told me that in football one pleasant memory was worth a thousand dreams. It's a quote I've used before and still holds true to this day.

The following Saturday, we hosted Forfar and won the match 1-0 thanks to a Roddy Grant goal – but that was a mere sideshow to the main event. The presentation of the First Division trophy was the main reason almost 8,000 people turned up at McDiarmid. We might only have scored a single goal in that match but it was our 81st of the season, which made us the highest scorers in the country. Only Tranmere Rovers scored more in the UK, and they played seven matches more. It proved that we had won the title by playing open and attractive football, and that was something that gave me a great deal of satisfaction.

When Don McVicar held the championship trophy aloft, the noise inside the ground was deafening. It was bedlam and that set the scene for yet another party. But that wasn't the end of it. Perth and Kinross Council organised an open-top bus for us to tour the city and thousands of appreciative supporters lined the streets to give us a rousing cheer. The Perth and District Pipe Band helped the day go with a swing. Then it was on to the old City Chambers for a civic reception and Provost Alex Murray paid a fantastic tribute to everyone involved 'in bringing St Johnstone back to life' before joining us on the balcony for a final bow.

It had been quite a season, but one of the highlights for me happened away from the park. When I went to Saints, most of the kids in the town wore Manchester United or Liverpool tops, but after clinching promotion, suddenly there were youngsters in Perth wearing St Johnstone tops, and that was a measure of how far we had come.

And promotion also meant I was a real 'man about town' thanks to car dealer Dickson's of Perth. When I joined the club they had given me a sponsored Rover car, but told me that if I took the club to the Premier League they would upgrade it to a Mercedes – and they were as good as their word. On the side, it said 'Alex Totten: Manager of St Johnstone' and that sounded really good.

15

In With The Big Boys

FOR me, being back in the Premier League was fantastic. It's where every player and manager wants to be, and I celebrated our return by signing a fresh three-year deal. The chairman kept his word and we were to be a full-time club. Things were looking rosy, even if the bookmakers – some of whom made us 500/1 to win the title – didn't agree. That didn't matter to me. We were free of debt and about to embark on a season of top-flight football. It was a great challenge for everyone at the club and we had all the so-called 'glamour games' to look forward to. Mind you, I was concerned only with St Johnstone and how we would fare.

And I got a helping hand in that direction from the board. When I came to the club, it was decided that we would adopt a sort of continental approach to bringing in new players. I would identify those that I reckoned could make the team stronger and the chairman would take care of the financial side of things such as contract talks, signing-on fees and wages. It was a weight off my shoulders and allowed me to concentrate on the playing side of the business.

Part of that 'business' involved making some tough decisions. Sure, we had just won the First Division, but that was the moment I had to sit down and plan ahead very carefully. We were in with the big boys and I was determined we wouldn't be left behind. Many of the players who had got us to the top league had been with me since the Second Division days and, if truth be told, perhaps weren't going to be playing much in the top flight. It was now a case of who was in and who was out. As Bill Shankly had done with me all those years ago, I decided to tell the players who were leaving face-to-face. It wasn't a pleasant task but it was the least they deserved.

I knew we had to match our rivals in terms of fitness, tactical awareness and preparation if we were to survive in the Premier League, and that was what I aimed to do. Nine times out of ten, the team promoted are hot favourites to go straight back down again, and I wanted to ensure that we would be the club to break the mould.

I moved quickly to identify players I believed were capable of keeping us in the top league, and the first player I signed was Lindsay Hamilton, who had been understudy to Chris Woods at Ibrox. Jock Wallace and I had looked at Lindsay during our time at Rangers and he was a goalkeeper I really admired. I felt he had been treated pretty badly at Rangers by Graeme Souness and when I made my move, I know he had other offers. Thankfully, though, Lindsay chose to move to Perth.

Next up was a player who had won four league titles with Dynamo Kiev and a similar number of cup gongs. He had also played for his country 45 times and won a host of other honours. Sergei Baltacha had a CV to match the very best, and I couldn't believe I was just about to get my hands on him.

Sergei would be the first Soviet to play in Scotland. Ian Redford recommended him to me and he was a player that I definitely wanted. Playing with a sweeper was a system I liked, and Sergei was one of the best in the business. We got him up to Perth and he did all his own negotiating. He was a pretty tough cookie to deal with and it took almost an hour to thrash out the details of his contract, wages and signing-on fee. He then said, 'I want one more thing, a car.' I looked at the chairman, and he looked at me. I thought to myself, 'Here we go, he'll be wanting a top-of-the-range Mercedes, or something similar.' Next thing, Sergei said, 'I'd like a Lada!' My immediate thought was, 'How many Sergei?' The chairman was also delighted.

I'll never forget my phone going late one Saturday night, and my wife telling me it was Sergei. I took the blower and he said, 'I not happy with you today. You swear at me.' I said, 'You're damned right I did,' and put the phone down and that was the end of the conversation, but years later, he got the manager's job at Inverness Caley, and we were appearing on a TV sports show together. There was Alex McLeish, Ally McLeod, Sergei and I. He called me up beforehand and asked for a lift, as he wasn't sure how to get to the studios. The first thing he said to me when he jumped into the car was, 'I know why you swore at me that time,' and we both started laughing. Welcome to management, Sergei.

He was one of the best passers of the ball I ever worked with, which was probably why he had almost 50 caps for Russia. He was also the consummate professional. He would look after every aspect of his life, from his fitness to taking his own boots away to be cleaned. He also went to his bed every afternoon for a sleep. He really was a great pro, had a lot of good habits, and we could learn a thing or two in this country from players such as Sergei. But the bottom line was his ability. He was a great player and was exactly what I needed at that time. I had been looking for a good sweeper to marshal the back four and he did the job perfectly. It was a fantastic recommendation from Ian, who had played with Sergei at Ipswich.

I wanted someone to play alongside him and John Inglis fitted the bill perfectly – but it meant Saints' record transfer fee would be broken again. We shelled out £115,000 to get him from Meadowbank Thistle but it was money well spent.

I paid out for other players, including another £100,000 for Morton midfielder Tommy Turner, but I also wanted to make sure that our fans' ambitions were realistic. I had experience of working in the Premier League but a lot of our players didn't. The impact of Graeme Souness on Scottish football, not only for Rangers, had stepped up the level of our game. He had brought in all these million-pound players from far and wide, but that meant the rest of us had to do what we could to keep up.

Our primary goal was to avoid relegation. When I said I would be delighted to finish ninth in the ten-team league I was deadly serious. It was shaping up to be one of our toughest seasons ever and while survival was the name of the game in Perth, we also wanted to enjoy it.

But there wasn't much to enjoy in the opening weeks of the campaign and we learned some pretty harsh lessons. Even when the First Division flag was raised before our opening home league game against Dundee United, we suffered a 3-1 defeat. There were a few more before we managed to beat Dunfermline and gain our first win of the campaign.

After that match, I'll always remember looking at the fixtures and thinking, 'My God, this is going to be tough,' as we had the Old Firm, Aberdeen, Hearts and Dundee United in successive weeks. I think most critics expected that run of games to cement our position as favourites for the drop – even that early in the season.

Then it happened. We absolutely ripped Aberdeen apart and thumped them 5-0. That's right, 5-0. Before the game, I remember telling the players that they were good enough to compete in this league, but they had to believe in themselves, it was as simple as that. That was a special day for me and everyone connected with the club, because it helped launch our season. The players certainly believed in themselves and as a result we were up and running. Some people said it could have been eight or nine, but I was happy enough with five. Mind you, I still felt for Alex Smith, a good friend of mine, who was manager of the Dons.

But we had little time to enjoy the result as our next match involved a trip to Celtic Park, although we showed different qualities that day and Lindsay Hamilton was excellent as we secured a 0-0 draw. It was another great result and when I saw Lindsay pull off a magnificent reflex save from Gerry Creaney, I immediately smiled and thought to myself, 'That save was created with the help of a Celtic legend.' I had asked Lisbon Lion Ronnie Simpson to come in and work with Lindsay and he was fantastic. He genuinely wanted to help us and I was really grateful for that.

I also enlisted the services of a guy called Jimmy Campbell in a bid to help the players with their pace. Jimmy might have been 71 but he was a fantastic coach and with us going full-time, I wanted to make sure we were as fit as we could be.

I was also able to start getting a bit of continuity with team selections – every manager's dream – and we went unchanged for seven games in a row. Nearing the end of the year, I was awarded the Tartan Special Manager of the Month trophy and that was definitely a 'special' moment. Perhaps I had been a wee bit too cautious at the start of the season but I was definitely growing into the role of a Premier League manager and it was really nice to be recognised in that way.

A real turning point for us was a win over a very strong Hearts side, who had just scored a terrific European victory over the Russians of Dnipro. They had some smashing players but I brought back a system that allowed our front three a bit more scope for attacking. It had worked well in getting us up from the First Division although I had been a bit concerned about whether or not it could be successful in the top league. The match was at Tynecastle but that didn't stop us going all out for victory.

At that point, Sergei Baltacha was getting a lot of the plaudits, and quite rightly so. He had proved a real inspired signing and his intrusions into midfield and ability to pick out the killer pass were real plus points for us. But it was as a team that we would succeed or fail and every single player gave everything he had for the cause that season. There was a fantastic togetherness about the place and that was our main weapon.

We had gone a few unbeaten when Rangers arrived in town. They brought with them their new signing, £1.4m man Oleg Kuznetsov, who was playing only his second match for the champions. I was besieged by people looking for tickets. Suddenly I had all these new pals. Everyone wanted to see the game. It was perhaps a combination of wanting to see all these big stars that Rangers had and also to see how the wee Saints would fare against them. It was inevitable that we would set a new crowd record for the match, but a bad injury to Kuznetsov, who twisted his leg after catching his studs in the turf, threatened to take the shine off what was another great performance by my players. We managed a 0-0 draw, which was the first point we had taken off Rangers in the Premier League.

But there was a heart-warming aside to that match. I'll never forget the moment little Fraser Waugh, who was eight, fulfilled a long-held dream by leading out St Johnstone as mascot before the game. The Crieff Primary pupil had collapsed during the glamour game against Manchester United and it was only the expertise and quick thinking of our medical staff that gave doctors a chance to save Fraser's life. He survived a critical brain haemorrhage, two cardiac arrests and complex surgery and went on to make a full recovery.

I remember going up to Ninewells Hospital in Dundee along with our skipper Don McVicar to visit the wee lad and praying that he would come through it all. He came from a lovely family and I also visited him at his home. He had been through so much and it really was fantastic to see him back in action again. We had always said that if we reached the Premier League, Fraser would lead the team out against Rangers, and I was so glad it was a promise we were able to keep. It really put football into perspective. But sadly there was to be no happy ending and the wee lad died. I attended his funeral and it was just such a sad time for the family. To lose their son so young must have been devastating.

And sadly the match itself was marred by comments made by Souness, when he made a thinly-veiled statement aimed at suggesting my players played the game a bit too aggressively. A few days later, Rangers went over to Belgrade for a European match and when asked about the loss of Kuznetsov, Souness was reported to have said, 'It's too tough in Scotland. We sign players because of their skill, not as hammer throwers.'

Baltacha, a good friend and international team-mate of Kuznetsov, was quick to defend his team-mate Harry Curran, the player who'd made the innocuous challenge on Kuznetsov and, after speaking to his fellow Russian, confirmed that he placed absolutely no blame whatsoever on the shoulders of Curran. 'Kuznetsov,' he said, 'insisted that Harry was definitely not to blame.'

Then it was reported in *Rangers News* that I had mounted a bitter attack on my former club, which was absolute nonsense. They took my comments the wrong way entirely. In comparing my team, which had cost around £500,000 to assemble, with the multi-million pound internationals of Rangers, I was merely trying to emphasise just how well we had performed.

We annihilated them that day. Chris Woods was in superb form, while Lindsay had just the one save to make. It was a shame that such a memorable occasion had been overshadowed in that way, but we simply moved on to the next task in hand – a match against table-toppers Dundee United, who were also putting together a great run in the UEFA Cup. It was yet another daunting prospect, although it was very pleasing to hear our fans sing 'There's only one team in Tayside' after leaving Tannadice with a 2-1 victory. It was a result that moved us up to fourth place, just three points off the pace, and I managed to complete the signing of John Davies, Billy's younger brother, on the eve of a draw with Hibs. He cost me £165,000, which was another club record, but we were getting a stylish midfielder that I had known from my time at Ibrox.

Next on the agenda was a trip to Pittodrie and I was delighted to hear Aberdeen boss Alex Smith say that the club wouldn't be caught up in any petty revenge stuff, which alluded to our incredible 5-0 win at McDiarmid Park. But that didn't stop a group of publicity-mad Aberdeen businessmen from offering the club £5,000 if they managed to avenge that defeat by scoring five against us. They were way off the mark and Lindsay Hamilton collected another shut-out, while we added another point to our tally. It was a good day at the office, although not for that particular group of businessmen!

We had a few indifferent performances before we pulled the big one out of the hat – a 3-2 win over Celtic at McDiarmid Park. Being able to compete with the Old Firm was great, but actually beating one of them was a fantastic achievement and the points ensured we were fourth at the halfway stage. Not bad for a newly-promoted side, and the fact that we were five points better off than Celtic was also a big plus. It had been a fantastic calendar year for us. We had won the First Division championship and enjoyed many good results in the Premier League. What pleased me most was that we were accumulating points while playing some nice football. In fact, after the win over Celtic, one of their elderly fans said to me that our play had reminded him of the old-fashioned Celtic style, which was a tremendous compliment.

I suppose I should tell you that I can be quite a superstitious person and that the sprig of 'lucky' white heather, which I had been given at the opening of McDiarmid Park, was still in its exact position behind my desk – and I continued to tuck my left sock into my shoe before the right.

I was delighted that we had secured our place in the following season's Premier League by the end of January. That was a fantastic achievement for a club of our size because unless you're one of the top four or five clubs, the spectre of relegation always haunts you, especially when you've just come up from the First Division and are especially vulnerable.

Then the Premier League voted to introduce league reconstruction and the top flight for the following season was extended by two teams. I felt that voting for something like that halfway through a season made a complete mockery of the Scottish game. I'm sure that had St Johnstone been bottom of the league at that point, reconstruction would have been the furthest item from the agenda. The others would have waved us goodbye without a second thought. It was all about self-preservation for those most in danger of going down.

*I'm two years old
and feeding cygnets
at the park in
Dennyloanhead*

*Can you spot me in my
class at Dennyloanhead
Primary School?*

*(Far left)
Playing the
accordion –
aged 8!*

*(Left) Mum
and dad pose for
the camera*

I was captain of the Denny High School football team

*Young Master Totten
was proud to play for
Scotland Schoolboys!*

With Scotland Schoolboys at Dens Park. I'm in the back row – third from left

At Sunderland's Roker Park before we played the English Schoolboys

We played England at Tynecastle, and I'm on the left

I still have the autograph from Bobby Charlton

Sitting pretty in my first car, a Morris 1100

Granddad and I admire my Hillman Minx outside his house in Bonnybridge

The great Bill Shankly teaches us the art of balance

Liverpool director, Mr Martindale, presents me with a prize for being the youngest member of the ground staff

A Liverpool player, and a proud one at that!

I was best man at Dundee team-mate Ally Donaldson's wedding

Running out at Highbury in Dunfermline colours

A match made in heaven – Jessie and I get married

My Pars mates, from left, Bert Paton, Tom Callaghan, Jim Thomson, me, wee Alex Edwards and John Lunn

Jessie and I with Kay and Bruce

With Rangers legend John Greig at Recreation Park

I was proud to manage Falkirk

This is one of my favourite family pics – with Jessie and the kids

I'm a Ranger now – with manager Jock Wallace

Looking smart at Ibrox Stadium in 1985

I steered Gers to Tennent's Sixes glory

Jessie and I celebrate an anniversary with a slice of cake

I'm the new boss at St Johnstone, with Geoff Brown and vice-chairman Ally Campbell

With Bert Paton, my Perth sidekick

Former Scotland boss Ally MacLeod and I shake hands before the last game at Muirton Park

Paul Wright and I

Winning the Manager of the Year title was a fantastic achievement

Davie Cooper and I show off our awards

Steve Maskrey hit the back of the net a few times for me at St Johnstone

Sir Alex Ferguson brought his Manchester United side up to open McDiarmid Park

With Jock Wallace at Perth

With Jessie at Christmas – and the half-finished tree!

Getting a ticking off from a referee

And another earful…

There is a pattern emerging here!

In charge of Kilmarnock

With Alex McLeish, left, and Craig Brown before a Killie v Motherwell match

I enjoyed working with Alastair Alexander for BBC Radio Scotland

I'm home! George Fulston and I at Brockville

Do you think I enjoyed beating St Johnstone on my return to Falkirk?

With wee Kevin McAllister, left, and big Crawford Baptie!

Brockville was my spiritual home

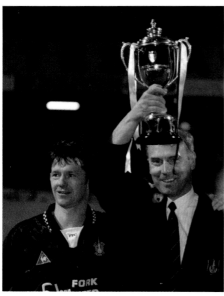

Kevin McAllister and I celebrate winning the Challenge Cup

With Marino Keith. I can't believe we almost lost him!

*At the Scottish Cup semi-final draw with, from left,
Tommy McLean, Bobby Williamson and Tommy Burns*

*Pouring a Scottish Cup Final pint in
Brian Flynn's Behind the Wall pub in
Falkirk*

Wearing my cup final kilt

*Bobby Williamson and I were fated to meet in
the cup final*

I never lost my passion for the game

*It was a sad day when I walked out of Brockville
for the last time*

My grandson Alexander and I at the site of our new stadium at Westfield

And we eventually moved into the new stadium

With Murdo MacLeod and photographer Harry Goodwin – note, he's wearing his Falkirk tie!

My hero, Alex Parker, left, and a very good friend, Andy Cameron

Alex Ferguson and I met up again at Stirling University when he was collecting his Honorary Doctorate

Think I'll leave the Superbikes to Niall Mackenzie

The family aren't long in growing up

With my grandchildren, Alexander and Jake

The grandkids are football daft. Here they are at the Nou Camp in Barcelona

I always did love working on the training ground

My testimonial golf day was very special

Being chieftain at Airth was a great honour

With the end of the season getting closer, we still had a small chance of qualifying for Europe, but lost by a single goal in largely forgettable matches against both Aberdeen and Dundee United. The first of those was beamed live on BSkyB, the first match to be shown live from the new stadium, and the club picked up a tidy cheque for £60,000, which was actually quite substantial given the match was under threat due to the big freeze. We lost count of the tons of straw that went on to the pitch!

In between the games against the so-called 'New Firm' we were given the opportunity to head out to Spain for a few days, which was fantastic, and showed just how much the club had been transformed in the previous few seasons. It was great for everyone although I especially enjoyed it as it gave me the opportunity to hook up with my old Rangers boss Jock Wallace, who was living on the Costa del Sol. We chewed the fat and recalled some great times at Ibrox and were joined by Terry Butcher, who had just been appointed as manager of Coventry City, and who had the same idea as me about getting the players away for a few days to 'foster team spirit!'

But we flew straight back into a storm – in a tea cup. Rangers were back in town and Allan Moore netted for us in a 1-1 draw. Once again, though, Graeme Souness wasn't a happy man.

One of our employees, Aggie Moffat, was so proud of the new stadium and always kept the dressing rooms immaculate. She always made sure there were flasks of tea in each dressing room after the match for the players and coaches. However, an angry Souness picked up the flask and threw it against the dressing room wall and smashed it to smithereens. It made such a terrible mess and Aggie was so upset. She was on her way upstairs to complain to the chairman when she bumped into Souness in the foyer, which was really busy, and the two of them had a go at each other in front of everyone. She got right into him about her new dressing room, and he was going on at her. It was ridiculous. It made all the papers and Aggie soon became the focus of attention. But reputations meant very little to her and she didn't miss him. I'm sure Souness met his match that day because Aggie didn't stand for any nonsense from anyone.

When she decided to retire, Owen Coyle was the manager. She called me up and told me the news and invited me up for lunch. The three of us sat and chatted about the good old days and it was fantastic. In fact, every Hogmanay, as soon as the bells chime, I call Aggie. It's an annual ritual now. I've always been really fond of her because she was great with me and the players, so we've always kept in touch.

At a lot of grounds, the players march straight into the dressing room with their boots still on, and the place is covered in muck, with tie ups and all sorts of rubbish left lying around. But whenever Dundee United visited McDiarmid Park, the away dressing room was always left immaculate, and that was down to Jim McLean. Whenever we played United, you found the dressing room exactly the way it had been before the game. He had a group of YTS players who cleaned it up after the team. You have to admire him for that and I followed his lead by always leaving dressing rooms the way I found them.

One thing that delighted me was the form of Lindsay Hamilton and I remember saying in the press that if there was a better keeper in Scotland I hadn't seen him. Ronnie Simpson also backed calls for him to get a chance with the national team – but the call never came.

In the Scottish Cup, we eventually saw off Berwick Rangers after a replay brought a win by the odd goal in seven. It wasn't the best way to begin our quest for national honours but we managed to beat Hibs in the next round, this time 2-1. Ayr United were next up at home and Allan Moore, not the biggest of players but with a good spring, scored a hat-trick of headers to see us through to only the club's fourth semi-final in 107 years.

The authorities took the decision to play the tie against Dundee United at East End Park, despite the players being desperate to play the match at Hampden. I was in two minds, though, as I knew we would get a much better atmosphere at Dunfermline. I took the players to Dunblane Hydro to prepare for the game and we knew that United were beatable, but we missed a few chances on the day and that cost us dearly. We were so near, yet so far. Perhaps it would've been better had we been easily beaten 3-0, or something like that, because to lose by a single goal, knowing we'd made plenty of chances, was a sore one to take, particularly as referee George Smith had made a horrendous gaffe when he missed Dave Bowman pushing a goal-bound Steve Maskrey shot over the bar with his hand. It's every manager's dream to lead out his team in a cup final and I'm no different. It would have been the perfect end to a great season for St Johnstone, but it just wasn't to be.

We finished seventh that term, after at one point occupying fourth for a spell. Had anyone predicted that – and suggested we would be challenging for a spot in Europe – they would've been laughed at. We beat every team in the league, with the exception of the champions, Rangers, and received tremendous recognition for our efforts which, in my mind, was fully justified.

On a personal level, I had been at the club almost four years to the day when I received a very pleasant phone call. 'You're Manager of the Year Alex, and we would like to invite you to accept your award at the Grosvenor Hotel, in Glasgow.' You could have knocked me down with a feather.

It was one of the proudest moments of my entire career. To think that you've outshone the managers of Rangers and Celtic, amongst others, is quite a feeling. There were around 400 people at the Grosvenor that night and I'll always remember Geoff Brown was sitting with Billy McNeill, and I said in my speech that if it wasn't for Geoff there would have been no St Johnstone Football Club, and that's something I still stand by. He put £300,000 in to save the club and worked hard to ensure it survived. During my acceptance speech, I also said that Shanks would have been proud of me, and I believe he was looking down that night with a wry smile on his face.

Davie Cooper won the Player of the Year award and it was a very proud moment when Coop and I lined up for the official photoshoot because we were great friends and had remained so even when I left Rangers. It was great.

But I'll never forget the year, 1991, because the next year I got the sack! One minute you're the best manager in the country and the next you're nothing. It really is a funny old game, although my mind drifted back to the day Jock Wallace came up to see me in Perth and said, 'I always knew you'd make a cracking manager Totts.'

We had enjoyed a good season, and played a lot of exciting football, but it never entered my head for a moment that I might win the award, it genuinely didn't, so it was a very pleasant surprise. I was always very respectful to everyone throughout my career. If a journalist phoned me for team news, and I couldn't take the call, I would always make sure I phoned back. It's just the way I've always operated. We all have a job to do and I don't see any point in making it harder for someone, just for the hell of it. I've always told journalists that I can take constructive criticism, 'Totten's a bad manager, Totten signed a bad player,' but don't print lies about me, I can't stand that. Be honest and above board with me and I'll return the compliment.

I found out the good news a couple of weeks before the ceremony and it was the cream of Scottish football who attended on the night. I had been sacked by Rangers a few years beforehand so this award proved to me, and probably a few other people, that I certainly wasn't a failure, so in that respect it was very pleasing.

Geoff Brown and I had travelled through to Glasgow for the event and we spoke on the way through about what had been an incredible five-year journey. It just didn't seem real, because a few years beforehand we were being tipped as the next Third Lanark, who had been forced out of the game in the 1960s due to financial problems off the park. But everyone at St Johnstone had worked hard and, financially, we must have been on as sound a footing as at any other time in our history, with a ground the envy of most. But I also felt that we were going places on the park too which, after all, is the only thing that concerns supporters.

16

Toe-To-Toe
With Wattie

I'VE always had the greatest of respect for those I worked alongside, and pitted my wits against, in dug-outs the length and breadth of the country. Walter Smith falls into the latter category. When I left Rangers, he got my job, but I felt no bitterness and left a note wishing him well. Our paths would cross several times and we soon became good friends off the park.

In October 1991, though, we were the best of enemies – St Johnstone v Rangers at McDiarmid Park and there was no quarter asked, nor given. At the time, we were in the bottom four and Rangers were second. Ally McCoist, a good friend from my time at Rangers, and a former Saint, had just put Rangers two up a minute before half-time when I gave him both barrels. I felt he had got away with murder earlier on by elbowing our centre-half, John Inglis, and I let him know. The goal was also a good bit offside and that was the final straw. Naturally, Wattie took exception to my comments and a war of words flew from dug-out to dug-out. It was quite heated but not really anything out of the ordinary, although just a few moments later, all hell would break loose.

Referee Sandy Roy sounded his half-time whistle and I headed straight for the dressing room – but I didn't get there. Wattie came in right at my back and there was a wee 'coming together'. Naturally we exchanged 'views' and as the players started to file past, and into the dressing room for their half-time orange and team talks, the match commander jumped in between Wattie and I. I didn't think it was necessary, but he obviously did. With the benefit of hindsight, perhaps he was trying to make some kind of point – or even a name for himself, which, if that was the case, was very disappointing as I had done an awful lot of good work for the police in Perth.

'Fair enough,' I thought but he then ordered one of his officers to 'book' us, and the constable looked at him to ask if he was serious. 'But they have to go into the dressing room and give their team talk,' said the officer. 'Book them,' came the reply.

Both Wattie and I suddenly realised that this guy was serious, and wasn't letting it go. But it had been nothing; handbags at dawn, and a difference of opinion from two guys whose only crime was showing a passion for their respective football clubs. We were given a stern lecture and told that our actions were unacceptable, could've influenced the crowd and led to trouble in the stands. I tried to point out that we were in the tunnel, and that no one could see us but he was having none of it. We had our names taken and were charged with a breach of the peace, while Wattie had the additional charge of assault added due to his 'shoulder charge' on me, which was a perfectly legal 'move' on the football field at that time!

Almost the entire half-time break had passed and we were both desperate to get back into the dressing room, but on the lecture went, and then the commander dropped his biggest bombshell. He said to the officer, 'Throw them out of the ground!' 'What?' I looked at Wattie, we both looked at the commander, and then at the officer. 'Are you serious?' I asked. 'Absolutely,' he responded. The next thing I know, we're being directed towards the emergency exit and quick as a flash we were both standing outside at the front of the main stand. It was a full house inside – although there were now two empty seats in the dug-outs – and tickets had been at a premium, so there were still a good number of supporters milling around outside the ground. They looked at us, we looked at each other and didn't know whether to laugh or cry. Seeing the managers of the two teams getting turfed out at half-time must have been quite a sight for the ticketless fans.

The door opened almost immediately and we both thought common sense had prevailed and they were going to let us back into the ground. Lesson learned. But no, one of the Saints directors, Davie Sidey, came out and ushered us straight into his car. We drove the short distance to his house and before long were sitting on his sofa watching the Dunhill Golf Championship and 'enjoying' a cuppa – but we were supposed to be at McDiarmid Park giving our half-time team talks!

It was all incredibly surreal and we were kept in touch with the match by telephone. Harry Curran and Paul Wright managed to cancel out Ally McCoist's first-half double but Scott Nisbet got the winner for Rangers with a quarter of an hour to play and there wasn't a thing I could do to try and help us pull back another equaliser. We were fourth from bottom and desperately in need of points but I felt totally helpless. It has to be the most incredible hour and a half of my football career – and perhaps even my life.

About an hour after the full-time whistle, we were bundled into the car and driven back to the stadium, in the belief that most supporters would be making their way home. They might very well have been but there was a posse of snappers and journalists awaiting our arrival, although 'no comment' was the order of the day as we were ushered through the crowd and back into the stadium.

Reading the papers the next morning was incredible, and the headlines were taken up with comments such as 'Police moved in at half-time during the Premier League game at Perth after a scuffle in the players' tunnel'. It continued, 'A police spokesman at Perth said later, "At half-time during the match an incident occurred in the players' tunnel involving two officials from St Johnstone and Glasgow Rangers. A report has been submitted to the Procurator Fiscal.'" The Procurator Fiscal. I couldn't believe it. What had started out as a normal day had quickly descended into farce. Sadly, it wasn't comical for Wattie and I. Thankfully, the police spokesman refused to confirm that the officials involved were Wattie and I, although everyone knew exactly who had been charged. Mind you, at least they didn't put us in orange jumpsuits!

And thank goodness for the proverbial 'football insider' who was able to tell the papers, 'A police inspector took the men into a side room and charged them with a breach of the peace. Then he asked them to leave the ground. A few minutes later, they were driven by a St Johnstone director to his home near the ground. The three of them watched the Dunhill Cup on TV. They were given updates on the football by telephone from the ground and both managers returned to the ground about an hour after the match finished.'

The following day, I still couldn't believe the furore which had followed an incident that would be mirrored in dozens of grounds around the country. Two managers having a disagreement. Big deal. I played golf on the Sunday with a few pals and we managed to have a laugh and a joke about it, but I also gave the incident some serious thought, and came to the conclusion that perhaps my passion on the sidelines was being detrimental to the team, so I decided to 'ban' myself from the dug-out for a short time to see if it made any difference. I always wanted to be in the dug-out close to my players, but decided I would only go down to the touchline if and when I felt I was needed on the spot to deal with an emergency situation. From then on, I would be in the stand and keep in touch by phone.

I also banned myself from talking to the media about my spat with Wattie. We were good pals, had known each other for a long time, and I didn't want that to change. Wattie said the same thing.

To be honest, I thought the charges would be dropped and that it was hoped we would have learned our lesson but, no, the

Procurator Fiscal decided in his wisdom that it was in the public interest for the case to go to court. We were both called to attend Perth Sheriff Court on Tuesday 23 October and Wattie failed to turn up. In fact, the court insisted they hadn't even received a letter from him, although his lawyer, Donald Findlay, insisted a letter had been sent.

My lawyer, Jock Brown, had definitely sent a letter, and naturally I denied the breach of the peace charge. We were accused of conducting ourselves in a disorderly manner at a match at McDiarmid Park on 12 October, and of shouting and swearing at each other and engaging in a stand-up fight. My trial was fixed for 10 February and Wattie's case was continued without plea until 12 November. On that date, a letter was read out in court on Wattie's behalf. He too pleaded not guilty to a charge of breach of the peace and Sheriff John Wheatley adjourned the case until 10 February when we would both be sent for trial.

I was confident I would be found not guilty but the whole matter was something I could've done without. We both believed we had done nothing wrong and that is was something that dozens of other managers do up and down the country every Saturday afternoon, but our fate would be determined at Perth Sheriff Court.

The big day arrived and it was like a circus outside the court building. There were supporters of both sides and lots of photographers and journalists present as both myself and Wattie, and our lawyers, Jock Brown, the football commentator, and Donald Findlay QC, arrived for 'Perth's celebrity trial' as one newspaper had dubbed it. Pity we weren't getting a fortune from one of the glossy mags like *OK* to tell 'our side' of the story!

Both Wattie and I sat in the courtroom – passing Polo mints to one another as an official read out, 'It is alleged that both Walter Smith, aged 43, and Alex Totten, 45, were involved in a fracas at McDiarmid Park.' The trial was delayed until 13 May after Donald Findlay asked that it be dealt with at one sitting covering two days. Mr Findlay, a Rangers director, said it was a case of considerable importance to both men that would have wider ramifications. Sheriff John McInnes, who would be taking the case, agreed and said, 'I think it's in the interest of justice to hear this trial in one.'

The season duly ended, we finished mid-table, and Rangers won the league – then it was time for court. I must admit to being really nervous stepping into the courtroom on the morning of the trial. It wasn't an environment I was familiar with and I'd only ever seen trials in films or on television. Once again a court official read out that 'tempers had flared', a saying I was getting used to. It was alleged that I shouted and swore at my opposite number. When Alastair Hood, operations executive for Rangers, took the witness stand, he said he moved to the tunnel mouth just before half-time. He said that initially his attention had been drawn to the St Johnstone dug-out, where the manager (me) was remonstrating with the linesman. He said I was using strong language, and also said that I was trying to indicate to the linesman to open his eyes. He then said that I turned my attention to the Rangers dug-out. He said, 'Mr Totten averred that perhaps Rangers were ruining Scottish football, and that some of the players or one of the players was a cheat. Mr Smith replied, using the same expressions, and told Mr Totten to shut his mouth.' Mr Hood also said that at half-time he put himself between the managers, to prevent a possible physical altercation, but at no time were any blows exchanged.

But that all changed when Chief Inspector James Adamson took the stand and claimed that Wattie had shoulder charged me in the tunnel, after he had warned both of us about our behaviour. Earlier, he said, he had led me off the park by the arm as I tried to argue with a linesman. It was then hinted that when Rangers scored, I turned to Wattie and shouted, 'You want every decision in the league.'

It was the end of day one, and I was drained. It was like reliving the afternoon every single time a new witness took the stand. I was glad to get home to Jessie that night and just have a cup of tea and a quiet chat.

The following morning, Wattie and I arrived at court at the same time and were once again met by a group of supporters from both sides asking for autographs. It was quite funny because we only had one pen between us, so we shared it and signed around a couple of dozen signatures before heading inside together. It seemed more than a little weird that we were laughing and joking going into court, where we were on trial for supposedly arguing and fighting with one another. It was to be another draining day.

The police insisted I had engaged in a stand-up fight with Wattie, which wasn't true, and I said that in court. I have never had a problem telling the truth, and this was another of those moments. When Wattie was asked about this so-called 'stand-up fight', he said he was 'worried that the police evidence could be so far from the truth'.

Later, the Crown deleted the term 'stand-up fight' from the charges and instead alleged that Wattie had struck me with his shoulder, but we both denied there was any physical contact between us. I agreed that I had been excited and probably swore during the match, and agreed that I had become angry when Ally McCoist elbowed one of my players and wasn't even warned about it. I had shouted, 'Hey Coisty, cut it out.'

I admitted that I became involved in exchanges with the Rangers dug-out but denied the use of 'specific words'. What I said at the time was, 'It worries me that you think you own the bloody league?' And a voice from the Rangers dug-out had replied, 'You won't win the league with the players you've got.' I entered the tunnel at half-time at the same time as Wattie but I definitely wasn't shoulder charged by him – and there was certainly no wrestling. Wattie agreed there had been exchanges between the dug-outs but said he had not cursed in the tunnel or assaulted me. It was left at that for the day and Sheriff McInnes promised to deliver his verdict the following Thursday. It would be a long wait.

When we did go back to court for the verdict, I was absolutely raging with the outcome. Once again we filed into court and when the Sheriff read out his judgement, I was completely shell-shocked. I was found guilty of a breach of the peace and fined £250 for the half-time bust-up with Wattie. And then, just to rub salt into the wounds, the Sheriff declared that he was clearing Wattie of all charges. Well, that's not strictly true, but it might as well have been. Wattie was not guilty of shoulder charging me, while a breach of the peace charge against him was found not proven. However, Perth Sheriff John McInnes, in his wisdom, insisted police were RIGHT to fear that we might have started fighting. And he said the incident might have been much worse if players had come down the tunnel and seen what was going on.

Both Wattie and I had been consistent from the start in our belief that we hadn't conducted ourselves in a disorderly manner in the tunnel, and that police hadn't told the truth, but Sheriff McInnes said, 'I prefer the evidence of the police officers to that of the accused. I am satisfied that the two accused shouted and swore at one another.' Crown claims that we had confronted each other, and that Wattie had shoulder charged me couldn't be proved because of contradictions in evidence. I decided that the only course of action left open to me was the right of appeal.

It was mid-November 1992 when the appeal was heard and once again I was to be left both frustrated and disappointed. I attended the Justiciary Appeal Court with my solicitor, Jock Brown, and the defence QC, Neil Murray, argued that the Sheriff had failed to take into account what normally went on at football matches. He said that managers regularly swore at each other, at match officials and at their own players.

Mr Murray said he was not trying to condone such conduct but, against that background, what had happened in this case did not amount to criminal conduct. Swearing in a tea room could be a breach of the peace but it might be something completely different if it happened in a public bar.

Lord Ross, the Lord Justice-Clerk, sitting with Lords Morrison and Prosser, said experienced police officers had given evidence at the trial about their fear that a fight might have broken out between the two rival managers in the tunnel. If that had happened, a much worse situation could have arisen as the players, on their way to the dressing rooms at half-time, saw what was going on.

Lord Ross said the Sheriff had been fully alive to the use of bad language at football matches but he had also appreciated that the circumstances at the particular time of this incident were all important. He had referred to the prevailing tensions. 'We are satisfied that the Sheriff was fully entitled to find the appellant guilty.' I was left to pay the £250 fine and, if the truth be told, I was happy just to put the whole sorry tale behind me. I still feel to this day that they arrived at the wrong conclusion, and while it's water under the bridge now, I certainly didn't think that way at the time.

Mind you, I just had to laugh when I heard what was going on at Ibrox during the court case. Apparently Ally McCoist got a boxing poster mocked up and pinned it up in the home dressing room, and it read 'Evander Holyfield Totten Vs Sonny Liston Smith', which is just typical Coisty!

17

Ruthlessly Axed

AS Christmas 1992 approached, my biggest worry was how to improve our away form. We were doing well at McDiarmid Park, where we had lost just twice in 11 games – but clubs were still spending big in an effort to keep tabs on Rangers and it was difficult for those with limited spending powers to keep up with the Joneses. On our travels, we had lost six of 11 games and next up was a trip to Ibrox to face the league leaders. To this day, I still can't believe I wasn't in charge for that match, and didn't get to wear the Saints scarf I'd been presented with earlier by the club – the one that said 'Alex Totten – St Johnstone FC'.

Prior to the morning of Tuesday 15 December we had been doing okay. We had lost just once in eight games in the run-up to the Christmas period and were seventh in the Premier League. On the Saturday we had drawn 1-1 with Hearts and I went in on the Monday morning for training and Aggie said to me, 'Aw, great news boss, Elaine [the girl in the office] is expecting.' She was married to Paul Smith, who did the programme, so it was fantastic for everyone at the club and we were all buzzing with excitement for them.

Next thing, though, Geoff Brown walked into the office, cloud of gloom hovering above him, and he genuinely looked as though he was in a lot of pain. I immediately thought there must be something wrong with him. He appeared to be breaking out in a cold sweat, so naturally we were all a bit concerned. We went into my office and he said, 'Oh, I haven't slept all weekend.' I was going to suggest he see a doctor immediately when he added, 'I just feel you've taken the club as far as you can.'

This had all happened in the blink of an eye, but I knew exactly where he was going with his comments, however difficult it might have been to comprehend – as I had been Manager of the Year at St Johnstone the year before. I took one look at him and said, 'What you're trying to say to me is that I'm sacked.' So, that was more or less it. He nodded his head and I walked straight out of the office and Brown wasn't far behind. I asked Jim Peacock, our physiotherapist, to get me a black bag, which normally means just one thing. I had some great photographs up on the wall and I said to him, 'I'm not leaving these behind.' He looked at me quizzically and I told him I had just been sacked. He was stunned. I asked him to gather the players in the dressing room and off he went. As surreal situations go, it was up there with standing next to Walter Smith after we had both been chucked out of McDiarmid Park at half-time. Yes, it was *that* surreal.

I walked along to have a word with the players and they just sat there, heads bowed. When I walked into the dressing room, you could have heard a pin drop, and I said, 'As far as I'm concerned, you have all done a brilliant job for me since I came here, but that's the chairman just been in to see me and I've been sacked.' They couldn't believe what they were hearing, and seemed distraught. I didn't say too much more, shook hands with every one of them, and just walked out and went back along to my office to start clearing it out. Next minute, the likes of Andy Rhodes, Allan Moore, Paul Wright and Mark Treanor came in, and said, 'I bet you any money that big bastard John McClelland has got something to do with this.'

Strangely enough, John McClelland was the only player absent when I told the guys what had happened. It was the only time in my career that I genuinely felt a colleague had stabbed me in the back, and I don't think there is any doubt whatsoever that he did. I had heard whispers that he was going behind my back to the chairman and that they were having hushed conversations. There was nothing I could do about it, though, but it was a sore one to take.

I gathered my possessions together, left the ground and drove home. I was numb. Getting the sack certainly wasn't a nice feeling. I had called Jessie and told her the news. She was shocked, but at least it lessened the impact on my arrival home. I told her that the chairman had felt a change was necessary. I pulled into my street and there was Chick Young and a BBC camera crew waiting outside my door. There were other journalists there as well, such as Lindsay Herron from *The Sun*. I've always admired these guys, and how they seem to know everything that's going on in the game before everyone else. My phone never stopped ringing for days and the postman soon grew to despise me as hundreds of letters from well-wishers arrived from all over the country, the majority suggesting that I had been badly treated and wishing me all the best for the future.

As I alluded to earlier, one guy wrote in to the *Perthshire Advertiser* and said, 'What have President Kennedy, John Lennon and Alex Totten got in common? I can remember what I was doing and where I was when I heard the tragic news.'

Once I had time to take everything in, I was gutted, because I felt I'd done a good job at St Johnstone, and had brought through some good young players – such as Callum Davidson and Phillip Scott – who eventually moved on for sizeable fees, with Callum moving for £1.75m. Not that long beforehand I'd had lunch with Andy Roxburgh and Craig Brown – both former team-mates who were with Scotland at the time – and they said to me, 'What a job you've done here Totts, you're here for life.' Prophetic words indeed!

McClelland got the job – no surprise there then – and he brought up Steve Harrison from England as his assistant. However,

Harrison was gone in days, and was reported to have said he couldn't believe the depth of feeling for me in the Perth area and headed straight back down south.

And McClelland didn't last too long either. I'd first got to know him at Rangers, and when he was at Leeds he used to come up to my house for a visit. I had initially tried to get Roy Aitken as my assistant at St Johnstone but he was on too much money at St Mirren, so I went for Danny McGrain, but he was in line for the Hamilton job. I then moved for McClelland, who came to the club as player-coach. I got on well enough with him at Rangers, even though he hadn't seen eye-to-eye with big Jock. When we went to Toronto on our world tour, he stood up and criticised Rangers about their wages policy (everyone was on the same basic). He said that big Jock had promised him more money, so the big man had a go at him. They certainly didn't have the best of relationships. Geoff Brown had got rid of my assistant, Bertie Paton, after five years at Saints, and that was when I brought McClelland in. He said he wanted someone with fresh ideas. I felt McClelland had vast experience on both sides of the border.

Brown made some stupid statements after he sacked me. He said things like if it hadn't have been for Allan Moore then we wouldn't have won the league. That was a silly thing to say, because if it wasn't for Alan Shearer, Blackburn wouldn't have won the league – but I had signed Allan for the goals he scored and made.

I was really disappointed with the way my time came to an end at St Johnstone. Shattered, really. To get manager of the year one season and the sack the next was weird. One of my mates was driving across the Kincardine Bridge when he heard the news and said he nearly ended up in the water. Straight out of the blue, Brown had come to see me at 9.15am, and one hour later I got a call from Davie Sidey, another director, to say that he'd just heard the news, so they didn't even have a board meeting. Brown took the decision off his own bat, although I heard later that McClelland had gone to see him. Strangely enough, I haven't seen McClelland since that day.

I was later told that at 8.45am, Geoff Brown told Henry Ritchie, who worked with him at GS Brown Construction, and who was also a director at the club, 'I'm going down to sack Alex.' To think that someone knew I was being sacked before me is incredibly disrespectful. Davie Sidey said to me later that day, 'I didn't know this Alex, he didn't even have a board meeting.' There were five or six people on the board, and they met once a month, but to not have a board meeting for such a big decision was pretty awful. But Geoff owned the club and did things his way. We have talked once or twice since he took that decision but I think you can guess that our relationship will never be the same again.

I was sacked just six months into a three-year contract which probably shows just how the owner operated while in charge of Saints. I don't think these are the kind of decisions most chairmen would take lightly, but I definitely reckon there was a lot of chit-chat going on in the background which influenced his decision.

I would later read in the papers that Brown thought my 'thinking was antiquated and for the Sixties', and that he blamed me for 'attendances falling to 3,000 and a soaring £1m wage bill', but our average crowd was 5,000, not 3,000. He also described some of my team's performances as 'diabolical, to say the least' and accused me of not bringing through enough youngsters.

I was left shattered and bewildered by the decision – and some of his remarks. I had no inkling that it was about to happen, but it was probably all about money. The chairman mentioned the attendances but I pointed out that there was a recession and that other clubs were suffering as well. However, his mind was made up, and shortly after my sacking, he said, 'When Alex Totten came to this club in April 1987 we were in the Second Division. Since then Alex has steered the team to promotion to the First Division, the championship of that league and three national cup semi-finals. These are significant achievements and we recognise Mr Totten's contribution towards them.

'However, we believe that the momentum has been lost over the last two years and results and performances, particularly in front of our own supporters, have not reflected the investment we have made in players and coaches. We are ambitious to challenge for the top honours in Scottish football and believe that a fresh approach in team management is the way forward for St Johnstone.'

Shortly afterwards, Alex Smith, the Clyde manager, and also chairman of the Managers' and Coaches' Association, said, 'We are extremely disappointed that this can happen to a manager who has achieved so much. This kind of treatment says a lot about the state of the game. St Johnstone's ambitions seem unrealistic.'

Morton boss Allan McGraw didn't pull any punches when he said, 'Alex is out of a job because the chairman – who claims to be his friend – is living in cloud cuckooland. Thank god I don't have friends like Geoff Brown. I wouldn't treat a dog the way he treated Alex. Brown believes St Johnstone should be up there winning titles and cups. He should come back into the real world. Alex achieved miracles at St Johnstone. Too many directors want to be big shots. When people who know nothing about football try to get their hands on it, we'll all be finished.'

And McClelland didn't exactly have his diplomatic hat on when he released the following statement to the press on the eve of the match at Ibrox against Rangers, 'I expect to get a good reception from the Rangers fans but I'm not sure how our own support will react to me. I know Alex was popular with St Johnstone fans and there has been a shock response to what has happened. But I would remind those people who are upset that changes happen all the time in this game. Perhaps they have forgotten that someone else was sacked when Alex Totten got the job here. The change has been made and now I am in charge.

'One thing that has disappointed me at Perth has been a lack of commitment from some players. They seem to accept a certain standard instead of wanting to improve. Maybe it has something to do with the Scottish nature. Having been with major clubs in England, I know how much good players want to better themselves. Careers don't last long and everyone in the game should be striving to reach his maximum ability. Players should aim to delay, as long as possible, the day when they become ordinary men in the street.'

As I said, just 48 hours after being appointed as assistant to McClelland, Steve Harrison walked out on St Johnstone after allegedly being told how much the fans resented my sacking. Brown said the Crystal Palace coach quit because of taunts over pranks which lost him jobs with England and Millwall, but Harrison said he made his mind up to leave when a hotel waiter told him how much fans in the town were incensed by my dismissal.

Harrison was quoted as saying, 'He told me the score on Saturday morning. That's when I realised I could not join the club – there was too much tension and too much emotion over Alex. The people up there obviously felt a great deal for Alex and it just wasn't right for me to suddenly come on the scene. I had a bad feeling when the waiter told me fans were petitioning for a boycott of home games. I had a certain amount of unease and anger at the situation. I came into it blind. I got a phone call from John McClelland asking me to join him – and jumped at the chance. I just wanted to work with one of my best and oldest pals in the game but I didn't do my homework.'

There is never a good time for anyone to get the sack, but a few days before Christmas was probably the worst time imaginable. We had a half-decorated tree in the corner of the living room and Jessie insisted she didn't have the will to finish it off. She wasn't alone. But I received so many pick-me-up messages from so many people in the football world, such as Jock Wallace, Andy Roxburgh and Jim Baxter, while the Provost of Perth was also quick to offer his goodwill. People from all walks of life offered their support and I received good luck messages from a host of Rangers supporters' clubs. It was really heartening to know they hadn't forgotten me.

Saints were due to play Rangers just a couple of days after I was sacked and I sent the players a good luck message before the match. I told them they had to play for themselves and their families at Ibrox, and just as importantly, to pay their mortgages.

After my sacking, I realised that I had to give myself a shake and try to get back into the game. It was all I knew but the terrible thing was, that were I to get another job, it meant someone else getting the sack and the unlucky man having to face the same anguish as me. I had the offer of a job outside football but wanted to see what else surfaced before turning my back on the game.

Reflecting on my time at Saints, I didn't think I did too badly at all. It was said that the club was 'sliding into oblivion' when I took charge in April 1987. We were in the Second Division when playing in front of crowds of around 700. In 1988/89 we finished sixth, got to the Scottish Cup semi-finals and almost beat Rangers. We then won the league by playing open, attractive football and scoring lots of goals in the process, and in our first season back in the Premier League we finished above Dunfermline, Hibs and St Mirren. We thrashed Aberdeen 5-0, beat Celtic a couple of days before Christmas, and then beat Hearts and Dundee United. There was another Scottish Cup semi-final appearance and I was named Manager of the Year.

In my final season in charge we reached the Skol Cup semi-finals, where we lost to Rangers, and were seventh in the 12-team table with just one defeat from eight games – and had just recorded four shut-outs in a row for the first time in 68 years. It was hardly the stuff of a dead manager walking!

The day I was sacked was the worst of my life – up until that point. For many years afterwards I was haunted by the ghosts of Christmas past. I had enjoyed five and a half wonderful years in Perth and I looked forward to going into work every day. Part of me definitely died when Geoff Brown sacked me. I saw every breeze block of the new stadium being put in place and felt as if I was part of McDiarmid Park myself. I couldn't believe what was happening to me that day and neither could anyone else.

I was invited to speak at a function in Perth a year later and was given a standing ovation by supporters, which was emotional. I'll always remember speaking to Tommy McLean not long after I was sacked, and he wondered what chance the rest of the managers had if I was bumped while doing a good job. His Motherwell team were at the bottom of the table at the time and the fans had been baying for his blood.

Later, when I started speaking at awards and dinners, I would say I was Manager of the Year in 1991, and the next year I got the sack. Geoff comes into the office and says, 'I haven't slept a wink all weekend, but I just feel that a decision has to be made. We're lying seventh in the Premier League, just about to play Rangers, and we've made a lot of money, but I think we have to part company,' and I say, 'I don't agree Mr Chairman, I think you're doing a great job,' and that's the bit where he says, 'I mean YOU!'

I remember John Litster, the secretary at St Johnstone, saying to me that Brown should have prepared a statement and given it to him to impart to the media, but he stayed all day answering the phone and telling different people different things. The things he said were daft. There was talk of a supporters' boycott, and broadcaster – and Saints fan – Stuart Cosgrove told me that he wanted to hold a dinner for me in Perth, which was nice, because they hadn't even done that for club legend Willie Ormond. It was a lovely night and I got some really nice gifts from supporters. We had a mutually good relationship and I used to take the players to visit hospitals and such, and I know I was a good ambassador for both St Johnstone and the city of Perth, but that's part and parcel of the job. It's not just all about football. Derek McInnes and Alan Gilzean have since told me that the people of Perth still talk about me positively, which is nice.

I will always remember Geoff Brown asking me if I'd lost my enthusiasm for the game – and that's something I still have to this day. I've never lost it – and never will. As the chairman, he had the right to make the decisions, but I still don't think sacking me was the correct one. In fact, when he retired after 25 years, he was quoted as saying, 'The most enjoyable time I had at St Johnstone was while we were playing flamboyant football with the likes of Moore and Maskrey,' but even though I was manager at the time, I didn't rate a mention. Says it all really.

18

Bayview And The BBC

I WAS still suffering the after-effects of my dismissal at St Johnstone when the BBC called just after Christmas to ask if I'd like to go to a few games and give my opinion, just like former Celtic and Dortmund star Murdo MacLeod is doing now. I didn't have to think twice. It gave me a whole new lease of life after what had gone on at McDiarmid Park and I absolutely loved it. On a Friday night, I would studiously look at the teams I was covering the next day to make sure I knew the players and likely formations inside out. I always knew that I had a good knowledge of the Scottish game but this helped me see things from a different perspective.

One week my commentator would be Alastair Alexander, and David Begg the next, and he would tap your leg when he wanted you to come in with your tuppence-worth. It was fantastic to see how the whole thing worked behind the scenes. It really was football from a whole new angle and I enjoyed every minute of it. I covered the Scottish Cup Final between Motherwell and Dundee United, which was a great advert for the game up here.

I was also fortunate enough to be asked to write a weekly column for the *Aberdeen Press and Journal* newspaper. It was another opportunity to get my opinions across to the wider public, and I did this for around four months at the beginning of 1993. It wasn't just all football but it was something I enjoyed immensely.

The life of a 'pundit' definitely agreed with me, but then the phone rang one day. It was Jim Baxter, although not that one. This Mr Baxter was the chairman of East Fife and had been at the club for more than 25 years. He was looking for a replacement for Gavin Murray, who had quit a fortnight previously. Mr Baxter had been speaking to Craig Brown and asked him if he thought I would be prepared to drop down a couple of leagues to join the Methil men. He said to me, 'I know you've been used to working in the Premier League with the likes of Rangers and St Johnstone...'

I told him I had been missing the game and every single aspect of managing a football club terribly, but my biggest miss had been working with the players. I loved my work with the BBC but really there was no substitute for involvement at club level. I told my bosses at the BBC that I was leaving and they were absolutely fine about it – but I owed them for helping me recharge the batteries. My last game for the BBC was Raith Rovers v Kilmarnock. It had been a short career in broadcasting, three months or so, but enjoyable nevertheless.

The following day I went through to Lower Largo to meet Mr Baxter and he offered me the job. I accepted and it was great to be back in the game. I went down to the stadium for a look about and the first thing I clapped eyes on was a big brown basket, which was used to keep the balls, of which there were only three. I knew I had to do something about it so the first thing I did was make sure we had a ball for every player. I then got them all a blazer and flannels so that when they were representing the club they would look the part. Rule number one in football is that if you look the part, you feel the part. And the smart rig-out was down to a guy called John McGregor, from Binn Farm, in Perth. He was someone I had become friendly with during my time at St Johnstone and he kindly paid for the jackets and trousers. It was a fantastic gesture by someone who had no affinity to East Fife. In fact, there were around a dozen Saints fans at my first game in charge of the Fifers, waving flags and singing my name, which was incredible.

I immediately appointed Kenny Thomson as my number two. Kenny had great experience with Dunfermline and Cowdenbeath and knew the football scene in Fife inside out. He was the right man for the job and we had nine games left to assess the squad. It wasn't a difficult decision to join East Fife because they were a club with a fine tradition and I was following in the footsteps of managers such as Scot Symon, who was a fantastic success at Rangers.

And while more than 53,000 supporters flocked to the east end of Glasgow to watch yet another enthralling Old Firm encounter, barely 350 bothered to turn up at Firs Park, home of East Stirling, to see my first game in charge of the Fifers, but I wasn't counting the crowd. I was only interested in the two points, and duly got them thanks to a fantastic second-half display. We were off and running – again.

After only a couple of games in charge, we went to Cliftonhill to take on Albion Rovers. Big Tommy Gemmell, the former Lisbon Lion, was back in charge of the Coatbridge side, and it was great to pit my wits against someone like that. In saying that, we were 4-2 down at half-time, thanks to four goals from Steve Kerrigan, who was obviously on a mission to impress the new boss!

We had some decent results in the final weeks of the season but still finished in the bottom half of the table. The players headed off for their summer holidays and Kenny and I set about planning for the new season. We brought in some fresh faces and were rewarded with an opening-day league win at Berwick Rangers. One of the guys we signed, Alan Irvine, made a huge impact on the team and we were top of the table after a couple of games. I had first signed Alan for Falkirk 11 years before he joined me in Fife. He had shown great potential while at Easter Road early in his career, but for one reason or another, failed to make the grade with Hibs and dropped down into the juniors. I snapped him up from Whitburn and he made over 100 appearances for the Bairns before snaring a £100,000 move to Anfield. He only played four times for Liverpool but one of them was against Everton in the Merseyside derby. After leaving Liverpool he had played for teams such as Dundee United and St Mirren, and I got him right at the end of his career, but he still did a good job for me at Methil.

John Reilly was another striker I admired and he was on target as we won the Fife derby against Cowdenbeath, which left us as the only team in the division with a 100 per cent record after three games, and after week four of the campaign, ourselves and Clydebank were the only teams in the country not to have dropped a point. It was a satisfying state of affairs – but we knew it was a case of if, and not when, the bubble would burst. When we beat Alloa 4-1 in our fourth match, the crowd was over 1,100, which was testament to the fact that we were trying to play football the right way. An astonishing near-1,600 crowd visited Bayview for our next match – against Queen of the South – but we lost 2-0 and were joined at the top of the table on eight points by the Dumfries side. It was the start of three successive losses but we finally got back on track with a narrow victory over Forfar, which moved us back up to fifth in the table.

A victory made going to meetings of the Technical Association for Managers, Coaches and Trainers (Technical Association for short) all the easier. I was president of the group at the time, and had Alex Smith and Andy Roxburgh as vice-presidents. It was a worthwhile organisation and we looked after the interests of those working hard for their clubs. Our aims included the pursuit of professional excellence in all aspects of football in Scotland, and to promote the position of Scottish managers. Alex Ferguson, Jim McLean and Walter Smith were among our many honorary members.

Meanwhile, over at Celtic Park, the situation had gone from bad to worse when Liam Brady quit as manager with the Parkhead side languishing in mid-table. There were fan demonstrations outside the ground in a bid to oust the board. It was late October 1993 and the repercussions of what was going on in the east end of Glasgow would have a direct bearing on my own future.

Naturally, I was concentrating only on East Fife's promotion push. We won a couple of games at the start of November to push us up to fourth – and then came a crackpot game at home to Queen's Park. Brian McPhee scored four times for the amateurs and with just a couple of minutes remaining, we were 5-3 down. The supporters weren't happy, and quite rightly so, but somehow we managed two goals in the dying moments to salvage a 5-5 draw. Who said we didn't provide value for money at Bayview?

We were doing okay in the league but just couldn't string together the few wins that would have seen us up there as genuine title contenders. We were there or thereabouts, but that wasn't good enough for me. And when we lost 1-0 at home to Queen of the South, in mid-April, the promotion dream was over. It was a frustrating season but there was still an awful lot to play for. League reconstruction was on the agenda and the top six teams would play in the new third tier the following season. We were hovering around the wrong side of the cut-off point and it all came down to the last day of the season. Avoid defeat at Alloa – the club that had given me my break in management – and we would be fine. Brian Kemp gave the Wasps a first-half lead but Allan Sneddon headed the vital equaliser a minute after the break. We would be playing football in the third tier the following season.

During the close-season, I got a call from Alex Cameron at the *Daily Record*, who told me on the quiet that Tommy Burns was going to Celtic. He then asked if I would be interested in taking over at Rugby Park, and I told him that I would. It was strange the way initial contact had been made but I suppose that was just the way of it in those days. Anyway, I was invited to a meeting at Killie director John Paton's house at Newton Mearns. All the Kilmarnock directors were present and I was offered the position. I had known Mr Paton from my time at Ibrox and of course I wanted the job.

It was a case of getting back into the SPL, and it was full-time, so I took it.

Don't get me wrong, I had thoroughly enjoyed my time with East Fife. The potential was definitely at Methil, and on our day we were one of the best teams in the Second Division. However, we had been dogged by inconsistency, which had left me tearing my hair out. We had won our first four games of the season then lost the next four and that was typical of the whole campaign. I tried different training methods and preparation and had long talks with the players but it was a common problem in football and there was no easy fix.

East Fife were a part-time club, which meant you only had the chance to work with the players twice a week, which was frustrating, but that was just the way of it. Given the opportunity to work with them five days a week, I think I could have made a big difference but the situation was what it was and, all things considered, I think I did a decent job in a short space of time, but the lure of Kilmarnock – and the Premier League – was too great and I was off on my travels again, but at least the Fifers were properly compensated for my departure.

19

Taking Over From Tommy

I HAD been all set to leave for a series of trial games south of the border with East Fife when the call came. I was soon changing plans and heading for the south of Ireland – with a three-year, full-time contract tucked away safely in my back pocket.

Once again, I had Kenny Thomson on board as my number two at Kilmarnock and we flew across the Irish Sea to begin our new adventure. It was August 1994 and Kenny, who had surpassed the late Sandy Jardine's then 643-game all-time Scottish League appearance record, was a good guy to have at my side. The first thing I did was have a meeting with the players. I told them that I had the greatest of respect for Tommy Burns not only as a manager and player, but as a person, and that I hadn't applied for the job, that I was invited. I knew Tommy was a popular guy, and that he'd done a great job at Rugby Park, so I wanted to let the players know how I felt about him and I think it went down well. I took them all out for a meal, which I think was also appreciated.

We started off with a win against Sligo Rovers, but I'll never forget the wisecrack that got my Killie career off to a flying start. There must have been around a thousand Killie fans present and there was a great atmosphere inside the stadium. Bobby Williamson and George McCluskey kicked off and this guy in the crowd shouted, 'That's you Alex, the honeymoon's over!' It was a fantastic one-liner and we smiled at each other. The ice was broken and my Killie career was up and running.

One of the first things I wanted to do was help shake off the unwanted tag we had received of being the 'Dad's Army' of the Premier League. I inherited players such as Bobby Williamson, George McCluskey and Bobby Geddes. They still had a lot to offer but I wanted to bring in new, young blood to complement the more experienced guys. We needed to lower the average age of the side quite considerably to make sure we didn't get left behind. I started the ball rolling by calling Alex Ferguson at Manchester United to see if he had any players that I could have, and he invited me down for a reserve match against Aston Villa at Old Trafford the following night.

A few players caught my eye but I wanted another look, and arranged to go down and see them against Wolves Reserves at Molineux. I was to call him after the game and give him the names of any players that took my fancy. I did, but when I asked about 'the boy Scholes', he said, 'No chance, he's a bit special.' On it went, with a few of their other quality kids, such as David Beckham, Phil and Gary Neville and Nicky Butt, and his answers remained the same. However, I was lucky enough to sign Neil Whitworth and Colin McKee for £500,000. The vice-chairman, Jim Moffat, who owned AT Mays, was fantastic and gave me his full backing. Kilmarnock had 25 supporters' clubs and Neil won every single player of the year award going at the end of that season. Sadly he contracted TB and was in and out of hospital, which was a great shame, because he was a smashing player. He was never the same after that.

Ironically, my first cup game in charge of Killie was against East Fife in the Coca-Cola second round at Rugby Park. I couldn't believe I would be going toe-to-toe so soon with the team I had just left, but that's the kind of anomaly that football tends to throw up on a regular basis. It was my first home game in charge and we had a good crowd in, and thankfully we won 4-1, with John Henry scoring twice. Steve Maskrey, whom I'd 'rescued' on a free transfer from St Johnstone, or at least that's the way the papers saw it, was also on the score sheet.

I had signed a handful of new players but I was delighted with the capture of number six – Dragoje Lekovic. The giant keeper – three years with Red Star Belgrade – was a Yugoslav international and he did a great job for me. I was trying to build a team who would be there or thereabouts for a few years to come, but it was the here and now that was throwing up the most problems. Celtic had just been fined £100,000 by the SFA for making an illegal approach to Tommy Burns and we were due to play them the following Saturday. One of the local papers whipped up a real storm before the match and called it 'the biggest grudge match ever'. The atmosphere at the game was poisonous and we were all just relieved to get it over with, none more so than the players, given the 0-0 scoreline. Personally I was delighted that the match was over, because there seemed to be daily rows between the clubs and that can definitely have an effect on what goes on with the players.

The squad was really taking shape, but I felt I still needed a striker and made quite a few sorties down south to continue the search. England was a much bigger market, with a wider choice and better value for money. Tom Brown was a good player with a lovely touch but we needed a goal poacher to partner him, and I was fortunate enough to sign Paul Wright from St Johnstone for £300,000.

We had just beaten Hearts 3-1, but regardless of how well you're doing, one of the events no manager looks forward to is the club's AGM. You can always be sure of a grilling, while Christmas always brought a mixed bag of memories flooding back. It was the time I got the sack from St Johnstone and even a few years later I was still getting Christmas cards from Saints fans. The Killie AGM was different, though, and the fans applauded me for the players

I'd brought in, which was all a bit different from that day at St Johnstone a couple of years previous.

The team was performing well and my thoughts turned back, as they often did, to the great Bill Shankly. He was a great believer in getting the spine of the team right. I carried on that philosophy and with Lekovic in goal, Whitworth in central defence, John Henry in midfield and Paul Wright up front, we were sorted.

We weren't yet in a position where we would be challenging at the top of the league, which was probably just as well as all the emphasis that season seemed to be on trying to dodge relegation from the Premier League. The likes of Kilmarnock and Partick Thistle had spent millions revamping their grounds to meet top-flight criteria, which had an adverse effect on playing budgets, but rules were rules and we just had to get on with it.

I always tried to pick the team on a Friday, which let the players prepare properly for the following day's match. One guy who was a special player for me was John Henry, who played for me at both Killie and Falkirk, but there was an occasion when he left me fizzing mad. One Saturday, he rushed into the dressing room, about five past two, out of breath and telling me he'd been held up in the Clyde Tunnel. I was furious, and he was straight out of the 16. The most important day of the week was a Saturday and everything had to be right. I wanted my players there at a specified time, not rushing in stressed out and gasping for breath. We had trained all week, and everything was geared towards 3pm on the Saturday, so it would annoy the life out of me when players didn't treat it as their number one priority. I don't think John made that mistake again.

During my time at Killie, I called up Kenny Dalglish to have a chat about one or two things and he offered to bring his Blackburn team up to Rugby Park to officially open our new stands. They were a smashing side and had just won the English Premier League. Big Gordon Sherry, the pro golfer, was a Killie fan and had played in tournaments such as the British Open and the Masters. We invited him out on to the park at the start of the game to take a bow, so we got both sets of players to line up, and there was about 16,000 at Rugby Park that night. Gordon walked out and the fans went crazy. He said to me later, 'Alex, I've played in some of the biggest golf competitions in the world, but that was the biggest thrill of my life.' His family and friends were all there and the noise was unbelievable, but we wanted to show that Kilmarnock had some really successful guys supporting the team from the stands.

I returned the compliment, not to Blackburn, but to Livingston when Jim Leishman was in charge there. Livi were in the bottom division and Leish called and asked if I would bring Killie up to open their new stadium, which I agreed to instantly. Leish was fantastic and phoned a few days before the game to say he had booked us into a nice hotel, and the following day we were to play golf at an exclusive course. The players were looking forward to it and, as you can imagine, 20 sets of golf clubs took up a lot of room on the team bus. However, the clubs would remain unused. We were absolutely woeful on the night and Livi thrashed us 5-1. It might just have been a friendly with nothing at stake to the players, but to me it was an embarrassment. I said to Leish, 'Sorry, but we won't be taking up the offer of golf tomorrow. My players were a disgrace and deserve nothing.' He said, 'You can't do that Alex, it's all booked.' I said to him, 'With the greatest of respect Jim, I'll look after my team, and you look after yours.' And they didn't get to play golf.

At the end of the season, Jessie and I were over in Puerto Pollensa, in Majorca, when this guy suddenly stopped me and said, 'You're Alex Totten, aren't you?' And I said, 'That's right.' He told me he was best friends with the vice-chairman, Mr Moffat, and invited me up to his house for a drink. I had a pair of Killie shorts with me so I handed them over that night, and we got some pics taken of him holding up the shorts. Anyway, at our next board meeting, I told the directors that I'd managed to sign a player while I was on holiday. They weren't happy, and the chairman said, 'You can't do that, Alex, you have to let us know first.' Anyway, I showed Mr Moffat the pic of his best pal and once it registered, he burst out laughing. It was the first board meeting I had attended and helped break the ice a bit.

On one occasion I went down to Newcastle to watch a player I had been tipped off about. I had arranged to see Tommy Craig, who was the assistant there, and got a taxi from the train station to St James' Park, but it seemed to be taking an awfully long time and I was convinced the driver was going the wrong way. I slid open the wee window in the cab and tapped the driver on the shoulder. He got an awful fright, swerved violently and hit a lamppost. We were both a bit shaken up and he turned to me, apologised instantly and said, 'I'm really sorry about that, I've just started as a cabbie – my last job was driving a hearse!'

During my tenure as Dumbarton manager I always had a soft spot for Owen Coyle. He was just a kid at that time but I knew he had a bright future in the game. He eventually moved to Bolton Wanderers, and it was then that I tried to sign him for Killie. He was playing for Bolton's under-21s and before the game he spotted me at the front of the stand. He came across and asked if I was going to sign him. I said, 'Owen, you can't come over just now and ask me this. I'll go in and see your manager after the game.' Bruce Rioch, my old pal, was the gaffer and I was sitting in his office after the game when the phone rang. It was Roy Evans, manager of Liverpool, and I offered to leave, but he told me to stay. Liverpool wanted to sign Jason McAteer and Alan Stubbs. Evans offered £5m for the pair but Bruce said, 'No, I'm not selling anyone, because I want to be where you are.' Bolton were in the league below Liverpool at the time but he was a fiercely ambitious young manager.

In the end, I didn't sign Owen because he started scoring goals in a great cup run with Bolton and the asking price rocketed. I must have tried to sign him about four times in my managerial career but he evaded me every time. On one occasion, while I was at Falkirk, I phoned Tommy McLean, who was the manager of Dundee United, and asked if he fancied a swap deal, Derek Ferguson for Owen Coyle. This was the Tuesday, and Tommy said,

'I think I might go for that one Alex.' On the Saturday, though, Derek got injured and that was that. I was obviously fated never to get Owen, which was a great shame. Ironically, he came to Falkirk with Ian McCall, just as I was leaving. Mind you, when he became a manager in his own right, he invited me down to Burnley, for their match against Arsenal, and to Bolton, when they played Liverpool, so we always had a special relationship. I paid £10,000 for his brother Tommy when I was at St Johnstone, so at least I managed to sign one of the family!

One of the most interesting periods of my Kilmarnock tenure was being invited over to South Korea to take part in a tournament. It was a fantastic experience. Seoul was an incredible city and we were really well looked after. It was great to experience another culture and try different food, because you're learning all the time. Thankfully we were based in Seoul and didn't ever venture too close to the north of the country. But the South Koreans were really nice people and took us to their hearts. I've always loved travelling as it broadens your outlook on life. The South Koreans were a good side and they beat us after a tough game. Given half a chance I would have taken a few of their players back to Kilmarnock. We also played against Costa Rica and Brazil and the whole experience was a very positive one.

Mind you, it wasn't a great trip for big Neil Whitworth. He was injured in the first minute against Costa Rica. He got a real bang on the nose and that was him out the tournament. We were invited to a party one night and big Neil was up dancing with this girl, although the rest of the players had their doubts about 'her' sexuality. They were saying, 'Look at the size of her Adam's apple.' It turned out it was a guy, and all the lads gave him pelters.

The beginning of the end for me at Killie arrived on the last day of November 1996. We went to Stark's Park to face a Raith Rovers side who were scrapping for their lives – as were we, of course. We were three points clear of them at the foot of the table but that all changed after 90 torrid minutes of football. It looked like ending up 0-0, which would have maintained our advantage, until Raith were awarded a free kick in the third minute of stoppage time. Danny Lennon floated the ball towards goal and it eluded everyone and ended up in the back of the net. It was a real sickener, especially as we had lost Jim McIntyre to a red card after just 36 minutes.

Mind you, my departure didn't just hinge on that game. The directors felt they had to act with the club lying joint bottom at Christmas. The season previous we had finished joint sixth with Hearts, and had an average attendance of just under 10,000, but football is all about the here and now. We were in a relegation scrap with Raith, Motherwell and Dundee United, although I would still insist to this day that we had the quality to escape the drop. But the new chairman, Ronnie Hamilton – a former team-mate of mine at Queen of the South – felt the need for change, and that was his prerogative. In the end, it went down to a vote by the directors and I lost 3-2, with all three new directors voting to sack me.

It was a sad moment and as I was clearing out my desk, memories of Christmas past came flooding back. I had been sacked by St Johnstone exactly four years before – in the run-up to the festive season. Before leaving my office for the final time, I scribbled down a note, which I left on the desk blotter. It said, 'This is a great club. Good luck. Alex.' I thought back briefly to immediately after the Raith Rovers match, when one of the directors had said to me, 'By God, these players put some effort in for you today,' and I was then sacked on the Monday!

The day had started the same as so many others. I drove the 52 miles from my house in Dunipace to Rugby Park, and the first thing I did was call Neil Whitworth's mum to see how he was, as he was suffering from TB. I was then called into the chairman's office and told the devastating news. I was out. But nothing surprised me any more in football. When I'd taken over, we were called 'Dad's Army', and I'd changed the squad from the oldest in the league to the youngest. We had managed our highest Premier League finish the season before, and were just three points off from fifth. I felt sore, but life is too short to be bitter. I left St Johnstone with my dignity intact and I did the same at Rugby Park.

I'll never forget the sports pages of the national papers the next morning, and they didn't miss the Killie board for the manner in which they had sacked me. They highlighted the press release that had been sent out – with the headed notepaper still showing me as manager, despite the contents of the letter saying I had been relieved of my duties. Oh, and they called me Mt Totten, which I was able to laugh about later. One journalist wrote, 'Whether or not Totten deserved the sack is up for debate. But he surely deserved a better epitaph than a few hollow platitudes in the style of a minister at a funeral who doesn't know the body.'

One of the first people to call me up after my sacking was Sergei Baltacha and if he was in my company, he would've thrown his arms around me, I know that for sure. He also backed me publicly and came out in the papers and said that Killie were wrong to get rid of me, citing the 'mistake' St Johnstone had made in doing the same thing, which was really nice of him.

But the harsh reality was that I was out of a job and Christmas was looming large. As always, Jessie was my rock and assured me that something else would come along – and she was normally right. Meanwhile over at Kilmarnock, Bobby Williamson was appointed as caretaker boss. I had appointed Bobby as my reserve team coach and we got on great together, and still do to this day. But life went on and the phone did ring again, Jessie was right, only the person on the other end of the receiver was asking me to manage a club – in Hong Kong!

20

Renewing Old Acquaintances

MY lawyer, Jock Brown, was keeping an eye out for a new club but even I thought he had taken leave of his senses when he told me that a team called Instant Dick wanted me as their new boss. They played in the Hong Kong league and their owner, a chap called Ken Gee, was apparently impressed with my CV. It was certainly an interesting proposition and I was keen to know more – after talking it over with Jessie and the kids, of course. They were offering great money, and a two-year deal, which I seriously considered, but eventually turned down when I got a call from someone I knew very well.

Mind you, the call came on the weekend when Scottish football went just a little crazy. Eamonn Bannon was sacked as manager of Falkirk and the chairman, George Fulston, offered me the chance of a quickfire return to the game. We met up at the Powfoulis Hotel, in Airth, and he offered me the job there and then. As a Falkirk fan it was my dream post so I had no hesitation in accepting. The club held a press conference on the Saturday morning to announce me as the new manager and as we had no game that afternoon, I decided to take in the Stirling Albion v Airdrie match at Forthbank after talking to reporters. I had just sat down when I got a tap on the shoulder. It was George Peat, the Airdrie chairman, and he asked for a quick word. He said, 'Do you fancy coming to Airdrie as manager?' I replied, 'But you've got a manager, Alex MacDonald,' and he said, 'No, he's getting your old job at Kilmarnock. It's all but signed and sealed.' When I told him I had just been given the Falkirk job he seemed really disappointed.

Apparently Killie had interviewed Mark Hateley, who was playing with Queens Park Rangers at the time, for the job at Rugby Park, but reneged on the deal at the 11th hour, which left Hateley raging. One of the national papers then announced that wee 'Doddie' was the new manager of Killie.

John Paton, who was still on the Killie board, had known Alex MacDonald from his days at Rangers and recommended him. But that day, while I was at Stirling Albion, Killie beat Aberdeen 3-0, and the supporters were chanting Bobby Williamson's name. Bobby was really popular at Rugby Park and the directors soon thought to themselves, 'We've already got this guy who is reserve team coach, and the fans love him...' It seemed a no-brainer for the board and they gave Bobby the job.

So, what would have happened if I hadn't got the Falkirk job, accepted the Airdrie post and wee Doddie didn't get the job at Killie? Airdrie would have been the only team in Scotland with two managers! Oh, and Billy Kirkwood got the Hong Kong gig. Mind you, I often wondered how life might have panned out had I gone to the Far East. There was definitely an appeal with working in a different continent with the different cultures. I wasn't sure of the standard of the league over there but I would always say that working abroad can only benefit you and broaden your outlook on the game. I'd never even been to Hong Kong but I was prepared to give it a go, although the downside was that Jessie and the kids would have stayed at home, which would have been tough for us both, but sometimes you have to go where the work is.

But I was manager of the Bairns, once again, and one of the first things George Fulston told me was that the club had no money.

He was up front, although it wasn't the first time in my career I had been told such a thing, and I certainly wasn't about to allow it to hold me back, nor use it as an excuse if things didn't quite go according to plan.

So I was back in the game after a mini break and, as often happens in football, the fixture list presented me with a nice easy start – with my first competitive visit to McDiarmid Park since being relieved of my duties as manager of St Johnstone. But it wasn't to be the happiest of homecomings as we lost 3-1. If I thought I knew the extent of the Falkirk job before taking it on, that afternoon – Boxing Day – merely confirmed the size of the task. There was a long, rocky road ahead, but I was ready for the challenge – and actually quite looking forward to it.

The first thing I did when I went back to Brockville was get rid of that god-awful chequered strip. It was horrendous and I always maintain that if you feel good then it's half the battle. I remember Dunfermline had this 'floodlit' strip which the players just loved wearing. It was silky blue shirts and shorts, and it made you feel every inch a footballer. But if you were asked to pull on something ugly, like the chequered strip, then I'm sure it would have had the opposite effect, so it went straight in the bin! But if that was the negative side of returning to the Bairns, then the positive was definitely signing Kevin McAllister from Hibs. We were reunited, which was a fantastic feeling.

In only my second day in the job, I had a massive bust-up with a big English lad, Andy Gray. He refused to base himself in Scotland and would fly up from London for training and games. He more or less suited himself. In fact, he wanted to fly up on the Tuesday for training and I told him he had to fly up on the Monday, because I wanted him fresh to start training on the Tuesday morning. It was probably the best thing that happened because after clearing the air, we got on like a house on fire and became really good friends.

We played Dundee United one Friday night and I was talking to Jim McLean in the boardroom after the game. I asked him if he was missing management and he replied, 'You must be joking

Alex, with boys like big Duncan Ferguson around!' I don't think Jim could handle big Duncan, who had lived just along the road from me. Duncan had just passed his driving test and on one occasion Jim wasn't happy with him, so called him up to his office and said, 'I want every car in that car park down there washed and polished. I want them all gleaming by the end of the day.' Big Duncan walked away whistling, and Jim shouted after him, 'And stop that bloody whistling!' An hour later, the phone went and the boss at the car wash said, 'Mr McLean, who is paying for all these cars to go through the car wash?' That was Duncan for you.

Taking over in December meant I was there for the start of the Scottish Cup campaign – and it would become one to remember for Bairns supporters. We got a scare in the first round, as Berwick took us to a replay, which we won – thanks to a fortunate penalty. We then played Raith Rovers and Dunfermline – two Fife teams from the top league. There was a fair bit of rivalry between ourselves and those two, and for us to beat both – while operating in the league below – was a smashing achievement. We had great crowds at Brockville for both ties and beating Raith and Dunfermline was fantastic for morale. I could sense that we were building up a real head of steam and that the momentum was with us. Our supporters were fantastic and while I wouldn't suggest for a moment that we were unstoppable, we were certainly on a roll.

Falkirk hadn't been to a cup final for 40 years and perhaps the fans were sensing that perhaps this could be our year – and then came the draw for the semi-finals. There were four teams left. Ourselves, Killie, who I'd just left, Dundee United and Celtic. The latter pair were obviously the strong favourites and when BBC celebrity 'Heather the Weather' made the draw, we were pulled out of the hat alongside Celtic.

I knew that if we were to have a chance of beating them at Ibrox, we had to prepare properly, so I took the lads down to the Marine Hotel, in Troon, and they loved it. They were well looked after and enjoyed being in a lovely part of the country, and while it cost the club a few quid, George Fulston was great about it. He said to me that he wanted to try and give the boys the best and, of course, I knew we had made a few quid by getting to the semis.

I remember the first game as though it was yesterday. Tommy Johnson had given Celtic the lead and I knew I had to do something to try and change the course of the game, so I put big Kevin James – all 6ft 7in of him – up front, and it paid off big time. Jamie McGowan sent in a superb cross and Kevin rose majestically to bullet home a header past Stewart Kerr. It was a fantastic moment but the first thing I did was pull big Kevin back into defence, and Gordon Smith, who was commentating for the BBC that day, said, 'I think Alex Totten has made a big mistake, because you don't beat the Old Firm in Glasgow in a replay.' I knew exactly where he was coming from, and he probably wasn't the only one who thought that.

But after just 19 minutes of the replay, Paul McGrillen – who is sadly no longer with us – scored a great goal and from that moment on we worked hard to thwart Celtic. They had about 20 corners and hit us with everything they had. We had players like Paolo Di Canio, Andreas Thom and Jorge Cadete bearing down on us from all angles but held firm to pull off one of the best results in the club's history. Willie Young was the referee that day and I was willing him to blow his whistle. I remember when we were into the third minute of stoppage time, Kevin McAllister getting the ball and running straight over to the corner flag to try and waste a bit of time. After it, I said to him, 'That was brilliant Crunchie,' but he replied, 'I know, but to be honest, it wisnae *my* legs that took me over there!'

I looked at my watch and we were in the 95th minute and Celtic were awarded yet another corner. Thankfully it came to nothing and when the whistle finally went, I didn't know what to do. It sounds crazy but I just stood there for a couple of seconds, perhaps in shock, and then it sank in – we were in the final. All hell broke loose and I looked over to where the Falkirk fans were and suddenly I felt incredibly emotional. It is a feeling that will live with me forever. Tommy Burns was the Celtic manager at that time and I'll never forget how humble he was. Despite the incredible hurt he must have been feeling, he came into our dressing room after the game and shook my hand and wished us all the best in the final. I always had a great respect for Tommy. Sadly that result cost him his job but I remember meeting him a few years later, at Hampden for a Scotland game, and I was over my illness. He told me he'd been saying prayers for me, which I thought was lovely.

We drank in every single moment of that win. We celebrated next to the fans and then popped some champagne and enjoyed a wee sing-song in the dressing room. Then it was back on the team bus for the trip back to Falkirk – but there was no way we were getting through Camelon. The main street was thronged with supporters and we were 'diverted' into the Roman Bar, which is a massive Falkirk pub – and the boys were treated like heroes. In fact, there was a function on that night but it's said that when the result came through, the band stopped playing and a massive cheer went up. It was a great night and I eventually left at 6am and Kevin McAllister was still there with his entire family. I got a taxi home but I wasn't drunk. I was still high with the feeling of the previous day. I was hardly in the door when the phone rang. It was Bobby Williamson and he said to me, 'So we meet in the final Alex.' Killie had beaten Dundee United in the other semi-final tie and we had the final no one had dared to predict.

To beat one of the Old Firm after two games in Glasgow was just incredible. There are certain moments in your life that stick with you forever and that was certainly one of them. To be honest, you really have to experience it because words simply can't do it justice. For you to take your team to a national cup final, against all the odds, was fantastic. But it's all about the supporters. Naturally you're delighted for yourself, your family, the players and the board, but at the end of the day it's all for the supporters. Managers and players come and go but for the supporters, it's their club for life.

Five months after being sacked by Kilmarnock, I was due to face them with my new club in the final of the Scottish Cup at

Ibrox. I had to pinch myself to make sure it was all for real. A fortnight before the final, we beat Morton 3-0 in our final league match of the season, and Kevin James, who had been an injury doubt, played and proved his fitness, but my abiding memory of that day is looking out of my office window at Brockville and seeing the queue of supporters stretching from our ticket office halfway round the stadium. They were all desperate to get their hands on a gold-dust brief for the big game. That was what we had achieved at the club. We had given supporters back their swagger.

And then the cup final build-up began. You could sense it every time you stepped out of the stadium and into Falkirk town centre. A local baker produced blue pies for the occasion – and reckoned they were even better than the famous Killie pies. The battle was on! Bunting was up, buses booked for Ibrox by the dozen. The place was buzzing.

Someone later suggested that I was the first manager to be in charge of BOTH teams at a cup final, as I'd signed seven of the players who appeared for Killie that day. The other four had been there when I arrived at Rugby Park. Mind you, I had enough to worry about with my own team, as I knew we could only strip 14 – and I had a pool of 20. My mind flashed back to 1968, when I'd played in a couple of rounds for Dunfermline before being left out for the final against Hearts. I'd sat in the stand that afternoon so I knew exactly how the six who were left out would feel. But there was nothing I could do about that and it was just part and parcel of the job, although definitely the worst part.

The week before the final was also a crazy media scrum, with dozens of journalists constantly on the lookout for a different angle. Some wanted to speak about that 1968 final, others the Falkirk side of 1957 who were the last Bairns side to win the cup, while the *Daily Record* even persuaded George Fulston to dress up as a cowboy in an effort to show that we were going to Ibrox to have fun, despite an SFA edict apparently 'banning fun at the final'.

Blue coloured drinks were the order of the day in Falkirk, and one bar even slashed 57p off the price of drinks, as a nod to the

1957 cup-winning team – and there wasn't a scarf, flag or rosette to be had anywhere in the town.

But there was one pilgrimage I undertook a couple of days before the final that meant so much to me. I headed down to the Ayrshire mining village of Glenbuck to visit a memorial – commissioned by Liverpool fans – of the greatest manager who ever lived, and a great inspiration to me personally – Bill Shankly. It was a time for quiet reflection and I left Ayrshire that day feeling energised.

Only one thing left to organise, and that was to pick up my kilt for the big day. That's right, I was about to become the first manager to wear Scotland's national dress at a cup final, and I couldn't wait. The feeling I had when walking out of the tunnel at Ibrox was among the most special I've experienced in my entire life. The noise was phenomenal although it was quite bizarre as one by one the Killie players all said, 'Hi Alex, hi Alex…' It was pretty incredible.

The game itself was over in a flash, but one moment – just one moment – will live with me for the rest of my life. Not the moment Paul Wright scored the only goal of the game for Killie, but the moment Neil Oliver equalised – and it was disallowed by linesman Sandy Roy. Andy Gray's throw-in was flicked on by Kevin James and Neil volleyed it home. There were 85 minutes on the clock and it was the goal that sent one end of the ground into raptures. Or at least it should have, but for some inexplicable reason, up went the linesman's flag and referee Hugh Dallas had no alternative but to chalk it off. It was a perfectly good goal and after watching it a million times since, I know it was a perfectly good goal. But that's football and sometimes it can be a cruel game.

We lost 1-0 and as soon as the final whistle went, Paul Wright came straight over and threw his arms round me and gave me a big cuddle. The following season, I was reading Paul's player profile in a programme and he said that everyone knew it was Alex Totten's team who won the cup that afternoon. It was a nice touch, but little consolation to the 22,000 Falkirk fans who attended Ibrox that day. Suffice to say I will never forget Sandy Roy's name.

Still, my players had given me everything they had, and we enjoyed an open-top bus ride from Bonnybridge to Falkirk after the game and there were thousands along the route to give us an extra-special cheer. In their eyes, we were still heroes.

21

The Darkest Days

THE early weeks of the new campaign were taken up with the Challenge Cup, which is for teams outside the Premier League. We had won it previously but I was like every other manager in the game and wanted to win every competition I entered. We beat Dumbarton and Forfar in the early rounds to set up a quarter-final tie with Stranraer, and we thumped them 3-0 at Brockville. After seeing off Hamilton Accies in the semi-finals, we would play one of my old clubs, Queen of the South, in the final at Fir Park. It was the first Sunday in November and we had a chance of silverware, so everyone was buzzing. Mind you, at the pre-match press conference two days before the game, I was asked the million-dollar question. Would I be wearing my kilt at the final? At the start of November, I didn't think so – and it wasn't because I was superstitious!

This time there was to be no cup final hangover and a David Hagen goal was enough to give us the trophy. We were delighted, and while it didn't completely make up for missing out on the Scottish Cup, it did go a little way to putting a smile back on the players' faces. Before the game I told them to remember the feeling of disappointment from the cup final against Kilmarnock and to go out there and win it for themselves and their families – and they did just that. I was delighted for my number two, Walter Kidd, who had lost four Scottish Cup finals in his career.

But tragedy was lurking just around the corner. Bob McCallum had been the physio at Dumbarton when I'd joined the Sons, and while I was at St Johnstone he had moved to Falkirk. It was great to see a familiar face when I walked back through the door at Brockville and something I appreciated was his penchant for keeping fit, and his fantastic attitude to life. Bob was a great runner, and was out all the time pounding the streets with his wife, Jackie, especially at night after work. Sadly, my mum was ill at the time and had cancer. She was resident in a hospice in Denny and I was on my way to see her one day when I met Bob and my assistant, Walter Kidd, coming back in after a run. They were both dripping wet and I thought it must be pouring outside. I soon realised it was sweat, and said my goodbyes.

Sadly, that would be the last time I ever saw Bob alive. I was sitting at my mum's bedside when a nurse came over and said, 'Mr Totten, you've to phone the club straight away.' I spoke to Walter, who told me Bob had collapsed. He had been rushed to Falkirk Infirmary and I was told to get there as soon as possible. I left the hospice and headed straight for the hospital but when I got there Bob was already dead.

I got on really well with him, he was a lovely guy. Before the Scottish Cup Final we went to Majorca for a spot of training, and to get away from it all, and Bob was my room-mate. I will never forget how excited he was, not just about the forthcoming cup final, but the impending birth of his grandchild. His daughter had been expecting but sadly Bob died just a matter of hours before the child was born, and that will always rank as one of the most tragic stories I have ever heard.

At the funeral, Jackie asked me to say a few words. There were around 500 people present at Linn Crematorium and I felt a bit overwhelmed. I was standing just a few feet away from his coffin, and I could see his daughter sitting in front of me with the wee baby that her dad had never seen. It was so sad and I broke down before finishing my speech. Bob was such a conscientious guy. He also looked after the kit and if the team had been playing in Glasgow on the Saturday, he would head back to Brockville and get the strips cleaned. He was an incredible man and his motto was, 'If a job's worth doing, it's worth doing right.'

I'm an only child so I was very close to both my parents, which means you can imagine how difficult it was when they were both ill. Watching my mum cope with her illness in that hospice was so tough. My dad was also ill. He had Alzheimer's and was in hospital for a year and I used to go and see him all the time. He followed my career religiously and would get the bus down south when I was playing for Liverpool, and when I was manager at St Johnstone he never missed a game in five and a half years, and he used to tell me how proud of me he was. But that feeling was definitely mutual. I loved both my parents with all my heart.

But my problems weren't confined to my family and alarm bells started ringing at the end of February 1998. Some of the players were due bonuses and signing-on fees and the club insisted they didn't have the money to pay them. It was a sorry state of affairs but when I went to the see the chairman, I was assured that everything was okay. I said at the time that if I won the lottery, I would buy the club and sort out the mess, and I 100 per cent meant it, but what we needed was action and not someone's romantic pipe dream. I had brought most of the players to the club but my hands were tied and I had to rely on others to get us out of the mess.

We were lying second in the league at the beginning of March and I have to take my hat off to the players for the manner in which they maintained such a high standard of performance, despite the rumblings off the field about the missing payments. We were eight points behind Dundee in the table and consolidated that position with a hard-fought 1-0 win at Airdrie, where the players had to really roll their sleeves up and get stuck in.

It was a tough position for everyone at the club to be in, because the football authorities in their wisdom had decided to scrap the play-off place which meant that only the winners of the league went up – and I felt that if we didn't top the table at the end of the season, our financial situation would determine that we would have to go part-time, which would have a serious impact on jobs. I had always been a big fan of a 16-team top league, simply because it helped safeguard jobs.

We were given a break from all the depressing stuff to prepare for our Scottish Cup quarter-final clash against St Johnstone at Brockville, and it was a tie that I was really looking forward to. We had an all-ticket, sell-out crowd of 6,000 in for the game and we gave the majority of them plenty to cheer about when we demolished Saints 3-0 to reach the last four of the competition for the second successive year. David Moss scored a couple and was fantastic – but that adjective could've been reserved for every single one of my players that day. They did us all, and most importantly, themselves, very proud indeed.

But it was back to work on the Monday morning and the realisation that even if I wanted to strengthen the team, I couldn't, as a transfer embargo had been imposed on the club because we still owed Dundee United £35,000 for the transfer of Marino Keith. Our former manager Eamonn Bannon had taken out a civil action against the club, which meant the cash we had banked after winning the Challenge Cup had been frozen. It was just a messy situation all round, but sitting moaning about it wasn't going to get anyone anywhere.

The club was in the red and desperate to find a buyer for Brockville which, in turn, would have allowed us to start developing a new ground at Westfield. But it seemed to be one thing after another and the planned development was placed firmly on hold.

A welcome break arrived through the post later in 1998. My old school, Denny High, announced it was staging a special dinner for me and the world superbike champion Niall MacKenzie. It was a fantastic gesture and a really great way to honour two of its old pupils. At the evening, I was invited up on to the stage and received a beautiful crystal decanter, with the Denny High School crest on it. I was being honoured for taking Falkirk to the Scottish Cup Final. It was a great occasion and Niall was a lovely lad.

Meanwhile, the draw was made for the semi-finals of the Scottish Cup and I'm sure Celtic were delighted to avoid us after we'd knocked them out the previous year. Seriously, though, we were paired with Hearts, which I'm sure they weren't too enamoured with either as, at the time of the draw, we had lost just one of our last 14 games. Derek Ferguson had battled his way back to fitness and was unhappy at not getting in the squad, but it was difficult for me to change a successful side, although I completely understood his predicament.

However, the situation at the club, from a financial perspective, was becoming messier by the day. But even with such a gloomy cloud hanging over Brockville, I knew in my heart that I had made the right decision to go back to Falkirk. It was my hometown club and one thing was for sure, life was never dull.

In my first full season we finished second in the league but were denied promotion due to a rule change at Christmas. Now, the rule at the start of that season had been that the team in second would enter into a play-off with the second-bottom team in the Premier League, but again the goalposts had been shifted. How can that be right? Dundee went up and we were left where we were. It was a real shame because the boys had been on a fantastic run, and while we got around £250,000 in compensation, we were still denied a place at the top table. I thought it was an absolutely shocking decision – one of the worst taken in all my time in football. When clubs received an email from Lex Gold, the chairman of the league, to say that there was only one up, it immediately snatched away the motivation to go on and finish second if, perhaps, the top team were running away with the title.

We still had a Scottish Cup semi-final against Hearts to look forward to but even that looked like it might not happen when I had a very brief conversation with George Fulston on the afternoon of Thursday 19 March 1998. In football terms, nothing will ever compare to the mood in my office that day.

George walked in and said, 'Alex, the liquidators will be in at four.' Just like that – boom! That was the first I knew the extent of our cash problems and it was just the start of an awful time for everyone connected with the club.

I went straight down to the dressing room to tell the players and they were devastated. I told them there might not be any wages, but they still went five or six games undefeated. They could quite easily have downed tools, but not one of them did. They were incredible, and that undefeated run took us up to second in the table, and ensured we got the £250,000 in compensation which, I'm sure, helped save the club. That should never be forgotten. What those players achieved under dreadful circumstances more than likely saved Falkirk FC from extinction. I would go as far as to say that what we have today is in no small way down to the players who gave every inch of perspiration that season, and did so knowing full well that they weren't being paid at the end of the week. It was a totally selfless act. We had a good, experienced dressing room at the time with players such as Scott Crabbe and Kevin McAllister doing everything in their power to keep morale up.

When George uttered these words I was completely shattered. The enormity of the situation hit me almost immediately but I couldn't quite believe it. We'd enjoyed the fabulous cup run just a few months before, which, I believe, brought in around £1.5m, so it was hard to believe that we were in such trouble. The club had obviously been quite badly mismanaged but that was something I didn't have an awful lot of knowledge about. I was the manager and my job was to manage the players and pick a winning team. We kept up our side of the deal but others quite clearly didn't. What was going on upstairs was nothing to do with me, although that doesn't stop me having my own thoughts. It's perhaps similar to the situation my old friend Ally McCoist found himself in when he was manager of Rangers.

The Inland Revenue had called in a provisional liquidator because it was owed £400,000 in tax – and that bill was increasing at a rate of £30,000 a month. It was a staggering debt. But the club were £1.5m in the red, with the chairman owed a fair chunk after apparently dipping into his own pocket to pay the players' wages.

We had the club management upstairs and me in the dressing room. I was the buffer between management and players and the person that was asked all the questions. To be honest, I didn't have the answers but always tried to do what I could to help.

One day in the dressing room, I told the players that if they needed financial help, to come and see me on the quiet. These guys all had mortgages and families and I was quite prepared to give them a small loan and do whatever I could to help them through what was a terrible spell. I told them just to pop into my office for a quick chat and I would get the money back once they had been paid. Whether or not anyone took me up on the offer will remain a secret until my dying day.

I remember one of the women, Barbara, who washed the strips, stopping Donald McGruther, the liquidator, in the corridor one day and saying to him, 'Excuse me, are you the liquidiser? Is there any chance of getting a new washing machine?' It was absolutely priceless, and proved that there was still humour around in those dark days. But Donald was a real gentleman and was so helpful. In fact, we still exchange Christmas cards to this day He was a big St Mirren fan, but we never let that get in the way of our relationship!

He was very up front and honest and spelled out the implications of provisional liquidation to the players in a face-to-face meeting which was attended by the Players' Union rep Tony Higgins. As a result of that meeting, the players agreed to take a 50 per cent wage cut to help stave off redundancies, which was a massive undertaking. I followed suit as I wasn't about to remain on full wages while some of my players had theirs slashed. We were definitely in it together.

A couple of days after provisional liquidation was announced, we went to St Mirren and won 2-1, that's how amazing the players were. Marino Keith and Scott Crabbe might have scored the goals but I had 11 heroes out there that day. The day after the game, it was announced that a fund had been set up to help pay the players' wages, which was a terrific gesture, and proved exactly what people in the town thought of the club.

Partick Thistle, themselves no strangers to financial trouble, offered to help out by bringing forward our match at Brockville to the Tuesday night. It was another fantastic gesture and a great opportunity for the fans to come out and show their support in what was our first home match since our troubles began. Just under 5,000 – almost double our normal home gate – came along and helped swell the bank balance, which was fantastic, but I was disappointed that we only drew the game. We knew there was a £250,000 compensation payment for finishing second, and we needed to get our hands on that cash. I could hardly blame the players for that, though, because they were emotional wrecks after the days previous.

When I walked out of the tunnel before the game that night, I filled up when seeing the packed terraces. I don't mind admitting that I shed a tear. I was very emotional. And the letters, cards and messages of support started to flood in from all over the world. People were sending cheques and postal orders to help us out, and that is something I will never forget. A supporters' group, Back the Bairns, emerged and they were selling merchandise to help raise funds. I have never seen a community pull together so much for a common cause. It was incredible. In fact, one woman even sent me a cheque for the amount she used to pay her heating bills, and while it was a terrific gesture, I didn't have the heart to cash it.

But with just five games of the season remaining, we dropped a point at Morton and Raith Rovers moved into second on goal difference, and they had a game in hand. It was a worrying time. Suddenly, though, it was time to turn our attention to the Scottish Cup semi-final tie against Hearts at Ibrox.

Once again the fans rallied round and we had superb backing in Glasgow, but sadly we couldn't give them a second successive cup final to enjoy, even though we were the better team on the day, a fact acknowledged by the Hearts management team of Jim Jefferies and Billy Brown. That day, Kevin McAllister turned in the performance of the century. He was up against Gary Naysmith, a real quality defender, and turned him one way then the other. He absolutely destroyed him, and topped it off with a wonderful goal.

Stephane Adam scored for Hearts in the fifth minute and it remained that way until Crunchie scored with five minutes remaining. In the 88th minute, we were denied a stonewall foul 30 yards from goal by experienced referee Hugh Dallas. Jim Hamilton went straight through the back of David Moss – and Dallas waved play on. I was incensed, especially as FIFA had just issued a directive stating that anyone guilty of a challenge from behind at the World Cup in France was to be shown a straight red card. But Dallas chose to do nothing of the sort and Hearts ran up the park and scored. A third goal 60 seconds later merely twisted the knife.

I was never lucky with Dallas – he was the cup final referee as well – but after the game against Hearts you could've heard a pin drop in the dressing room. The players were so down, because they knew we were the better side, and then the door opened and in walked Kevin with a bottle of champagne, which was almost as big as him. There was simply no way another player could have got the man of the match award that afternoon, but even that was scant consolation in the face of defeat. When we went up to the lounge for a bite to eat afterwards, I was approached by Bill Dickie, the Motherwell chairman, and he said to me, 'The referee made a terrible decision not to give you that free kick. It was a nailed-on certainty, and I say that even though the referee is my cousin!'

It was back to the bread and butter of the league, and we focused all our efforts on finishing second. We knew it would be a tall order, but the players had to pick themselves up for a match against Stirling Albion at home, and this time David Moss had a broad smile on his face as he scored the only goal of the game. We were back in second place with just four games remaining. We then won at Hamilton – and again at home to champions Dundee – to remain in the driving seat for the quarter-of-a-million pay-out – but nothing was guaranteed. Seven days later it was, and the relief among the players and management team was palpable. We beat Ayr United 3-1 at Somerset Park to clinch second place.

It had been quite a season and at one point I genuinely thought the key was going in the door and the club was dead. Falkirk Football Club RIP. What happened though was that a consortium came in and paid £100,000 each to save the club, and that cash paid off all the debts. The members of the consortium – Martin Ritchie, Douglas McIntyre, Colin Liddell, Ann Joyce and William Moffat – really do deserve a huge pat on the back. Campbell Christie also put money into the club, while Colin McLaughlin represented Eddie Healy on the board, and is still a shareholder. Douglas McIntyre became chairman, and he is the best I ever worked under.

And then there are the unsung heroes, like Ronnie Bateman, who has supported the club all his life. He comes into the club every day and works with the girls in the accounts department. He has never received a penny for his efforts, and never misses a game. He was a buyer with Norboard, in Plean, for 30 years and is a true gentleman.

But the fans also played a massive part in helping Falkirk rise from the ashes. We had primary schoolchildren baking cakes to help raise money, car boot sales, everything you can think of, the fans came up with it. George Craig was in charge of our youth set-up at the time and they raised around £90,000, which was an astonishing sum of money. Everyone rallied round and played their part.

Falkirk genuinely is a real community club and the support we received from everyone in the town – even the people who didn't really have a great interest in football – was extra special. There was one last surprise, though, in a season that had taken my breath away – and that was when wee Crunchie and I had whiskies named after us. His was The McAllister, which was described as 'an exciting balance of flair and poise'. My tipple, A Tot of Totten, was apparently 'matured to perfection – adventurous and full of passion'. They were produced by Back the Bairns and were available at £20 a bottle – a snip at half the price!

22

Thank God It's Crunchie

THE makers of Kevin McAllister's whisky got it spot on when they described him as 'an exciting balance of flair and poise', but he was so much more than that to me. If Falkirk was my local club, it was also Kevin's. He was a Bairn born and bred and was also the best player I ever signed – twice!

Kevin played for Camelon Juniors and was recommended to me by a chap called Bill Parker. Bill was my scout at Alloa and had a fantastic eye for a player, so much so that he gave me a couple of good ones and we got promotion. I took Bill to Falkirk and again he pointed out a number of good players, including Brian Irvine, who moved to Aberdeen, Alex Rae, and Peter Hetherston.

He also recommended Kevin and that was good enough for me. Normally I liked to see a player before I signed him, but Kevin came along and I snapped him up straight away. I'd built up such a great working relationship with Bill that I trusted his judgement implicitly. Kevin was brilliant for me and for Falkirk. He was only 19 when he came to Brockville and made his debut against Leeds United. He was up against Frank Gray, who was the Scotland left-back at the time, and we drew 2-2 at Brockville in front of about

5,000, with Peter Houston and wee Kevin getting the goals. As soon as the game finished, Eddie Gray, the Leeds manager, and I shook hands and the first thing he said to me was, 'Who's that little lad, he's got the lot!' I was also thrilled with his display and you could see how he got people up off their seats with his trickery. He was such an entertainer and that was right up my street. He was different class for me and made such an impact on the Scottish game, and when I went back to Falkirk the second time he was my first signing – from Hibs.

But I'll never forget Kevin's first night at training with Falkirk. He was this young, raw talent but seemed at ease from day one. We had this exercise where a forward took on a defender, then the goalkeeper, and there was this lad called Brian Brown, who is now in Australia, and he was getting twisted further and further into the ground, like a corkscrew, and wee Kevin was in his element, ball glued to his feet and all the skill in the world. He was just such a joy to watch and one night I thought to myself, 'I'm glad my playing days are over if this is the type of player that's breaking through!'

Later on, Falkirk hosted a Rod Stewart concert at the new stadium, and organiser Andy Thomson thought it might be a good idea to try and make a few quid for the club while the stadium was set up for such a big event. We had a hospitality marquee on site and he came up with the idea for a fun *This is Your Life* event. Realistically there was only one player who fully merited such an accolade and that was Kevin. There was a great turnout of former players, such as Scott Crabbe and Marino Keith, and everyone had a ball.

I remember watching Eamon Andrews presenting the programme on television and seeing some wonderful personalities being handed that famous red book at the end of the show. It was an emotional programme and a real trip down memory lane for the celebrity in the spotlight. But I didn't realise just how emotional it could be and it wasn't just wee Kevin who was in tears that night – half the audience were reaching for the Kleenex as we watched clip after clip of the wee man in action. We showed footage of Kevin at Chelsea, Falkirk and Hibs and we all realised just what a special and talented footballer he actually was.

During matches, I used to get really annoyed when big defenders kicked lumps out of him – because he was my boy! But the list of people who turned out for him that night was endless, although to be honest, I think you would struggle to find someone in the game who has a bad word to say about Kevin.

I made him my assistant at Falkirk and when I moved on I wanted Kevin to get the manager's job. That was out of my hands, though, and Ian McCall got the job, but I just feel that Kevin should have been at the club in some capacity, because he truly is a Falkirk great. And he had experience of managing, at Albion Rovers, but as I say it was something that was out of my hands. He's a Camelon boy but lives in Grangemouth now.

He was also a fantastic influence in the dressing room but an equally nice lad off the pitch as well. The boys in the dressing room all looked up to him not only as a player but as a person. I was his manager a couple of times but I would have paid to watch him, he was that good. When I left to go to Rangers, Chelsea paid £60,000 for him and he was definitely Chelsea class. He fitted in well at Stamford Bridge but would've fitted in anywhere. Centre-forwards get lots of plaudits and become the top guys in the game for the goals they score, but who makes them look so good – wingers. Kevin played football with a smile on his face and I remember one wee shimmy that left Lorenzo Amoruso on his backside. As a kid, Kevin went to all the games on the supporters' bus from the Roman Bar. He was a Falkirk man through and through and I was delighted when he was voted the club's Player of the Millennium at a big ceremony in the Inchyra Hotel, in Falkirk. He was definitely a worthy choice.

Another player who I think about from time to time is Marino Keith. We had signed him from Dundee United for £35,000, a transfer that would ultimately prove almost fatal to the club because we didn't pay United the fee and were hit with a transfer embargo, which prevented us from signing new players for what seemed like an eternity. While our rivals were able to strengthen in the run-in to the title, we were forced to plough on with what we had.

But on Saturday 21 November 1998, talk of transfer embargoes and provisional liquidation paled into insignificance when we travelled down to Greenock to play Morton. We were joint second in the First Division with Hibs, and three points behind Ayr. We won the match 3-0, but that was all but forgotten because just a minute into the second half, there was a sickening clash of heads between Marino and Derek Collins. Both players collapsed to the ground in a heap but Marino was knocked unconscious and immediately started convulsing quite violently.

Clashing heads is something you see quite often on a football pitch as players jump up to win the ball, but there seemed something entirely different about this one, although it was no one's fault. Marino was in a bad way – he had swallowed his tongue – and had to be rushed to hospital. Thankfully, once at hospital, the injury didn't seem as bad as first feared, but believe me when I say there were people inside Cappielow that day who feared the worst. Several players wanted the game called off and I don't think there would've been too many dissenting voices had the referee gone along with their wishes.

We all got a terrible fright and it was all I could think of the entire second half. I tried focussing on the game but it proved impossible. I went straight up to the hospital after the match and thankfully he had improved tenfold. After the game I spoke to the players closest to him, and they said he had turned blue. They were waving frantically for the doctor to come on and when he did he could see that Marino was fitting. They took him up to the first aid area, but a second fit meant he had to go to Greenock Royal Infirmary, and after the game we had it confirmed that he had almost died.

If it hadn't have been for the quick thinking of our doctor, Gillies Sinclair, I believe we might have lost him. That's how serious it was. Dr Sinclair has been involved with Falkirk for more than

50 years and he realised the severity of the situation straight away. I also ran on to the park and I could see exactly how ill Marino looked, and it was quite clear that he was choking. When I saw the colour of him I realised that something had to be done very quickly to save him. I don't mind admitting that I was terrified of what might happen.

We thought the game might be abandoned but when Marino came to, the referee decided that play should continue. To be honest, I couldn't really concentrate on the rest of the game. All I could think of was Marino. You just hope that he is going to be okay, so it was a case of get the game finished and get up to the hospital to check up on him. One of the first things Marino did when he came back to the club was to thank Dr Sinclair for saving his life.

Of course, like every dressing room up and down the country, the players had a bit of banter about it, although every time I go back to Morton the first thing I look at is the centre circle, and where the incident took place. I always get an eerie feeling.

Marino was a good player. He was a big, strong forward who did a really good job for us and scored a few goals. On one occasion we played Huntly in the Scottish Cup and Kevin McAllister went on this amazing run, where he beat five players before sticking the ball in the top corner. It was arguably the goal of the season but Marino was annoyed with Kev for not passing to him – but that's strikers for you.

As with my first spell as manager of the Bairns, it was a really enjoyable time. Sure, there were lots of ups and downs, but isn't that what's so good about football? No two days are ever the same and as a manager you are presented with new challenges all the time. It's a fantastic line of work and I feel so blessed that I had so long in the job, and with so many great clubs.

My last season at Falkirk was once again an action-packed affair, although why should it have been any different from the rest? The players had achieved their objective by getting third place in the league but we were denied a place in the play-offs because the league decided we didn't meet the criteria, as we didn't have a 10,000 all-seater stadium. So that was that. Promotion was a distant memory and, as a result, I lost all my best players. I was left with a bunch of kids.

My last game as manager of the Bairns was against Everton. David Moyes had just taken over the hot seat at Goodison Park, so it was his first game for them, and my last in the game – definitely a case of two managers at different ends of the spectrum. It was our 125th anniversary and David brought his top team up to Brockville, which was a cracking gesture.

A few weeks before that match, I had gone to a board meeting and told the directors that I wanted to retire from football management. I just felt that six years was enough and that it was time to step aside. I had been 22 years in the hot seat and there were other things I wanted to do. That was on the Thursday night and the chairman, Campbell Christie, called and asked if he could see me the next day. We met up at the Falkirk Wheel and he asked me to stay on at the club. He had this vision of me working on the commercial side of the club, bringing in money for the academy and such. I thought it was a great idea. That was 2002 and I'm still doing the same job to this day. It was the perfect compromise as far as I was concerned because it meant I didn't need to sever my ties with the club. I had been over 20 years at my local team as a player and manager, twice, and this meant I could stay with the Bairns.

I'm the only guy to get a lifetime achievement from Falkirk, as well as a testimonial, so it was a good opportunity to stay on without remaining at the sharp end. During my tenure we had twice finished second and third, but in my last season, we finished second-bottom. Normally that would've meant the drop, but we were saved by Airdrie going out the game. It might have proved our saviour but it was a terribly sad time for Scottish football, and the first time since Third Lanark, in 1967, that a club had died. Ian McCall had been manager of the Diamonds and, ironically, he moved to Falkirk as gaffer. I had wanted Kevin McAllister to replace me, and I wished him all the best before he went for his interview, but also warned him that it wouldn't be my decision. The likes of Kevin, Brian Fairlie, John Hughes and McCall were interviewed through in Glasgow, and the latter got the nod.

We had lost an entire first team and I had been left with a bunch of pups. I'd had four or five promotions during my managerial career but had never been relegated, although I came mighty close that season. But even then, the fans were brilliant with me, and left the guys in the dug-out alone!

I was at an event with the supporters round about that time and I'll never forget the story wee Kevin told. The upshot was that I was shouting and bawling at the referee and screaming, 'Cassidy, Cassidy [a reference to Brian Cassidy], you're absolutely hopeless.' And the referee eventually came bounding over and said, 'Will you stop that at once, my name's no' Cassidy, it's McGarry!' We then started shouting, 'Hey McGarry, you're worse than Cassidy!' He took it very well indeed.

But my time as a manager was definitely up and I was happy with my new role as commercial director. I was finished with management and had no desire to get back into it. I felt it was a younger man's game. Mind you, I did have one stint back in the dug-out, just before McCall was appointed. John Hughes and Owen Coyle were in temporary charge and they asked me to look after things on the touchline as they were both still playing, so I did that for a while to help out.

My last game was against St Johnstone and, wait for it, I had yet another bust-up with Hugh Dallas. He gave what I believed was a wrong decision and I responded by giving him a mouthful. He stopped the game, walked calmly across to the dug-out and motioned for me to approach him. He said, 'Alex, I have a great respect for you, but please just shut your mouth.' He walked away laughing, I started laughing, and that was that. I suppose it was the best way to end my time at the coalface of football. Brian Rice then came in as coach, which allowed Yogi and Owen to concentrate on playing.

On reflection, I didn't have the best of relationships with referees, but I appreciate and respect that the job they do is far from easy. My only concern as a manager, though, was my players, and I liked to treat them all the same. You can't afford to have any favourites. If you're not playing, then I feel for you. I wanted to play as a player, I didn't want to sit on the bench or in the stand but a manager can only pick 11 players and there can be no room for favourites.

I signed Kenny Ward for St Johnstone and Falkirk and we had a great relationship but when we beat Queen of the South 1-0 in the B&Q Cup Final, he didn't make the 14, and I remember Scott Crabbe coming up to me and saying, 'Oh gaffer, he's so disappointed.' We went to the Scottish Cup Final and again he didn't make the 14. Kenny was pig sick, but I had picked the team I thought could do the business on the day. When I had my testimonial dinner at the Inchyra Hotel, all the players, including Kenny, were there. The next day he sent me a text saying, 'Great night gaffer, you thoroughly deserved it. Love you to bits, Wardy' and that showed his class. Leaving players out – especially on the big occasions – is one of the hardest parts of the job, but it's something that has to be done. It's great that Kenny and I still meet up for a game of golf to this day and there are no hard feelings.

I've made a lot of friends in football but management is a tough business and you can't afford to let sentiment get in the way of your decision-making. I had this young lad Andy Seaton, who was a smashing player, but in one game down at Morton, he gave the ball away in the last minute and it led directly to us losing. I was furious with him and when the players walked back into the dressing room, I gave him a swift kick up the backside. I wasn't messing about and that was my way of letting him know that I wasn't happy with him. Of course, you couldn't get away with that kind of thing nowadays!

Another tough aspect of the job is when you have to release kids at the end of the season. You've maybe worked with them for two or three years, and watched them grow and develop, and then you have to tell them they can go. That's something I don't miss. It's different with the older players, as a lot of them have experienced getting a free transfer before. But when you're told for the first time, it can be devastating for a player.

But everything I've done has always been for the good of Falkirk Football Club. I have been a shareholder since 1983 and have enormous feeling for the club. I'm not the only one, mind you, because the directors who saved the club should never be forgotten. The club continues to be run on a sound footing and there are no Billy Big-Timers in the boardroom.

One abiding memory of my time as manager at Falkirk was Scottish Television's old *Football First* programme. It used to focus on the second tier and I watched it every Sunday – and not just for the trailer, which had this guy saying, 'I'm going for a meal with Alex Totten.' It was hilarious and I always laughed when it came on – and some folk still rib me about it to this day.

Signing players and recognising who will fit into the way you want to play can be quite difficult. It's all about your judgement as a manager, although Shankly used to say, 'You go and watch a player, and then you go and watch him again, and if you think he'll do a job, you sign him. But you don't actually get to know him until you work with him every day.' It's very true, but initially you really have to go on instinct. Your team is like a jigsaw puzzle. You're always searching for the bit that will make it complete.

On a Friday morning I'd pin a sheet of paper up on the dressing room wall with the team on it and we would talk briefly about the opposition before chatting about how we would play. The players knew the starting XI and once we'd covered the theory behind how we would play, we would go out on to the park and work on everything such as positions at set pieces, defending, attacking. We would leave nothing to chance and the players knew exactly what was expected of them the following day. But then a player would make a calamitous error in the first minute – or someone would get sent off – and everything was up in the air.

It was very frustrating for a manager – even though players are only human – and I would kick lumps out of the dug-out. There were holes all over the home dug-out at Brockville. On one occasion there was this wee boy leaning against it supping his drink when one of our players made a bad error and I rattled the dug-out. Next minute, the wee boy was covered in juice. It was all through his hair and his clothes. Everyone round about started laughing but I didn't know what they were laughing about until I saw this wee lad standing there. I felt really bad afterwards.

People have told me that I'm very mild mannered, but I definitely changed on a Saturday afternoon. If you've got a run-of-the-mill 9-5 job then the chances are you're doing the same thing most days, but with football everything you do from a Monday to Friday is geared towards 3pm on a Saturday. That's the be-all-and-end-all. It's all about winning that game and if you do it's a great feeling because obviously all your preparations have been worthwhile and you've enjoyed the match. Lose the match and you can't wait until the next one for the opportunity to rectify it. I always got too engrossed in a game.

But I've always loved to play football. I remember Tommy McQueen's dad telling me that he enjoyed watching my teams because of the way we played the game. Tommy was a smashing left-back for Falkirk, and went on to play for West Ham. I always played with wingers and used to love watching the likes of Garrincha with Brazil, but where are the wingers now?

Wingers were all but a distant memory when the bulldozers moved in and razed Brockville to the ground. The old stadium that I had watched my very first game of football from was gone in a flash. A lifetime of memories reduced to a pile of rubble. Lots of people missed Brockville when it finally went. It was a special place because the fans were so close to the action. If I was in the lounge you would see the players walking past – and smell the wintergreen rub. It was a proper old football stadium and while I was well aware that it was way past its sell-by date, it was still sad to see it go. I saw virtually every brick go in at

McDiarmid Park, and I was there when three stands were developed at Rugby Park.

When Brockville became the latest 'stadia casualty' of Scottish football, I just wanted to see Falkirk have a proper replacement at Westfield. Many years ago, Martin Luther King had a dream – but seeing the Bairns have a nice new ground was mine, and thankfully it came to fruition.

John Hughes was the manager when Falkirk played for a season at Stenhousemuir. The only thing we did at Ochilview was play games. We had portacabins at Brockville and ran the club from there. I was director of football at the time, and one Saturday we had a march from Brockville to the new site at Westfield to try and highlight the length of time it was taking to get planning permission for the new ground. It was a distance of about three miles but spirits were high and about 1,000 supporters took part. That was a memorable day because when we reached the site, we decided to have an impromptu game of football, about 21-a-side, and we put jackets down for goalposts. We were soon ankle-deep in mud, but we were enjoying ourselves and no one seemed concerned about the cleaning bill.

In all honesty, Brockville was, and always will be, my spiritual home, but it was still a fantastic feeling when we were eventually given the go-ahead to start constructing our new stadium. We knew there was no leeway to build a new stadium on the site of Brockville, because of the houses on Watson Street, but we did look at every permutation available to us.

So, a new stadium it was, and I went down to places such as Bolton's Reebok Stadium to have a look at the type of facilities they had incorporated into their stadium. We were also considering an astroturf surface so off I went, with Brian Rice, to check out the surfaces at Bayern Munich and Salzburg. We took our boots over and kicked a few balls about on the pitch. We headed back to Falkirk, recommended a specific surface, and then the SPL said they couldn't guarantee us promotion if we installed a synthetic surface. It brought back bad memories of missing out on previous promotions to the top flight so we had to go with grass, initially, although we now have a synthetic surface and, as a result, our ground is well utilised.

The only thing missing from the new ground is a fourth and final stand. I've said it myself that if I win the lottery I will finance it, because you definitely miss the other stand. The initial plans were for four stands AND for the corners to be filled in with offices and a hotel on the other side, but then the recession hit and the plans were up in the air. When I was assistant at Rangers, we went across to Spain to play Osasuna, and the atmosphere was incredible. The corners were filled in and Osasuna's ground was like a bullring. That was the initial plan for the Falkirk Stadium but, as usual, these things are all governed by finance, although we were fortunate enough to have our South Stand paid for privately. Sandy Alexander, who owned the footwear company Schuh, paid for it, and it cost him around £2.5m. He is a fantastic man and a massive Bairns supporter. I used to speak to him a lot when I was manager and he was always offering his help. But despite only having three stands, there is no doubt that we have a lovely stadium. When you approach the car park it's like a miniature Hampden, but it's not Brockville, although that's something I *will* get over! Mind you, I still have the key to the home dressing room at Brockville to remind me of all the good times I had there.

23

Facing My Biggest Fight

BILL Shankly didn't get too much wrong when I was at Liverpool. He was the master of his craft and we hung on his every word, but when he coined the immortal phrase, 'Football isn't just a matter of life and death, it's more important,' I'm afraid he was wide of the mark.

I had been going over to Portugal every year on a golfing holiday with a bunch of mates and the summer of 2007 was no different. I always found the trips a great way to unwind from the stresses and strains of football and with a group of about 16 of us, you were always guaranteed a good laugh – it was the ideal boys outing. As always, I enjoyed the break that year but when I came back I didn't quite feel right, although I couldn't put my finger on it.

I had been back for about ten days and was still feeling sweaty and warm when I was invited to a barbecue at Glenbervie Golf Club, which is in Larbert. I'm a member there and always feel very comfortable, although not that day. I wasn't eating, which isn't like me, but I just didn't feel hungry. I went home feeling all strange and decided to have an early night. Naturally, Jessie was worried but I thought a good night's sleep would shake off the mystery feeling.

I couldn't have been more wrong. I awoke at five in the morning, rolling around in agony. I had so much pain coming from my hand and arm and it was like a really bad case of toothache – but not in my mouth. I went to the surgery as soon as it opened, and spoke to my doctor, Bobby Deuchar, whose son is Kenny, the footballer, and he wasn't happy. He didn't mess about and packed me straight off to Stirling Infirmary, where they took one look at me and knew that something pretty serious was going on. They admitted me and ran tests. One of the first things I did was to call George Craig, the chief executive at Falkirk, and told him I might be off for a day or two as I wasn't feeling well. My calculations were a wee bit out and I was in hospital for five weeks.

My head was all over the place and all I could think about was Jessie and the kids. I knew I was unwell but simply didn't know to what extent. I had loads of visitors, such as Andy Cameron and his mate Andy Bain, who came up and did their best to put a smile on my face. I also had a pal, Rab Duffin, a nurse at the hospital, who later told me that one of his colleagues had said that I had been fighting for my life that first night in hospital. The colleague then said to Rab, 'Hopefully he's turned the corner now.' When you hear that you realise just how serious the whole matter actually was.

I had never been ill in my life but it turned out I had septicaemia and that wasn't something to be sniffed at. A couple of years ago I was reading a feature on the condition and the headline was 'The Silent Assassin'.

When I told doctors I had just been in Portugal they asked if I'd been bitten by an insect, but I couldn't recall anything like that happening. They opened up my arm to run tests and I ended up with 40 stitches – but what a small price to pay. They decided to operate and afterwards the surgeon phoned Jessie to say there had been an improvement, but that I wasn't yet out of the woods. Any improvement was slow and I eventually came to after a few days.

I was in the intensive care unit for a while and also the high dependency unit so by all accounts I was very fortunate to come out the other side. I was also in a coma for a while, which I can only imagine must have been terrible for my family. The one thing I know is that I'm a lucky boy still to be here and I'm very grateful for that.

While I was in hospital I had to use a zimmer to get walking again, and the nurse would tell me not to walk too far because inevitably I would struggle to get back. While you don't realise just how ill you are, the staff know exactly what stage you're at.

Mr Ritchie was my surgeon and I'm not exaggerating when I say that I owe him my life. I went back up to the hospital to see him and gave him a pen. At first he didn't realise the significance of it, but it was from my testimonial and he wrote me a lovely letter and said it was great to see me looking so well, and signed off by saying, 'Thanks so much for the pen, I didn't realise it was from your big day.'

I also popped in to see the nurses because they were always asking if I knew of any rich, single footballers they could marry! I got out of hospital on the Thursday and my testimonial was just 48 hours later against Rangers, so when I went back to see them my photograph was up on the noticeboard in the ward. They had the match report and pictures from my testimonial pinned up and I felt really humbled. They were brilliant with me.

I remember Andy Cameron speaking at my testimonial dinner and looking over to Jessie and saying, 'You can put the insurance documents back in the drawer then!' To be honest, and with the benefit of hindsight, he probably wasn't that wide of the mark.

Two days before I was due out of hospital, a physio hit me with the bombshell news that she was refusing to discharge me. She told me that my balance still wasn't quite right and that it might do more harm than good if I was to get out. I was devastated and told her that I had to get out as it was my testimonial a few days later, but she wasn't for budging.

On the Thursday, Mr Ritchie re-assessed the situation and decided to discharge me – but on one condition, that I didn't attend the testimonial match. He was banning me from going to the game. He said I would end up completely drained, but I couldn't miss it, and he probably knew that. I was sensible and curtailed my visit to just 40 minutes. I got to the ground at 2.30pm and left again just after three.

In total, I was off work for ten months, and it was the same again before I played a game of golf, which also illustrates how unwell I was, as anyone who knows me will tell you exactly how much I love my golf. But Falkirk were brilliant with me, and continued to pay my wages, even though I wasn't giving anything in return. They really looked after me and I still get very emotional to this day when anyone mentions this dark period in my life. It was at that time I realised just how much family and friends meant to me.

When I was ill, I received so many letters, and Jessie had loads of telephone calls, and you really do appreciate what people do for you. It's fantastic and it gives you such a lift. I found it incredible that so many people had these types of feelings for me.

While I was in a coma in hospital, I had this awful dream, and I still haven't been able to make head nor tail of it. When I eventually woke up it was as though I had left my body and all I remember was lots of turmoil going on around me. It was terrible and I seemed to be coming and going and nothing really made any sense. I'm not sure if that was me recovering from my ordeal, or crossing over from one side to the other. I really don't know, but it was like nothing I had ever experienced before – or want to experience again.

It was a dreadful time for my whole family. My wife lost a stone in weight and I lost a couple, but people rallied round and I have no doubt that also helped aid my recovery. The staff at the hospital couldn't do enough for me and were different class. I'll never forget the role they played in my journey. Ten months was a heck of a long time to be ill and you don't realise the stress and strain on your body and what it has been through. But throughout the ordeal

I can safely say there was never a time when I felt like throwing the towel in. It's just not in my nature to give in, and perhaps that attitude also had a bearing on me making a full recovery.

When I eventually got out of hospital, one of my neighbours, Brian Moffat, came over to the house and he had a couple of cans of stout with him. As we sat chatting, he said to me, 'Just look in the mirror Alex and you will realise you're still here,' and he was so right. I couldn't even begin to imagine looking into a mirror and not seeing a reflection. How awful would that have been?

I'd worked all my life so the natural thing to want to do was get back to raising money for Falkirk – and repaying everything they had done for me. And even though Jessie and I get on great, I think she was glad to see the back of me, because I was starting to get under her feet. I love my job. I enjoy going round all the different clients and customers. I've known most of them for years and we have a wee chat and a cup of coffee, and they sponsor the club. It's the perfect job for me.

Since the illness, though, I think I've started to appreciate life more. You realise how lucky you've been and you think the world of your grandkids, and your family. I don't mind admitting that I have questioned my mortality on a number of occasions since then. But football is a great profession and I know that I could phone any one of the players or managers I've worked with in the past and they would be there for me. That's just the way it is.

Peter Houston is now the manager of Falkirk. I signed Peter as a player for the Bairns and we still have an excellent relationship. We play golf together and I count my blessings every time I walk on to the first tee. Now and again I take him out to meet clients and they all love it. I know that Peter was sorry he never applied for the job when Gary Holt got it, but the board remembered that and called him up. There were 40 applicants for the manager's job but Peter was always the favourite, and I really enjoy seeing him around the club again.

But my brush with death is never far from my thoughts and a couple of years after the scare, I was at the Airth Castle Hotel in

Falkirk one day when this well-heeled gentleman came across to my table and said to me, 'Alex, I'm one of the surgeons who looked after you when you were ill. You know, by rights you shouldn't be here today, you should be six feet under. Seven folk out of ten don't survive what you had but your level of fitness helped a great deal.' I stood there open-mouthed as he was talking. It was incredible to hear that, and straight from the horse's mouth, so to speak.

Looking back, it's frightening to think that I was at death's door. I was unconscious for four days, hooked to a ventilator and clinging to life while Jessie worried herself sick. I've since been told that sports editors in newspaper offices around the country were asking reporters for obituaries. My testimonial match looked like it might have to be replaced by something far more morbid. It was touch and go but I'm a fighter and I had no intention of giving in. It simply wasn't my time.

24

My Testimonial Year

WHO was that frail old man leaning on a walking stick at the back of the stand applauding both sets of supporters and players? That was my first thought when I looked at the papers the morning after my testimonial match between Falkirk and Rangers. Sadly, it was me, although I wouldn't have missed that game for the world, despite being told not to go by the doctors and nurses who had been treating me at Stirling Infirmary.

Being granted a testimonial by Falkirk Football Club in the first place was a real honour – and the perfect pick-me-up as I lay ill in hospital. It was an unusual testimonial, awarded for working for the club for ten years, although I'm sure the time I spent as a player and manager with Falkirk was also taken into consideration. And don't forget my spell as a supporter on the Hope Street terracing – which started as a passionate ten-year-old Bairn! But, seriously, I appreciated the gesture so much, and it meant an awful lot to be recognised by 'my club'.

I was laid up in hospital prior to the event but thankfully I had a hard-working committee – headed brilliantly by Brian Flynn, a local businessman – who put in so many hours, days and weeks to ensure everything went well. Others who played a key role in organising my testimonial year were Davy Lapsley, Craig Richardson, Iain Mitchell and Peter Brown.

What my period in hospital had done, though, was to allow me the time to reflect on my relationship with Falkirk. As I said, it started out as a young fan but to play for the club at Brockville was just such an honour. Thousands dream of pulling on their favourite club's shirt, but I was one of the few who actually managed it.

As manager, leading the Bairns out in the Scottish Cup Final against Kilmarnock really was the stuff of dreams. I would think back to that afternoon at Ibrox and me with my kilt on. Unfortunately it didn't bring us the luck to go on and win the game, although just making it there was fantastic in itself I suppose.

Another highlight was to guide Falkirk to promotion from the First Division, although to see it snatched away from us because of bureaucracy gone mad was so disappointing. The powers that be had decided that Brockville didn't meet the criteria for the Premier League and that was that.

But my testimonial year more than made up for any disappointments during my career, although it was a 12-month period that unfortunately coincided with one of the lowest points of my life. Mind you, it started off with a superb golf day, in which so many celebrities, such as big Derek Johnstone and Andy Goram, turned up to play alongside supporters and businessmen. It was a great success and as long as I live I will never forget one of Jim Leishman's quips. He is hilarious, and acted as MC that day and said, 'I know Alex is unable to speak today, but he needn't worry, because I'll pay his f****n tax!'

There is a rule that forbids the beneficiary from speaking due to tax reasons, but that line from Leish brought the house down. And big Tommy Gemmell insisted that I'd had more press than he and his Lisbon Lions had received even when they won the European Cup in 1967. The football fraternity really are a close-knit group and they rally round for colleagues, and I know I appreciated every single person that turned out for the many events in my testimonial year.

We also had a fantastic dinner, and that gave me the opportunity to invite one man in particular, a player who had been my hero when I first started watching Falkirk. I was delighted that Alex Parker was able to make it along to the event and he sat at my table. Alex was a big part of Falkirk's 1957 Scottish Cup-winning side and won 14 caps for Scotland. He was a legend at the club and I was privileged to become his friend.

The comedian Andy Cameron was a speaker at the dinner, as was Len Murray, a lawyer. They were both fantastic, and I had a smile on my face when Len said, 'I don't think Alex has ever had the credit he deserves for what he has done for Scottish football. Achieving promotion with so many clubs was quite a feat,' which I thought was a really nice thing for him to say. He also said everyone knew that Kilmarnock's Scottish Cup-winning team of 1997 was my team. I suppose it was because I had signed seven of the players and the other four were already there when I went to Rugby Park.

But the focal point of the testimonial year was the challenge match against Rangers, and I was delighted that Gers boss Walter Smith brought his first-team squad through to the Falkirk Stadium for the match. To see players of the calibre of Barry Ferguson, Carlos Cuellar and Kris Boyd turning out for me was a massive boost.

It was a real family affair and despite attending the match against medical advice, I did try and be careful not to overdo it, although how can you keep a low profile when so many people have made the effort to turn out to pay tribute to you and your career?

Jessie, the kids and I went along to the stadium, where the committee had arranged a pre-match meal. I was sitting with the likes of Andy Cameron, Alex Parker and Andy Goram. 'The Goalie' was going on at half-time for a penalty kick competition and said to me, 'Come on, I'll take you down to the pitch,' but I knew I couldn't make it that far and I went out and stood at the back of the stand. I hobbled out but was completely drained when I got there and my daughter had to get me a glass of water. I was standing there with my walking stick and I could tell by the way people were looking at me that I still had a long way to go before the recovery was complete.

I later saw photographs of the afternoon and they merely confirmed that I had just come through something truly awful. But the ovation I got from both the Falkirk and Rangers fans was simply incredible, and is something that will live with me for the rest of my life. They were fantastic and will probably never know just how much their ovation and applause lifted my spirits.

Unfortunately I had to leave the stadium after just 40 minutes or so because I simply wasn't up to it, but Jessie and the kids stayed on to present the players with their testimonial gifts. My mate called me to tell me it had been a really good game and that it had finished 1-1, with Pedro Moutinho equalising for the Bairns after Lee McCulloch had scored for Rangers inside the first minute. I was so glad that everyone had enjoyed themselves. Of course I was disappointed that I couldn't play a bigger part in it but I had a greater battle on my hands at that time, and I know everyone appreciated that. I was later given a video of the afternoon and thoroughly enjoyed watching it.

Football is a very emotional sport, and when players and managers face one another on a Saturday afternoon, there is an incredible amount of rivalry, because everyone wants to win – that's the name of the game – but when the chips are down there is no better sport for people coming together and helping out a colleague.

The following day, I read in one of the Sunday papers, 'While illness prevented "Mr Falkirk" Alex Totten from making an on-pitch appearance at his testimonial match, his mere attendance in the stands confirmed he's on the mend.' It was nice to read that. Being called 'Mr Falkirk' might have been a bit of an exaggeration, but it's incredible how just reading some words in a newspaper can give you such a lift.

John 'Yogi' Hughes was Falkirk manager at the time and after the game he said, 'Alex has always been there for me to offer advice and that's something I really appreciate. At this time of year you are working behind the scenes trying to bring players in but when we heard he was getting back on his feet it was the best bit of news we could have had. He is a remarkable man, full stop. It was nice seeing him at the game and it was a proper tribute, deservedly so for all his years in football and what he has done for Falkirk Football Club.' Yogi is a gentleman, and someone I have always had lots of time for.

Walter Smith was also full of praise for me, and said, 'Anyone that knows Alex knows that football is his passion. He is always enthusiastic, even when he was "attacking" me that day in Perth. It was a bit over the top but that happens to us all. I have known him for a good number of years through the football, so the illness he had was a concern to us all but it looks like that has run its course and he can get back on the golf course now.'

I remember sitting on my sofa reading Wattie's comments in the following day's papers and, just for a moment, I was transported back in time to that afternoon in Perth in October 1991. After what I had just come through, and was still enduring to a certain extent, the bust-up in the McDiarmid Park tunnel seemed almost incidental. The shouting and bawling at the sidelines, almost coming to blows in the tunnel at half-time, and then appearing in court on a breach of the peace charge. It was all crazy. I thought back to where I had been, and where I was 16 years later. Sitting on the sofa recovering from a life-threatening illness, but in a really strange sort of way, I probably wouldn't have changed a thing. That's the way football gets you, and the driving force behind grown men striving to achieve their goals and ambitions. It's addictive, infectious, and many other such adjectives, but it's our national game, and it grips us in a way that no other can. It's that simple.

I played football until I was about 60. I used to play five-a-sides with a bunch of mates on the astroturf pitch at Comely Park Primary School, in Falkirk, but this lad tackled me one night and I broke my finger, so I decided it was time to call it a day. You can't beat playing football – at any level – and it was always my intention to play as long as I could, but I needed an op on my pinkie and that was that. My best days in football were undoubtedly my playing days, although being a manager, while pretty stressful at times, is also a great job.

25

Family Ties

FOOTBALL has been my passion ever since the day and hour I was old enough to kick a ball without falling over, and it will remain that way until I draw my last breath. It's an infectious game and, for many, when it grabs you, it never lets go. But family, now that's a different ball game altogether. When you put the two side by side there really isn't any competition, because family would win hands down every time. I've been blessed with a great family: a fantastic wife, kids and grandchildren. They are the reason I managed to stay sane in the often insane business of football.

My wife Jessie and I were in the same class at high school. We were friends, and perhaps even boyfriend and girlfriend for a while, but I left school at 15 and went down to Liverpool. We remained in touch and would write to each other but, if the truth be told, I got fed up writing and that was it. The big romance was off. In those days, I only got home twice a year – at Christmas and again for the summer holidays, so there was little time for rekindling old romances. But when I went to Dundee, I got down the road every weekend and Jessie and I met up again in Denny – well, it wasn't the biggest town in the world so it wasn't too long before we had bumped into one another.

We started going out again and this time it was a 'proper' courtship. We decided to get married, and named the big day as 22 June 1968. But just before it, I was shipped off to America on tour with Dunfermline, and I was to be away for five weeks. Sadly it meant I missed all the preparations which, as you can imagine, I wasn't too unhappy about! We were married at Westpark Church, in Denny, in a beautiful ceremony, and then had our reception at the King Robert Hotel in Bannockburn and a few of my team-mates were present. It was a fantastic day and I was the proudest man alive.

Jessie and I decided to head for Spain on our honeymoon: destination Lloret de Mar. We had a fortnight in the sun and got on like a house on fire. It was a magical time and we were looking forward to spending the rest of our lives together.

While on honeymoon, we were sitting in the hotel bar one night and got chatting to another young couple, who were also on honeymoon. It turned out to be Bruce Rioch and his wife and we became good friends. He asked what I did for a living and I told him I was a professional footballer with Dunfermline, and he said, 'I'm a footballer as well, with Luton Town.' At that point I hadn't heard of him but we went about together for ten days, and they were a lovely couple. Before we left, he said that Tommy Docherty, who was manager of Aston Villa, had been in touch to try and sign him. We had only been home a few days when I read in the paper that Bruce had moved from Luton to Villa in a £200,000 deal, which was an awful lot of money in 1968. We kept in touch, and he played for Scotland before eventually becoming manager of Arsenal.

Marriage certainly agreed with Jessie and I, and we settled down in our new home in Dunipace, which isn't too far at all from where I was brought up in Dennyloanhead. We had a lounge, one bedroom, bathroom and kitchen. My claim to fame was that I helped to tile the bathroom – and did a pretty good job. In fact, our new home was in Milton Row, the very same street where the great Billy Steel was born. Billy played for the likes of Derby

County and Dundee. When he moved from Morton to Derby, the transfer fee of £15,500 was a record at the time, and when he signed for Dundee, the £22,500 fee was another record.

Despite coming from the same area, and being in the same profession, I only ever met Billy once, and that was when I was in Los Angeles with Dunfermline. He was working over there and our gaffer George Farm knew him. I told him where I lived and he really was taken aback. It was great meeting him and we enjoyed a lengthy chinwag. I hadn't seen him play but knew all about him. I've stayed in Dunipace ever since I was married although we've moved since then. Jessie and I have been in our current house just under 40 years and we're very happy there.

We weren't long married though when one day I got home and Jessie was lying in her bed – and she was as white as a sheet. I phoned Dr Fleming immediately and he came out to see her. He took one look at her and phoned the 'flying squad'. Their response was immediate and she was rushed to Falkirk Infirmary by ambulance. She was pregnant at the time and it seems her fallopian tube had burst and poison was coursing through her body. It really was serious but the medics were fantastic and got to her just in time. Jessie required an emergency operation and after a week or two was back on her feet, but it genuinely was the most worrying time of my life. I asked the doctor if we could still have kids and she said we could, although at that time my main concern was for my wife.

One thing that suited me down to the ground was that she has never really had an interest in football. The extent of Jessie's involvement has been to attend a couple of big matches, such as cup finals, while I was at Rangers and Falkirk, and I'm glad about that because when I left the ground on a Saturday, irrespective of who I was playing for or managing, I could go home and didn't get all the 'he said this or that' which can be so common behind the scenes at football clubs. I was away from it all which was really great.

Football is very seldom discussed in our house, and even nowadays I have a TV in the extension and can watch all the live games that I want. Jessie, on the other hand, will watch whatever she wants if there is football on. Don't think for a moment, though, that we live in our own separate bubbles, because nothing could be further from the truth. We are very much a team and have been since the day we were married. She is the love of my life and for that I am eternally grateful. As for my career, Jessie has always taken a keen interest, but just not in the game itself.

Five years after we were married, our first child was born. When Kay made her grand entrance into the world, it was such a happy occasion. I'll always remember I was in East Kilbride at my work, and knowing that the birth was imminent, emptied all my change into the telephone box to call Falkirk Royal Infirmary. I said to the nurse on the other end of the line, 'I'm enquiring about Mrs Totten' and she told me to hold the line. The money was running out but she came back and told me that Jessie had just given birth to a wee girl, and that mother and baby were both well. I walked out of the phone box and there was a man waiting to use it. I had this big grin on my face and I said to him, 'See the money that's left, just you use it, I'm off to the hospital,' and he just looked at me blankly. I ran to the nearest shop and bought a bunch of flowers and headed straight to Falkirk. It was the greatest feeling I had ever experienced, and better than anything I could have achieved in football. I was a dad, and an awful proud one at that. It was a magical moment.

And just under three years later, Bruce arrived. I wasn't in for either of the births as it wasn't really the done thing in those days, but you can't beat having a boy and a girl, so Jessie and I were delighted, and now we all live in the same area of Dunipace, which is fantastic. We also have two grandkids and Jessie is never slow to put her hand up to babysit. Because we all live quite close to one another, it means we have remained a close, tight-knit family, and see each other often.

When it came to naming the children, Jessie and I chose Kay and Bruce. They were just names we fancied – and they were our decisions, not the grandparents', because I always remember how influential they were in naming me.

When I was manager of Falkirk, Kevin McAllister and I were on our way to watch Hibs v Celtic as we were set to play the Easter Road side in our next game, when I got a call from my wife to say that Kay was in labour, and that the birth was imminent. I immediately about-turned the car, dropped Kevin off and picked up Jessie and we headed straight for Stirling Infirmary. We got there and Kay's partner came rushing out and said, 'It's a boy, and we are going to call him after you Alex.' I felt really honoured and had a big lump in my throat. It was a really proud moment for me, and it kept the family name going, but it was Alexander's parents' decision, and that was important.

I also have a grandson, Jake, who is Bruce and Natalie's son. That meant another trip to Stirling Infirmary, and another really proud moment. You can't beat family and when a new life comes into the world it is just magical.

Both boys have been involved in playing football for a team called Milton, in Bannockburn, and they also like a game of golf. I've always tried to encourage them to get into sport, although I'm mindful not to be too forceful, and not to meddle too much. They play their football on a Saturday morning and I always try to get to watch them before I go to the Falkirk game in the afternoon. I never miss a Falkirk game home or away, but it's also very important to me that I take an active interest in the lives of my grandchildren.

But in March 2006, I was able to sit back and look on as the proudest granddad in the land when my grandsons were the mascots for a match involving Falkirk and Rangers. It was a special day for me, not just because it was my 60th birthday, but because for one day only ALL my family were at the football – and my two lovely wee grandchildren were walking out at the Falkirk Stadium with the love of my footballing life – Falkirk!

My 60th birthday was fantastic. Jessie and I went to Dubai to mark the occasion and we had a great time, and when we came back we arranged the day out at the football. In fact, the afternoon was complete when I found out that Alex Parker was also a guest of the club that day. We talked about the 'old days' when I watched Alex and the 1957 Falkirk team win the Scottish Cup and taking a step or two down memory lane was fantastic. The day of my 60th birthday is one I won't forget in a while.

But back to my grandchildren and my son helps out with their team. It's a very well run outfit and has allowed Bruce to stay in touch with a game he also enjoyed playing very much. He played to a really good level with Camelon Juniors, where he had former Falkirk and Dunfermline player Jack Ross as a team-mate. He also played amateur football with Cambusbarron, Milton and Tullibody and now helps coach the kids at Milton. He loves the game as much as me. It definitely runs in the Totten blood.

My family are incredible and have been my bedrock throughout my life – and never more so than when I was ill. Knowing they were there for me was a great comfort, and no doubt the main reason I pulled through. I have always valued family highly but they became priceless at that time. It soon struck me how fortunate I was to be surrounded by so much love and affection. It's worth all the trophies and promotions in the world – and a wee bit more.

26

Still Involved In The Beautiful Game

I'M still involved with the Bairns, although on the 'other side of the fence' trying to raise money for the club in whatever way I can. This involves organising events such as sportsmen's dinners, golf days, getting shirt sponsors and the like. The events we run are always sold out because I have built up such a good relationship with so many people in the community over a long number of years, and my golden rule has always been if a job's worth doing then do it properly. With me, what people see is what they get, and I think they appreciate that.

While I was working as a salesman for Goodyear, I had to be persistent – and that approach has helped pay dividends for the Bairns. There is a prominent tyre firm in Cumbernauld which I thought might be interested in taking our products at one time. I went in twice to see if they wanted to place an order. Twice the gaffer said no, but I went back a third time and he said to me, 'Good to see you again. I love your persistence and was trying to find out if you were genuinely interested in my company. Okay, let's do business.' It just shows what you can achieve when you persevere.

Looking back, 1979 was a 'good year' for me, if you'll pardon the pun. I was voted the best area sales manager in the United Kingdom and received a nice plaque – and a Caribbean cruise – for my efforts. Being part-time for quite a large part of my managerial career means I have needed a 'real' job to supplement my income, and the sales job with Goodyear was perfect. I needed a job, they were very flexible with me and as long as I met my targets then I was able to get on with my football.

When I won the best sales manager title, I was invited down to London to pick up my award. It was a glitzy bash and when I heard 'Top area sales manager in Britain…Alex Totten' I went up to the stage to collect my prize and the boss kept it brief. I was thrilled and shook hands with him and he turned to me and said, 'Well done, Alex, fantastic – do better next year!'

I was flabbergasted. It felt so callous, but at the same time, having been in sales for so long, I knew exactly what he meant. You can't afford to rest on your laurels, and must keep striving to improve.

But Jessie and I were thrilled with the reward and flew from London to Miami where we boarded the ship, the *Song of Norway*, and cruised round the Caribbean. We visited the Virgin Islands, Puerto Rico and a host of other great places. It was a fantastic holiday and it was all-expenses-paid for a week. Every day at 7.30pm they would host the Goodyear Cocktail Party. It was fantastic and definitely the trip of a lifetime.

The company were incredibly flexible, but I'd left them twice to go full-time and the boss said, 'There won't be a third time Alex,' but when I went part-time again in my football career I was invited back, so I must have been doing something right. They were a good company to work for and I enjoyed my time with them. Getting out and about suited me down to the ground because I'm not good at constantly being surrounded by four walls. There is nothing better than being out all day in the fresh air and that was the case when I was a player, manager, salesman and even now as business relationship manager at Falkirk.

The job I'm doing at the moment is right up my street. It's like an extension of my position at Goodyear, although the only difference is I get to talk football as part of the job! I have made some fantastic contacts in the central Scotland area and we have some really loyal sponsors at the club. And that award I received from Goodyear isn't the only one that has come my way, although the *Falkirk Herald* Business Award for Sales and Marketing, which was awarded to Falkirk FC in 2010, was as a result of some great 'teamwork'. I was very proud to share that accolade with Sharon McGuire and David White.

Any football club would find it nigh-on impossible to survive without a steady stream of sponsorship money so my job is important and I'm under no illusions about the need to keep the cash coming in.

Asides from football, my other great sporting passion is golf. I started playing when I was 20 at Bonnybridge Golf Course, which has just nine holes. A lad called Campbell Ferguson, who is a postman, taught me, although it took me quite a while to start 'delivering' decent scores. The first time around I had more 'fresh air' shots than anything else, and three old worthies were giving me a bit of stick. After that, I went round like Benny Hill – all speeded up, although the fresh air shots were still there! I practised most afternoons and got my handicap down to four. I even reached the final of my club championship at Bonnybridge in 1976 and 1977, and while I may have lost out in both, I did manage to win the Spring Cup and a Pro-Am tournament soon after.

I stayed at Bonnybridge for around 15 years before joining Glenbervie, simply because it was an 18-hole course, and I'm still a member to this day. When I was manager of St Johnstone the easy option would've been to move to Perth but we remained in situ because of my love for Glenbervie, although I'm now playing off a handicap of 12.

One of my big pals is Gordon Sherry, who is a member at Loch Lomond, and I've been invited to play that course a few times. When he was given honorary membership of his local club at

Barrassie, he invited Dougie Donnelly and I down to the event, and it was a great day. To be honest, I don't know where I would be without my golf.

But I always make time for the family and Jessie and I have taken our grandkids on holiday a few times, although one of the most exciting was to Lapland to see Santa Claus about eight years ago. We all absolutely loved it and, as you can imagine, there was plenty of snow everywhere you went. We booked a sleigh ride and we had huskies pulling us along. It was magical not just for the kids, but also for Jessie and I. When we actually got to meet Santa Claus, he called Alexander and Jake forward and said to Alexander, 'And what would you like for Christmas young man?' And Alexander replied, 'A Rangers top!' His dad is a Rangers fan and everyone present thought it was hilarious.

I've managed to do a lot of fantastic things throughout my life, and most have been connected with the beautiful game, but one day I received a phone call and the voice on the other end invited me to be Chieftain of the Highland Games in Perth. I was told that I should be very proud because the previous year they had invited Lord Mansfield. To be honest, though, it *was* a great honour and naturally I wore Scotland's national dress, and went there and opened the games. It was a fantastic day – and the sun shone – and everyone seemed to embrace the whole concept of the games. It was the first time Jessie and I had attended such a gathering but it was made easier for me because I always had a special feeling for the people of Perth. They were fantastic with me when I was manager of St Johnstone and it was great to be able to give something back.

But that wasn't my one and only time as Chieftain. A few years ago I received another call, this time from Councillor Craig Martin, who was on the committee organising the Airth Highland Games, which takes place near Falkirk. I was again asked to open the games, and once again I accepted the honour with great pride – although on this occasion I took the opportunity to wear the kilt that I had on when Falkirk made it to the Scottish Cup Final. That was another fantastic day and, due to previous experience, I knew exactly what was expected of me. Once I had declared the games open, I went on an official walkabout – like a member of the royal family – and spoke to lots of folk before presenting prizes to those who had won races and the various competitions held throughout the day. It was really nice to be asked because Highland Games are a fantastic tradition in Scotland and it's not something that you get invited to take part in every day of the week.

I've had a lot of recognition, especially from people in the towns and cities in which I've managed. It's nice to be recognised and we all like praise from time to time. I think I've done pretty well during my career, and to be honest I really couldn't have asked for much more. I think my record as a manager stands comparison with most, but there is no shortcut to success. Everything is down to hard work, although I would agree there is an element of good fortune in there as well.

When I'm signing a player, I'll look him straight in the eye and say, 'If there is one thing I hate, it's laziness.' I was always straight with players – and I would also ask them that if they were the manager, where they would play themselves. Apart from in the case of an emergency, what's the point in playing a player in the left-back position if he's naturally right-footed? I would always try and play a guy in his most comfortable position. Getting to know your players is everything, and man-management is crucial. I've learned from an awful lot of good managers over the years – that has been invaluable. It's also vital that you have a Plan B in case things aren't quite going your way. For me, that's what Friday nights were for!

Mind you, one of the highlights of my time in football took place in the year 2000. The Millennium Dinner at the Inchyra Hotel was something else. There were 500 people there and that wasn't including Falkirk legends such as Alex Parker and Kevin McAllister. It was like a who's who of the Bairns. The MC went through Falkirk's Team of the Millennium– as chosen by the supporters – and then it was between Kevin McAllister and Simon Stainrod for Player of the Millennium, and I was delighted that wee Crunchie won it, even though I also love Simon to bits. I was there with my wife and kids and when Bill Leckie, of the *Scottish Sun*, got up and started talking, it soon became apparent who the subject was.

He mentioned that 'this chap' had been a supporter, manager, player, twice, and I'm thinking, 'That must be me.' He then invited me up to the stage to collect a Lifetime Achievement award – the only one ever given out to anyone connected with Falkirk Football Club – and I was chuffed to bits. I don't think there was a prouder man in the whole of Scotland that night and when I collected my trophy, which resembled the claret jug given to the winner of the British Open, I just stood and stared at it for a while. It was beautiful.

One of the first people off his seat to congratulate me was Alex Parker, and he knew a thing or two about football, so that meant a lot. He had just been named in Falkirk's Team of the Millennium, to go with his place in the Everton Team of the Millennium and the Sir Matt Busby World XI. He had absolutely everything. He could pass the ball, read the game, he tackled well. He was the complete player, but most important of all, he was a true gentleman.

Something I've always enjoyed is a bit of after-dinner speaking. I started over 20 years ago, at Dunfermline, when I was asked to speak one night at a Sportsmen's Dinner. Mr Abie, the comedian, was there and said that if I polished one or two things up, I could make a good career in public speaking. I now speak at the likes of Rotary and Probus clubs. I enjoy talking about my career, and throw the odd joke in here and there. I talk about an Asian boy that Bill Shankly signed for Liverpool. His name was Anwar and he was a really good player, and a lovely lad. He was only 17, originally from Pakistan, and I said to him one day, 'I see your country is at war with India, will you be going to fight?' And he replied, 'That all depends if they attack my village.' I asked him where he stayed, and he said, 'Wigan!'

When Graeme Souness first arrived at Rangers he had this really conceited attitude, and I tell the story about how he was so arrogant he wouldn't even get into the same car as his chauffeur!

On one occasion, I was asked to speak in front of about 700 people at the Thistle Hotel, in Glasgow. The likes of Peter Cormack, who played for Liverpool, and the comedian and presenter Tom O'Connor were also on duty that night. I was asked to speak for 20 minutes and was quite nervous, being in such exalted company, but the organiser was soon tugging on the bottom of my trousers and telling me my 20 minutes were up, so it went by really quickly, which was a sure sign that I was enjoying myself.

I've spoken at all sorts of events and it's definitely something I want to keep on doing. I like telling stories about Shanks and my time at Liverpool, and by all accounts people like hearing them. But while I enjoy a gab, both playing and managing was my 'thing' and I will forever be grateful for all the wonderful opportunities I was given in football. As for management, there is much more to it than merely picking the team on a Saturday afternoon. You are an ambassador for the club 24/7 and it's equally important that you fulfil both roles with an equal amount of passion and dignity. I had a great career in the game and played for, and managed, some smashing teams. Is there much I would change about my time? Perhaps I wouldn't have travelled in Paul Breslin's car when Alex Ferguson was teaching him to drive. Mind you, I think I would just keep everything else the way it was…

Bibliography

Shankly: The Lost Diary

Playing for Rangers: No. 16 – Ken Gallacher

Saints Alive – Gordon Bannerman

And It's All Over – David Francey with Phil McEntee